UNDERSTANDING EMPLOYEE ENGAGEMENT

Employee engagement is a novel concept that has been building momentum in recent years. *Understanding Employee Engagement: Theory, Research, and Practice* exposes the science and practice of employee engagement. Grounded in theory and empirical research, this book debates the definitions of engagement; provides a comprehensive evaluation of empirical findings in the engagement field; including a focus on international findings; and offers implications for science and practice in organizations. Employers can learn how to foster and drive engagement to increase productivity and happiness, and researchers can master the existing engagement literature and begin to study the many propositions and new models that Zinta S. Byrne, PhD, proposes throughout the book.

Zinta S. Byrne, PhD, has more than 10 years of work experience at Hewlett-Packard as an engineer and manager, worked for Personnel Decisions International as a regional manager, and is currently Professor of Psychology at Colorado State University and President of Atniz Consulting, LLC. She has published in top psychology and management journals and books, presented internationally, reviews for and serves on a number of editorial boards, is a co-editor of *Purpose and Meaning in the Workplace*, published by the American Psychological Association, and is the author of *Organizational Psychology and Behavior: An Integrated Approach to Understanding the Workplace*, published by Kendall Hunt.

SERIES IN APPLIED PSYCHOLOGY
Jeanette N. Cleveland, Colorado State University
Kevin R. Murphy, Landy Litigation and Colorado State
University
Series Editors
Edwin A. Fleishman, Founding Series Editor (1987–2010)

Winfred Arthur, Jr., Eric Day, Winston Bennett, Jr., and Antoinette Portrey
Individual and Team Skill Decay: The Science and Implications for Practice

Gregory Bedny and David Meister
The Russian Theory of Activity: Current Applications to Design and Learning

Winston Bennett, David Woehr, and Charles Lance
Performance Measurement: Current Perspectives and Future Challenges

Michael T. Brannick, Eduardo Salas, and Carolyn Prince
Team Performance Assessment and Measurement: Theory, Research, and Applications

Zinta S. Byrne
Understanding Employee Engagement: Theory, Research, and Practice

Neil D. Christiansen and Robert P. Tett
Handbook of Personality at Work

Jeanette N. Cleveland, Margaret Stockdale, and Kevin R. Murphy
Women and Men in Organizations: Sex and Gender Issues at Work

Aaron Cohen
Multiple Commitments in the Workplace: An Integrative Approach

Russell Cropanzano
Justice in the Workplace: Approaching Fairness in Human Resource Management, Volume 1

Russell Cropanzano
Justice in the Workplace: From Theory to Practice, Volume 2

David V. Day, Stephen Zaccaro, Stanley M. Halpin
Leader Development for Transforming Organizations: Growing Leaders for Tomorrow's Teams and Organizations

UNDERSTANDING EMPLOYEE ENGAGEMENT

Theory, Research, and Practice

Zinta S. Byrne

Routledge
Taylor & Francis Group

NEW YORK AND LONDON

First published 2015
by Routledge
711 Third Avenue, New York, NY 10017

and by Routledge
27 Church Road, Hove, East Sussex BN3 2FA

Routledge is an imprint of the Taylor & Francis Group, an informa business

Library of Congress Cataloging-in-Publication Data

Byrne, Zinta S.
   Understanding what employee engagement is and is not : implications for
theory, research, and practice / Zinta S. Byrne.
   1. Employee motivation.   2. Employees—Attitudes.   3. Employees—
Psychology.   I. Title.
   HF5549.5.M63B97 2014
   658.3'14—dc23
   2014003981

ISBN: 978-0-415-82086-8 (hbk)
ISBN: 978-0-415-82087-5 (pbk)
ISBN: 978-0-203-38594-4 (ebk)

Typeset in Sabon
by Apex CoVantage, LLC

Printed and bound in the United States of America by Publishers Graphics,
LLC on sustainably sourced paper.

To Jon Byrne, Naja Stofberg Mocek,
and Anna C. Stofberg.

CONTENTS

CONTENTS

FIGURES AND TABLES

Figures

Tables

SERIES FOREWORD

The goal of the Applied Psychology series is to create books that exemplify the use of scientific research, theory, and findings to help solve real problems in organizations and society. Dr. Byrne's *Understanding Employee Engagement: Theory, Research, and Practice* is one of those rare books in which the title says it all. Her book helps us understand what engagement is, why it is important, and how a clearer understanding of employee engagement advances theory, research, and practice in applying psychology to organizations.

After setting the stage with an introductory chapter that documents the growing importance of employee engagement, coupled unfortunately with growing confusion about what engagement really means, Dr. Byrne dives into the challenge of pulling together and making sense of the growing literature on employee engagement. Her first section puts engagement under a microscope, and defines what engagement is and how it is related to and distinct from other concepts used to understand the experience of work. Her next section lays out the forces that allow organizations to attract, develop, and retain an engaged workforce, as well as those that stand in the way of building and maintaining employee engagement. Her third section examines the proposition that employee engagement can be (but is not always) a competitive advantage, and discusses ways of using employee engagement to improve organizations. Her final section explores the future of research and practice in employee engagement, highlighting two topics that have not yet received sufficient attention: the similarities and differences in engagement across cultures and the dark side of engagement.

Understanding Employee Engagement: Theory, Research, and Practice comes at precisely the right time. *Employee engagement* is becoming a buzzword, and Dr. Byrne's book shows how a rigorous and thoughtful application of psychological research and theory can be used to understand, advance and make use of employee engagement. Developing employee engagement can be a win–win for employees and organizations, but making it work requires a clear understanding of what engagement is, how it is developed and maintained, and how it can be channeled to improve both the individual employee's experience at work and the health and welfare of the organization. Dr. Byrne's book provides a road map to accomplishing these goals. We are happy to add *Understanding Employee Engagement: Theory, Research, and Practice* to the Applied Psychology series.

Jeanette N. Cleveland
Kevin R. Murphy

ACKNOWLEDGMENTS

The following individuals each played a valuable role in the writing of this book: Jeanette Cleveland, Kevin Murphy, Anne Duffy, Lynn Shore, Maria Kuznetsova, Kurt Kraiger, Dirk Steiner, Jackie Coyle-Shapiro, James Weston, Samantha Stelman, Amos Engelbrecht, Kathryn Rickard, and Janet Peters.

Special thanks and acknowledgment to Elaine LeMay, who many years ago asked me, "What do you know about employee engagement?" Additionally, special thanks to Jennifer Anderson, Gaynel Tanner, and Rachel Lee.

1

THE STORY OF ENGAGEMENT

I don't know how to describe it—I just feel alive. I feel ener-gized, excited, stimulated, almost on edge, and yet I can focus as if nothing else exists. When I'm engaged, I feel connected and feel like I'm doing something that matters; I'm making a difference, even if in a small way. It's a choice, really, to be that 'into' my job—I wasn't always this way and I'm not always 100% in this mode.

—Interview 45

Employee engagement is a motivational state that, thus far, has been associated with a number of positive and desirable consequences for organizations. It is about investing oneself, being authentic in the job, and delivering one's work performance with passion, persistence, and energy. It has become a widely discussed topic in both popular and aca-demic press, with practice outpacing the research necessary to validate the hundreds of solutions offered as "the answer" to the *disengagement* dilemma.

Many books and articles define and discuss engagement in terms of what it looks like (as opposed to what it is), and most refer to engage-ment by describing what disengagement looks like (a loss of money), all trying to invoke fear—fear of what happens when you lack engagement. For example, the Gallup Organization (2002, 2013a, 2013b) reports that upward of $355 billion is lost in annual revenue in the United States, all due to unengaged workers, and that 87% of employees in 142 countries are disengaged. A 2009 Kenexa Research Institute report states an analy-sis of 64 organizations indicates engaged employees are responsible for twice the annual net income than that of their unengaged contemporaries. Finally, a 2007 report from the Dale Carnegie Organization suggests managers should care about engagement because (a) high engagement results in employee retention (they say this is because there is a close rela-tionship between company image and self-image), (b) engaged employees

1

are productive, and (c) high engagement workplaces attract people who want to work hard for the organization. Thus, according to these reports (and many others I did not cite here), the fear of not having engaged employees or losing out on the benefits of engaged employees are the key instigators for why you should care about engagement.[1]

Another reason to propel you into caring about employee engagement might be peer pressure—everyone seems to be focusing on engagement; therefore, it must be important. Employee engagement is a relatively novel concept in both the popular and the academic press, and novelty often draws tremendous interest. Simple searches on the Internet, online bookstores, and electronic research databases reveal thousands of hits. Of the engagement books available on the market today, nearly every one is targeted at the practitioner audience, explaining how to get engagement and, as a consequence, high performance. Thus far, only a handful are targeted for a mixed (higher education, practice) or academic only audience, suggesting that organizations and the practitioners and consulting firms for whom they work are running full steam ahead with the idea of employee engagement; researchers need simply to catch up. Indeed, it has been suggested that researchers are attempting to legitimize engagement, an "intuitive construct" (Newman & Harrison, 2008), which requires significant theory, debate, and empirical studies for clarifying its uniqueness and validity in causing the effects heavily marketed by human resources and consulting firms (Macey & Schneider, 2008).

Perhaps more compelling than fear or the novelty for caring and reading about employee engagement include the following: First, engaged employees *choose* to be engaged—so what is it that is driving them to work hard, commit to the goals of the organization, and deliver desired performance in their jobs? Second, studies examining the relationship between engagement and performance, job satisfaction, and commitment suggest engagement uniquely contributes to explaining and predicting organizational behavior (e.g., performance, innovation), the ultimate goal of both practice and science. Third, engagement is related to the health of employees—engaged employees report positive health outcomes and well-being; a substantial number of studies report negative relationships between engagement and burnout, stress, and psychosomatic illness (Halbesleben, 2010). Billions of dollars are pumped into the U.S. economy to thwart illness and to improve individual health and well-being. Paying attention to engagement is paying attention to the health of employees. Fourth, focusing on employee engagement may be considered a feature of attending to corporate social responsibility and of efforts to reestablish the trust of the public in the ethical practices and intentions of organizations. By paying attention to the well-being and welfare of employees through fostering their engagement levels at work, organizations may be able to send the message they care about profits and not at the expense of their employees' health (physical and psychological).

Employee engagement is a challenging concept to describe and study because it seems to manifest itself in many ways, defying initial attempts to box it into a single and simple definition. The following are a few illustrative excerpts taken from actual interviews I conducted within the last few years, targeted toward understanding what is employee engagement and what does it look like. Names and personal information have been changed to protect confidentiality.

DeWayne is a 40-year-old associate professor in the social sciences at a mid-sized university on the East Coast of the United States. His answers to questions about how he felt about work initially indicated that he was burned out. One of the dominant approaches to employee engagement started with the assumption engagement is the opposite of burnout—if you feel burned out, you cannot also be engaged. But DeWayne tells a different story:

> Well, a few years ago, I would say I was getting burned out at work. I hated going to staff meetings and when there, I would just crawl into a corner and focus on my own thoughts and notes. I avoided people by working from home as much as I could—just so I didn't have to be in that environment. So much back-stabbing and so little accountability [*he looks disgusted*]. They expect a ton of you and never recognize how much you do. I felt so different, so energized when I could work at home for a couple of days in a row. Just being away from my coworkers— don't get me wrong, I'm sure they are good at what they do. I just don't really like them all that much. They do nothing to make me feel supported. [*paused for a while as if collecting thoughts*] I really like what I do—I feel so intellectually stimulated, writing, and problem-solving in my research. It's a challenge to me to figure out how to convey our field in simple terms to the students, so that they can see how exciting the material is and . . . well, I like to find ways to make it come alive. [*paused for a moment*] My wife complains that I work too much—I get lost in what I'm doing, ya' know, lose track of time and then I'm late for dinner, finding excuses for why I couldn't tear myself away from my research. I just really like what I do—it invigorates me.

Becky's story conveys how important the people at work are to her and the value of relationships in promoting her engagement at work. Becky is a 55-year-old mental health care worker at a nonprofit organization in the Midwest of the United States.

When I started, the organization was a tiny version of its current self, and so in those days people were much less specialized and did a lot of different things; had a lot of different roles. We had more variety. [*She paused for a few moments as if collecting her thoughts*]. Things have gotten much more bureaucratic. There were fewer levels to go through for decisions, we had easier access up the ladder, power used to be delegated downward more, we had more say in decision-making. It doesn't feel like the camaraderie is happening [*she started crying*]. Relationships are different now and it used to be easier to talk through things—now it's all e-mail; so distant between people, even with people sitting a desk away.

So why are you still here, what keeps you going?

I love my job. I love the clients. What I do matters in their lives—I've known some of them for years and when they come in, it's like seeing a good friend. Having a long-term perspective helps me. I don't always feel like everything is engaging for me, but I like the big picture and it helps me know that it's valuable in the long run. I like what we do, I like our vision and I like what we provide. I think we do a really good job for our clients. There's a lot of wonderful people here.

Petrus is a 46-year-old consultant in South Africa. He used to work for a large corporation, but when the government instituted new policies for selection and promotion in efforts to rectify many years of apartheid oppression, he left and started his own consulting firm. I asked him about his consulting work, because he specializes in helping organizations with promoting engagement:

I really liked my work at [*organization*]—I was there for at least 20 years before I decided to leave. I don't begrudge the organization for what it was doing—they had to follow the law. I do a number of different things now, which makes my work so interesting. I work with a variety of organizations all around South Africa—none are the same. I develop leadership training programs—I focus a lot on communication, conveying clear vision, and basic management principles. There's such a large pay discrepancy here between the lowest level worker and the managers, a problem that I can't solve. So we focus on developing employee appreciation programs, finding ways to match employees' skills to the right jobs, and teaching them how to work together in teams. I use both surveys and focus groups to measure engagement—I wouldn't say everything we do works every time, but for the most part, we make a difference.

4

Finally, Valerray is a 30-year-old businessman in Russia who responded to my questions about engagement in the following way (we conversed through translators):

> I'm not sure I understand your question. Happiness? You want to know about happiness? Look at us, we're very happy. We love to have fun. [*we discuss how happiness is not the same as engagement*]. Involvement, engagement? [*the translator offered that she thinks they are all the same word*]. I don't know. The older workers are struggling with what it means to be independent—they grew up in a government where they knew their place at work and felt pride about doing something the government needed and wanted. The younger workers don't know that system so we experience work differently. We are challenged and excited about making our way in this new world. We are happy; we work hard; I work hard. We do as much as we can and feel good. We are passionate about what we do and find ways to make it good for the people—I have nice offices for my employees, give them time off when they need, have work they like to do and we talk a lot about work. I send my employees to training programs; they like to learn and then they do better on the job.

Road Map for This Book

Employee engagement is about investing oneself, being authentic in the job, and delivering one's work performance with passion, persistence, and energy (Chapter 2 provides detail on this definition). Engagement is generally characterized as a positive state, associated with positive performance, which is different from important organizational attitudes and constructs frequently mentioned such as job satisfaction (Chapter 3 reviews differences and similarities). It is something most believe organizations can promote not only by providing the right environment and good leadership (Chapter 4) but also by removing inhibitors (Chapter 5). Of course, fostering engagement means being able to assess how often employees report being engaged and by how much (Chapter 6 reviews measures of engagement).

Given the many benefits associated with employee engagement (I review many in the earlier chapters), organizations seek to use engagement for competitive advantage (Chapter 7 discusses how to do so). Although one of the benefits associated with engagement is improved health for the employee, I introduce in Chapter 8 the possibility engagement can improve the health of the organization through engagement contagion. Most of the benefits associated with engaged employees have been studied and demonstrated in the United States and in several other countries. A gap exists in that few, if any, have examined engagement across cultures—comparing one culture to another (Chapter 9 reviews engagement on the international landscape). In addition to this gap in the literature, engagement has to date been considered a positive and very desirable state for employees; more seems to be better. However, there may be a dark side to engagement—an unexplored paradox that should be considered before assuming more is better (Chapter 10 introduces the dark side of engagement).

This book offers a comprehensive review and a discussion of employee engagement as we know it today. In his introductory chapter to the *Handbook of Employee Engagement* published in 2011, Albrecht puts forth 10 questions he believes are facing researchers today. The questions are great, and although Albrecht brings together a number of authors to contribute more than 30 chapters and 400 pages of information, few actually address the questions. This book addresses his questions completely and objectively. Specifically, he asks what defines engagement, what makes it unique, what are the theories that explain engagement, is there such a thing as too much, what is the story on the measurement of engagement, how do we foster engagement, and what should we research next.

The book is grounded in theory and empirical research, yet it also includes, when appropriate, references and reviews of efforts in the practice realm of employee engagement. The first few chapters in Part I are devoted to setting the stage for where we are today with the literature—what is engagement? There are many different definitions to engagement; therefore, making progress in identifying predictors and consequences of engagement requires understanding what perspective you want to take. Criticisms challenge whether engagement is different from existing constructs that are already staples in the organizational behavior literature. Therefore, I provide a good review of the empirical findings demonstrating the uniqueness and similarity of engagement to existing constructs such as job involvement, satisfaction, and commitment.

Part II focuses more on the applied side of understanding employee engagement in the sense of how does one get engaged employees, what prevents them from being engaged, and how do you know if they are engaged? Thus, these chapters focus on application, with a strong grounding in theory and research. What empirical evidence do we have or are we missing to feel confident the solutions being recommended do and will work in organizations? Much of the attention in organizational sciences is on how we use theory and research to make a difference in organizations—to not only advance the sciences but also, importantly, how to apply what is learned. These chapters were written while keeping these objectives, advancing science and furthering its application, in mind.

Parts I and II bring you up to speed on what is currently known about engagement. Part III focuses on how engagement serves as a competitive advantage and not just because of high-performing employees. Instead, I focus on building an organizational culture to improve competitive advantage and on how employees themselves grow the organization's engagement capacity. Part IV is dedicated to what is not known at this time about employee engagement and why it should be known—what are the new frontiers in engagement? In this part of the book, I shine a light on the gap in knowledge about engagement across cultures. Although studies are being conducted in many countries around the globe, the lack of a clear definition of engagement makes many of these studies difficult to compare or use in advancing the science of engagement. I was raised bilingual and in a non-U.S. country and culture; therefore, I was already exposed to the subtleties in translating colloquial speech. However, made especially clear to me in my interactions in Russia in 2012 and 2013 was that translations of scientific ideas are more complicated and that the exact word choice is critical. I only scratch the surface of the gap in international studies in Chapter 9, but hopefully this "scratch" will lead to rigorous efforts to promote the study of engagement cross-culturally (and not just engagement in a different country). Additionally in Part IV of the book, I turn several ideas on their heads to expose other perspectives of engagement. By reviewing theories and literature that may be brought to the study of the topic, these chapters have immediate utility as opposed to just being a presentation of possible ideas for future research.

Although many researchers and practitioners may not agree on a single definition or approach to employee engagement, perhaps the one thing we can agree on is engagement is not a simple concept. Engagement is not easily transported from practice to science. Yet, the concept of employee engagement holds promise for generating much conversation, even more than it has already, about employees in organizations. I hope you find the book helpful and inspiring.

NOTE

1. These reports provide few, if any, details on how the studies were conducted, including essential information about the samples and how engagement versus disengagement were operationalized.

Part I

ENGAGEMENT UNDER THE MICROSCOPE

2

WHAT IS EMPLOYEE ENGAGEMENT?

Employee engagement, referred in practice to a state in which employees give 100% or more to their jobs, is fiercely growing in popularity among practitioners, organizational leaders, and researchers in the organizational sciences. *And why not?* According to an article in *Business Week* magazine,

> companies with engaged employees boosted operating income by 19% compared with companies with the lowest percentage of engaged employees, which saw operating income fall 33%. What does that mean in real dollars? For S&P 500 companies, Watson Wyatt reports that a significant improvement in employee engagement increases revenue by $95 million. (Irvine, 2009)

Similarly, disengaged workers are reportedly costing the British economy between £37.2 billion and £38.9 billion per year (roughly $58.8 to $61.5 billion; Flade, 2003).

Although astounding financial gains and losses are attributed to engaged and unengaged workers, there seems to be little consensus on what exactly engagement is, whether it is a new topic or one comprising a combination of existing topics (Newman & Harrison, 2008). Furthermore, a review of websites, books, and trade magazines, as well as academic journals, reveals a reasonably large disparity between research and practice concerning the definition and use of the phrase *employee engagement*. For example, practitioner writings (e.g., white papers, consulting firm websites, blogs, books) refer to engagement as an umbrella or overarching term that subsumes many different concepts (e.g., attitudes, behaviors, dispositions) relevant to the performance of the individual or the organization as a whole (see Mone & London, 2010). In contrast, researchers push for parsimony, specificity, and uniqueness in their definitions of the concept, distinguishing attitudes from behaviors and dispositions (i.e., personality), with a tendency to focus at an individual unit level. To confuse matters more, the word *engagement* is sometimes used as a verb signifying behavior and performance (e.g., to be engaged or involved in an activity; Miles, 2001; R. Miller, Greene, Montalvo, Ravindran, & Nichols, 1996), as an adjective whereby engagement describes a person in a particular state of being or energy level (e.g., *self-engagement* as a form of personal responsibility: Britt, 1999), or as a noun representing a certification (e.g., *Community Engagement, Curricular Engagement*: classifications of the Carnegie Foundation for the Advancement of Teaching, 2009). So what is employee engagement?

Defining Engagement as the Opposite of Burnout

The most widely used definition of engagement in the research literature was proposed by Maslach and colleagues (e.g., Maslach & Leiter, 1997; Maslach, Schaufeli, & Leiter, 2001), and later by Schaufeli, Salanova, González-Romá, and Bakker (2002). Maslach and Leiter (1997) originally defined engagement as a concept composed of three elements—energy, involvement, and efficacy, each being the direct opposite of one of three burnout dimensions: emotional exhaustion, depersonalization, and lack of efficacy. Burnout has been traditionally defined as a three component construct: *emotional exhaustion*, emotionally drained; *depersonalization*, detached and often cynical; and *reduced personal accomplishment* or *lack of efficacy,* experienced as an overwhelming internal feeling of failure (Maslach, 1982). Maslach and Leiter proposed the Maslach Burnout Inventory (MBI) could be used to assess engagement, with low exhaustion and cynicism scores and high efficacy scores reflecting high levels of engagement. Their perspective was that engagement was a positive state—the opposite of burnout. They relied on their years of scholarship in studying burnout to determine that when people were not burned out, they were often in this positive state of energy, involvement, and efficacy.

Schaufeli, Salanova, and their colleagues (2002) also defined engagement as the opposite of burnout but modified their definition somewhat to specifically refer to engagement as "a positive, fulfilling, work-related state of mind characterized by vigor, dedication, and absorption" (p. 74). *Vigor* refers to high levels of energy while working and persistence when confronted with challenges. *Dedication* refers to experiencing enthusiasm, pride, inspiration, challenge, and significance. *Absorption* refers to "being fully concentrated and deeply engrossed in one's work, whereby time passes quickly and one has difficulty detaching oneself from work" (Schaufeli et al., 2002, p. 75). Schaufeli et al. argued because engagement and burnout were opposite constructs, hence perfectly negatively correlated, using the same instrument to measure them was psychometrically and conceptually problematic (Schaufeli & Bakker, 2003). Therefore, Schaufeli and colleagues modified the MBI and created the Utrecht Work

Engagement Scale (UWES) to assess vigor, absorption, and dedication. The researchers showed that although correlations between the MBI and the UWES were moderate to high between and across dimensions, the two scales appear to assess distinct constructs (the UWES is reviewed in Chapter 6). This view of engagement from a stress model perspective has been quite popular (see Bakker & Leiter, 2010); however, it is considered only one approach to understanding engagement.

Defining Engagement as Investing in One's Work Role

Another well-known definition of engagement also used in research literature was proposed by Kahn (1990). Kahn introduced personal engagement as "the harnessing of organization members' selves into their work roles; in engagement, people employ and express themselves physically, cognitively, and emotionally during role performances" (1990, p. 694). He clarified his definition of engagement by also defining disengagement as the opposite point on an engagement continuum, where disengagement or "unemployment of the self" (Kahn, 1990, p. 701) is akin to detachment and self-defense. Grounded in Goffman's (1961) work on symbiotic relationships, Kahn suggested the more people draw themselves into their various work roles (i.e., engagement), the better their performance and the more happiness they experience. Drawing on oneself means *self-employment*—effort, involvement, flow, mindfulness, intrinsic motivation, and psychological presence—and *self-expression*—creativity, personal voice, emotional expression, authenticity, nondefensive communication, playfulness, and ethical behavior. Kahn developed his definition using a qualitative study in which he observed camp counselors at an athletic summer camp for adolescents and employees of an architectural firm. His focus on engagement was primarily as a moment-to-moment concept (W. A. Kahn, personal communication, May 6, 2012; Kahn, 1990), although many have applied his idea of engagement as a general stable state (e.g., May, Gilson, & Harter, 2004). A recent publication of a measure designed to assess employee engagement using Kahn's definition (see Rich, LePine, & Crawford, 2010, which is reviewed in Chapter 6) illustrates this perspective of stability. Although not quite capturing the construct Kahn had in mind, the advantage of an existing measure that assesses the three-part conceptualization as Kahn noted is that it may facilitate the explicit application of his perspective, which has previously been slow to occur.

Other Definitions

These two most popular definitions of employee engagement in the research literature describe it as a motivational state; however, many others refer to engagement as a form of performance. For example,

Macey and Schneider (2008) proposed engagement represents a process, whereby *trait* engagement (a predisposition to view life and work with enthusiasm) determines *state* engagement (feelings of energy and absorption), which subsequently leads to *behavioral* engagement (discretionary effort), the ultimate goal. Thus, for Macey and Schneider, employee engagement is a process that subsumes several preexisting organizational constructs (Newman & Harrison, 2008) and results in a specific type of performance. Recent empirical work has built on Macey and Schneider's framework (see Christian, Garza, & Slaughter, 2011), and consultants (besides themselves) have applied the model in organizational interventions (Mone & London, 2010).

Other definitions of engagement exist, though a search of the Web of Science® citation database (database of citations of scientific and conference publications offered by Thomson Reuters) reveals few, if any, have been used by anyone other than the original authors. These additional definitions include engagement as a combination of commitment and organizational citizenship behaviors (i.e., extra-role or discretionary performance behaviors facilitate organizational productivity and teamwork; CIPD, 2009; Matthews, 2010), a form of happiness or satisfaction (Edwards, 2009), positive attitude (Robinson, Perryman, & Hayday, 2004), discretionary effort (Hay Group, 2010), and a connection with the company, accompanied by a willingness to demonstrate extra-role behaviors (Towers Perrin as cited in Gebauer, Lowman, & Gordon 2008).

A Unifying Definition

Similarities between previous academic definitions of engagement (namely, Kahn, 1990, and Maslach & Leiter, 1997, or Schaufeli et al., 2002) are the investment and the display of three components of the self: affective, cognitive, behavioral or physical. What makes Kahn's (1990) definition particularly distinct from the others is his focus on engagement as a moment-to-moment experience that includes presence and authenticity. The distinction in Schaufeli et al.'s (2002) definition is its origination in burnout and the inclusion of a variety of other constructs such as satisfaction, job involvement, and pride in the dimensions of engagement. Compared to other definitions, both Kahn's and Schaufeli et al.'s are multifaceted and incorporate the notion of the entire or whole self employed in the engaged state. So how do we move productively forward when there appears to be a few different definitions of employee engagement?

We do so by (a) creating a unifying definition that combines the similarities of concepts across definitions, (b) capturing the key components that make engagement unique from other constructs, (c) integrating key perspectives from science and practice, and (d) separating the antecedent and consequence constructs from the definition itself. What remains is employee engagement is *a moment-to-moment state of motivation, wherein one is psychologically present (i.e., in the moment) and psychophysiologically aroused, is focused on and aligned with the goals of the job and organization, and channels his or her emotional and cognitive self to transform work into meaningful and purposeful accomplishment.*

Let me break the definition down and examine its parts. First, employee engagement is a *state of motivation*. Motivation is not directly observed (Kanfer, 1990); rather, it is inferred by observing the direction of one's attention and energy, the intensity with which one persists on a task, and the effort one exerts in working toward accomplishing a task (J. Campbell, Dunnette, Lawler, & Weick, 1970; Kanfer, 1990; Ployhart, 2008). Engagement, however, is more than just motivation because one can be motivated in a direction that fails to support the organization's goals, be directed with manipulative or purely instrumental intent, or be motivated without skill and thus counterproductive. Employee engagement is motivation focused on meeting organizational goals. Several existing approaches to engagement refer to it as a motivational state or use the language of motivation to describe engaged employees (e.g., Bakker, Schaufeli, Leiter, & Taris, 2008; Halbesleben, Harvey, & Bolino, 2009; Kahn, 1990; Maslach et al., 2001; Schaufeli et al., 2002). I retain the moment-to-moment aspect of Kahn's (1990) definition because engagement is not a nonstop continuous state, lasting for hours on end and day in and day out. I agree with others (see Kahn, 1992; Macey & Schneider, 2008; Maslach et al., 2001) that one cannot be engaged at all times. The degree to which it fluctuates and how long it can be sustained are empirical questions (see Chapter 11).

The next component, *psychological presence*, refers to a state in which one is focused on the task at hand and wherein one directs all attention and psychological energy to what is currently happening. Kahn (1992) defines psychological presence as a state wherein one is fully attentive to the present moment, connected, integrated, and focused. Psychological presence is similar to mindfulness (K. Brown & Ryan, 2003; Dane, 2011; Herndon, 2008), which is essential to what engagement means; one is *in the moment* rather than thinking about other events or people, either in the past or in the future (K. Brown & Ryan, 2003). Daydreaming or mind wandering on the job is a sign of a lack of psychological presence; hence, focusing on the current task and being psychologically present can also mean losing track of time similar to flow (Csikszentmihalyi, 1996). Csikszentmihalyi and Rathunde (1993) described flow as "the subjective state that people report when they are completely involved in something to the point of forgetting time, fatigue, and everything else but the activity itself" (p. 59).

My definition of engagement refers to *psychophysiological arousal* rather than to physical energy, because many jobs do not require people express themselves physically, yet they can report high levels of engagement. One can be physiologically aroused without demonstrating physical movement and action (Duffy, 1957; Lacey, Bateman, & VanLehn, 1953; Shipman, Heath, & Oken, 1970). Research in psychophysiology (i.e., physiological bases underlying psychological processes) has determined that people respond with physical arousal (e.g., increased heart rate and/or electrodermal activity) to psychological experiences (e.g., enjoyment of music, chess, gambling) without necessarily demonstrating overt physical movement and action (e.g., running, jumping; Alpers, Adolph, & Pauli, 2011; Studer & Clark, 2011). That is, people can be involved in a nonphysically demanding task, such as playing chess, but can place "metabolic demands on their bodies that begin to approach those of athletes during the peak of a competitive event" (Sapolsky, 2004, p. 5). Psychophysiological arousal incorporates physiological arousal. Physiological arousal refers to the excitation or activation of biological functions such as cardio activity, as indicated by blood pressure or heart rate, brain activity, concentration of blood sugar or lactic acid, or body temperature. One cannot have physical activity without physiological arousal.

Kahn's (1990) illustrations of the physical component of his conceptualization of engagement are all observably physical activities like "darting about checking gear" (p. 700), and "flying around the room" (p. 701). His examples imply that physical activity is required for engagement. In contrast to Kahn, Schaufeli et al.'s (2002) concept of vigor may be more similar to what I refer to here, in that vigor is the feeling of energy rather than the expression of physical activity. Heightened arousal levels are characteristic of the state of engagement, and I suggest the derivation of energy from goal progress and achievement accounts for this heightened and sustained arousal.

Focus is a concept incorporated in nearly every definition of engagement and, likewise, is in mine. I specifically include an alignment of employees' focus with the organization's goals, because including focus with no target leaves this component of engagement a little vague and fails to incorporate an important aspect of what practitioners note is critical for engagement. When discussing employee engagement with other consultants, corporate and office leaders and managers, and human resource representatives, they all refer to employees focused on achieving organizational goals (see also Robinson et al., 2004). Those employees whose engagement seems focused elsewhere are those considered challenges or sometimes called "problem" employees. These employees advance great energy toward a goal that is not in the organization's current vision and not where the organization wants employees to expend their efforts or enthusiasm. Such an employee, in the worst case, may have great focus and motivation toward fulfilling his or her own goals and, as a result, may even be considered as misusing organizational resources or as creating a performance issue. For example, in one of my consulting projects, a few employees whom the organization considered unengaged were actually, by all other definitions, engaged, just were not focused on the tasks of the job—they had found a side project of great interest to which they were completely absorbed. Engagement outside of work is great, but it is not what organizational leaders are primarily invested in promoting—their objective is to enhance engagement at work, and employee engagement is a construct that I agree includes focus in alignment with organizational goals.

My definition of engagement is similar to existing definitions through the incorporation of *affect and cognition*. Not every job requires the same amount of emotional or cognitive energy, nor does it require employees invest themselves affectively or cognitively to the same level at all times. Therefore, when employees are in a state of engagement, they employ and combine varying levels of their emotional and cognitive selves as they transform their work tasks and specific activities into meaningful accomplishment. In a recently published book *Purpose and Meaning in the Workplace* (Dik, Byrne, & Steger, 2013), Ashforth and Kreiner (2013) write about finding meaning in dirty work. Dirty work, they suggest, refers to occupations society views as socially unclean or physically ugly, such as funeral service, trash or maintenance service, or hospice care. They suggest workers in dirty occupations create a cognitive shift in what work means, enabling them to derive new meaning and to essentially transform their work into work that is meaningful and purposeful.

Not only do different jobs or occupations require different investments of one's cognitive and/or emotional self; people are also different in how they approach their work and interpret the world around them. Specifically, some people tend to be more logically focused, opting for a cognitive explanation for sense-making and decision making. Others are more driven to decisions and understanding through their emotions. This distinction has been referred to as thinking versus feeling, often ascribed to the Myers-Briggs Type Indicator (Myers & McCauley, 1985), but has been long debated, discussed, and supported in scholarly literature (see Ochsner, 2007; Zajonc, 2008). That means that some individuals prefer to view and respond to their job tasks from a more emotional base, where they allow their emotions to lead their decisions and they invest their affective selves through emotional expression into their work. Others prefer to view and respond to their job task from a thinking base, where they think through what the work means to them and they invest their cognitive selves through the thought they put into their work. Their preferences may vary by the task and are not exclusive of one another; some people balance their affective and cognitive investments relatively equally, as can best be determined by how they express themselves in their work.

My incorporation of the emotional and cognitive self into a definition of engagement is not completely different from other conceptualizations of engagement. For example, Schaufeli et al.'s (2002) definition incorporates enthusiasm and absorption. Similarly, Kahn (1990) refers to engagement as an investment of the self into the work role, an investment that includes drawing on one's self-employment: effort, involvement, flow, mindfulness, intrinsic motivation, and psychological presence; and self-expression: creativity, personal voice, emotional expression, authenticity, nondefensive communication, playfulness, and ethical behavior (see Kahn, 1990, p. 700). The distinction between self-employment and self-expression mirrors that between cognitive and affective investment, respectively. Self-employment seems to be drawn from our thinking selves, whereas self-expression could be argued as being drawn from our affective selves.

Finally, the synergistic mix of these aspects of oneself is directed toward a *transformation* of tasks or activity into accomplishment, which is meaningful or has significance to the individual. Classical motivation theorists proposed individuals have innate needs for work that is meaningful. For example, Alderfer (1972), Maslow (1968), and Rogers (1961) all developed theoretical models describing the inherent need of individuals to seek higher order values that translate into meaningfulness and purpose. In contrast, diminished accomplishment or lack of successful achievement at work is considered a component of job burnout (e.g., Maslach & Jackson, 1981). Thus, employees enter a state of engagement to fulfill their need for purposeful accomplishment, and they do so by transforming the meaning of their work through the full expression of themselves.

Kahn (1990) and Schaufeli et al. (2002) both incorporated antecedents (e.g., significance, challenge) and consequences (e.g., involvement, pride) into their definitions. Because I wanted a definition of engagement only such that when a respondent was asked, "What is engagement?" one could answer without also saying what it causes and/or what triggers or promotes it, I did not include the antecedents or the consequences of engagement into the unifying definition. The exclusion of antecedents and consequences of engagement into their own definitions is a distinguishing difference between the unifying definition and most others.

Is Engagement the Same for Every Organization?

While writing a few book chapters and a review paper of engagement, I read every existing document I could find on engagement, including published books not based on the academic or research literature. It appears that no one yet has explored whether the existing conceptualizations of engagement hold across all organizations—that is, most seem to run with an existing definition of engagement even though only one or two qualitative studies have been completed exploring what engagement really is. Additionally, it was not clear in the literature or books as to which definition was best or captured engagement at most organizations, because no one asked the question, "What does engagement mean and look like *here*?" Therefore, I explored these ideas in a couple of consulting projects that offered me the opportunity to conduct research in parallel, otherwise known as action research (Lewin, 1946, 1947).

In one of my consulting/action-research projects conducted in 2010, my team and I interviewed employees (32 one-on-one interviews and six focus groups of eight people each) from across a variety of jobs, departments, and locations of a medium-sized not-for-profit community health care system ($N = 4,985$ employees). The focus of the project was to understand what engagement is and what drives engagement for these employees. About two-thirds of the individuals we interviewed were identified by the organization as engaged, whereas the other third were considered as not engaged. We analyzed the content of the interviews and extracted several themes for how people described their own engagement and for what drove their engagement. In their own words, employees said being engaged meant experiencing work as invigorating and energizing, feeling that time moved faster and they got lost in time, feeling a self-imposed need to accomplish their tasks—to push themselves harder and faster, to take the initiative, to switch into a mode, to thrive, and to choose to be rather than be told to be engaged. In a follow-up survey of a representative sample of the same organization ($n = 517$, using proportionate sampling techniques), I confirmed this was indeed what engagement meant across the entire organization.

In another consulting/action-research project conducted in 2012, also directed toward identifying what engagement means to employees and what drives their engagement, my team and I again interviewed employees (46 one-on-one interviews and four focus groups of eight people each) from across a variety of locations, jobs, and departments of a small not-for-profit community mental health care provider ($N = 437$ employees). I also interviewed representatives of three partner organizations who each play a role in providing mental health services, in conjunction with the focal organization. For example, one partner organization makes referrals to this organization, another handles the medical and insurance claims, and another partner organization offers a supporting medical service. We transcribed all the interviews and conducted content analysis resulting in the extraction of several themes. Themes for what engagement meant included focusing on the work, getting a job done, caring about how what a person did helped the organization, energy, curiosity, and, as a manager, feeling of accomplishing the removal of roadblocks and giving that big perspective to give context and meaning to work. Again, these qualitative results were validated with quantitative results.

The interviewees' responses to the question, "Does engagement look the same in every organization?" and the quantitative data from just the two organizations noted earlier suggest that engagement may be similar across organizations. However, in the second organization, employees used a broader scope to define *job* than did those in the first, which affects how one defines and refers to what employee engagement is. Specifically, they defined *job* as "what my organization needs me to do," "what my team needs me to do," and "what I am hired to do." Not everyone in the organization defined *job* as incorporating all three emphases when referring to engagement. Thus, to some, engagement referred to being focused on and energized about just the tasks one is hired to perform, but not also toward what the team needs and/or what the organization needs (i.e., demonstrating an alignment with the organization's goals). In contrast, for others, engagement to them included it all; they described engagement as being fully committed to this all-encompassing expenditure of self towards all three aspects: tasks, team, and organizational needs. Thus, how *job* is defined may influence what engagement means across organizations.

The multiple conceptualizations of what it means to do one's job are similar to some degree to Saks's (2006) *job engagement* and *organization engagement*. Saks proposed employees reciprocate (following the tenets of social exchange theory; Blau, 1964) benefits and resources from the organization with job and organizational engagement. Saks argued employees occupy two roles: a work or job role and an organizational role or the role of a member of the organization. Therefore, employees can be engaged in more than one work role, resulting in two forms of engagement. Saks's delineation of engagement is akin to supervisory and organizational commitment (e.g., Cheng, Jiang, & Riley, 2003) or to perceived supervisory and organizational support (e.g., Eisenberger, Stinglhamber, Vandenberghe, Sucharski, & Rhoades, 2002; Kottke & Sharafinski, 1988), where the construct can be expressed across two foci or beneficiaries of the exchange. I did not find the two-foci model in the second organization; however, what is somewhat similar between my findings and Saks's idea of multiple expressions of engagement is that there could exist an overall concept of having multiple work expectations that can be incorporated within an umbrella of the focus of one's engagement. Thus, one's investment of self, one's transformation of work, and one's energy can be toward whatever *job* is defined to be, and how this is manifested apparently varies by organization.

These projects, in addition to others, led me to conclude that although both Kahn's (1990) and Schaufeli et al.'s (2002) definitions of engagement each contained many of the key components shared in these interviews and seemed to make up engagement (as did a few other not so popular definitions; Dvir, Eden, Avolio, & Shamir, 2002; Macgowan, 2000; Seijts & Crim, 2006; Vansteenkiste et al., 2007); neither alone was enough to provide a unifying conceptualization. Furthermore, both were missing the ideas of alignment with organizational goals, transformation of work, and accomplishment, which have all been described to some degree in the practice literature and also revealed themselves in my own qualitative work.

If we use my proposed unifying definition of engagement, it would appear the construct of employee engagement is the same from organization to organization. The scope of one's engagement varies from organization to organization, which by definition suggests how it manifests itself (or what results from engagement) varies to a degree as well. Because organizations differ and industries differ, what fosters the right culture to allow employees to choose to enter into a state of engagement naturally must also vary. My data from just the two projects described earlier support this assertion. The two organizations referred to previously differed significantly in what fostered or promoted engagement, a topic I discuss in Chapter 4, yet the essence of what employees experienced when engaged seemed similar.

What Does Employee Engagement Look Like In Organizations

Most descriptions of employee engagement capture how it manifests itself—what it looks like when seen by others. In organizations, employee engagement looks like high-quality/high-quantity job performance, discretionary effort, high energy, enthusiasm, commitment to the organizational mission, and expressions of passion, initiative, and collaboration. Engagement in organizations looks like employees loving their jobs. These employees are so into what they are doing that they forget to take their breaks and ignore the clock on the wall that says it is time to go home. They block everything out so they can focus on the task at hand. They ask what else they can do to help the situation improve or to relieve someone who is overwhelmed. They look for what is missing or out of place and fix it without being asked and without expecting to be rewarded or recognized. Descriptions of engaged employees include they deliver improved business performance (CIPD, 2009); they are aware of business issues, improve performance, go the extra mile, believe in the organization, and respect others (Robinson et al., 2004), and they have higher productivity, innovation, stay longer, have higher quality discretionary efforts, are energetic, enthusiastic, and solve more problems than disengaged employees (Scarlett, 2009).

Engaged employees transform nonmeaningful work into something meaningful. For example, the nurses we interviewed talked about performing

21

"grunt work" (e.g., "wiping poopie butts") as being required regularly—the job is not all glamorous. Instead of describing it as the hassles of the job, they referred to their job as promoting mental and physical health in all aspects of each patient's life. They transformed the negative aspects of the job (e.g., paperwork, sometimes cleaning up after a patient who cannot control him- or herself) into important parts of the mental and physical health recovery chain. Likewise, some of the case workers in the mental health organization talked about how important they were to providing the clients stability—they felt their job was to be the stable relationship in their client's life, rather than adding to the requirements, stressors, and constant changes that some mental health patients endure when trying to deal with their illness. Thus, they did not refer to work as the job of providing therapy, prescribing medicine, or tracking their patients; instead, they transformed their work from providing mental health care to offering the stability and support of a long-term relationship.

In organizations, employee engagement does look like a combination of constructs some researchers have spent considerable effort delineating from engagement (e.g., Demerouti, Bakker, de Jonge, Janssen, & Schaufeli, 2001; Hakanen, Bakker, & Schaufeli, 2006; Hallberg & Schaufeli, 2006; Rich et al., 2010; Richardsen, Burke, & Martinussen, 2006; Saks, 2006; Schaufeli, Taris, & Bakker, 2006). A strong work ethic can masquerade itself as high engagement. However, although engagement may result in outcomes that appear similar to engagement such as citizenship behavior, commitment, job involvement, and job satisfaction, what it is, what triggers it, and how it is defined as a state of motivation appear different.

Conclusion

The field of employee engagement is in its infancy, which means debate over how to define it is normal and to be expected. The notion of engagement started in practice and application in organizations, and researchers have since been making great strides in translating the intuitive ideas from industry into theoretical and empirical works of organizational and social sciences. At the present, we may be better at describing what we think engaged employees look like than we are at explicitly stating what it actually means to be engaged or what constructs make up engagement.

Chapter 3 focuses on what engagement is not, providing evidence for how it is similar and different from other constructs associated with engagement. Thus, this chapter and Chapter 3 should be considered together when understanding what we currently know about engagement.

Walk-Away Points

- Employee engagement refers to a state of motivation, wherein one is psychologically present (i.e., in the moment) and psychophysiologically aroused, is focused on and aligned with the goals of the job and organization, and channels his or her emotional and cognitive self to transform work into meaningful and purposeful accomplishment.
- Employee engagement appears to be quite similar across organizations; however, how it manifests itself and how it is fostered vary.
- You cannot see engagement, but you can infer from people's emotional expressions, their talking about their work, and their behavior on the job whether they are likely engaged.

3

WHAT MAKES ENGAGEMENT DIFFERENT FROM OTHER CONCEPTS?

Some researchers have referred to engagement as an attitude (e.g., Dalal, Baysinger, Brummel, & LeBreton, 2012; S. Fine, Horowitz, Weigler, & Basis, 2010; Newman & Harrison, 2008). An attitude is a tendency to evaluate a psychological object's attributes, typically resulting in value-laden labels such as pleasant–unpleasant, good–bad, or likeable–dislikable (Ajzen, 1991; Eagly & Chaiken, 1998, 2007). A specific attitude is generally part of an associative network, wherein beliefs, feelings, and thoughts are connected within and between attitudes; the activation of one attitude can spark an associated attitude (Eagly & Chaiken, 2007). Attitudes do not exist until an individual perceives an object, after which an initial evaluation occurs and leaves mental residue to be reactivated on a second encounter. The attitude is separate from its expression (Eagly & Chaiken, 2007). In contrast, employee engagement is a multidimensional construct comprising moment-to-moment psychophysiological arousal, absorption, focus, mindfulness or psychological presence, self-expression, self-employment, and intrinsic motivation (Kahn, 1990; Schaufeli, Salanova, González-Romá, & Bakker, 2002). When employees become engaged, they generate positive emotions about their work experience (Kahn, 1990).

Distinguishing whether engagement is or is not an attitude is both a theoretical and an empirical question. To understand a construct, it often helps to be clear on what the construct is and is not and to what it is related or not related; in other words, it helps to map out the construct's nomological network (Cronbach & Meehl, 1955). A nomological network is the pattern of relationships between the focal construct and other constructs, and information about how those constructs are or are not related to one another; this information can be in the form of theories or statistical data such as correlations (Cronbach & Meehl, 1955).

As a sequel to Chapter 2, which explains what engagement is, this chapter focuses on what engagement is *not* with the intent of distinguishing engagement from other potentially similar concepts (see also Schohat & Vigoda-Gadot, 2010, for another type of comparison to commitment, job involvement, and citizenship behavior). Constructs similar to employee engagement include job performance and organizational citizenship behavior, job involvement, job satisfaction, and organizational commitment (Newman & Harrison, 2008), yet evidence suggests that engagement is not the same as any of these concepts (see Hallberg & Schaufeli, 2006; Rich, LePine, & Crawford, 2010; Saks, 2006).

What Engagement Is Not

Job Performance and Organizational Citizenship Behavior

The study of job performance has a long history and large research domain; thus, the review here is focused explicitly on what makes job performance similar to or different from employee engagement, as opposed to a complete review of the job performance literature. Job performance is what people do on the job toward completing tasks assigned by the organization or tasks that contribute to achieving organizational goals— job performance is what an employee is actually hired to do (J. Campbell, McHenry, & Wise, 1990). Job performance may be considered most closely tied to people's behavior that contributes value to the organization (i.e., Motowidlo, 2003), their readiness to do the job (e.g., military personnel, police, or firefighters), or the result of on-the-job behavior (e.g., when the job is primarily cognitive such as analyst or strategist; Murphy, 1989). Another view is to consider job performance as a process or outcome, whereby process refers to the actions or behaviors taken to complete work tasks and outcome refers to the product or result of actions taken (Roe, 1999).

The job performance construct has been delineated into a number of dimensions or factors, with some common to most, if not all jobs, and other dimensions specifically aimed at certain types of jobs. For example, J. Campbell's (1990) model of job performance comprises eight dimensions and was derived from a study of U.S. army personnel. In contrast, Murphy's (1994) model of job performance comprises four dimensions and was derived from a study of U.S. navy personnel. Although both are based on military institutions, the models are quite different. For example, Campbell's model has eight different dimensions, whereas Murphy's model has only four. The eight levels of Campbell's model were intended to describe the top of the hierarchy of all jobs listed in the *Dictionary of Occupational Titles* (1991) and focus primarily on positive or productive job performance. In contrast, Murphy's model covers a large and diverse set of jobs, is meant to be both broad and general, and includes inconvenient job performance-reducing behaviors, as well as destructive counterproductive performance behaviors. Dimensions of the models include types of specific tasks employees perform or the technical aspects of the job (e.g., welding, typing, driving, surgery, communication), employees' management of themselves on the job (e.g., whether acting within safety guidelines or carelessly; emotion regulation), and how employees interact with others (e.g., interpersonally, through others).

Another classification system for the performance domain includes *task* versus *contextual* performance (Borman & Motowidlo, 1997). Task performance refers to behaviors considered part of the selection and performance management system that transforms raw materials into finished products of value to the organization (e.g., actual production, selling, teaching, banking). Contextual performance includes activities that are ignored within the selection system but facilitate the production of organizational goods, yet do not in and of themselves result in the final goods (e.g., planning, coordinating, social support). Contextual performance describes performance in terms of the support the expressed behaviors provide toward the functioning of the organization, more so than in terms of the type or the quality of behavior displayed (such as whether it is discretionary).

A similar classification to the task versus contextual performance is one that divides job performance into *in-role* performance and *extra-role* performance, when considered within the organizational citizenship behavior domain (e.g., Bateman & Organ, 1983; Katz, 1964; Motowidlo & van Scotter, 1994; O'Reilly & Chatman, 1986; Organ, 1988; Williams & Anderson, 1991). In-role job performance refers to prescribed behaviors such as completing assigned tasks and attending required events or meetings, as outlined in a formal job description (when that exists; not all jobs or organizations provide job descriptions). In-role job performance is the work expected of an employee within a given work role. In contrast, extra-role behavior is described as contributing to the effective functioning of the organization and may or may not be formally expected of employees or recognized within the reward system. Organizational citizenship behavior's definition has morphed over time from being "individual behavior that is discretionary, not directly or explicitly recognized by the formal reward system, and that in the aggregate promotes the effective functioning of the organization" (Organ, 1988, p. 4) to being synonymous with contextual performance (Organ, 1997); although many still use the in-role versus extra-role categorization (e.g., Salanova, Lorente, Chambel, & Martínez, 2011; Sosik, Juzbasich, & Chun, 2011; Tremblay, Cloutier, Simard, Chênevert, & Vandenberghe, 2010; Walumbwa, Morrison, & Christensen, 2012).

Perhaps the most defining characteristic of job and/or task performance and citizenship behaviors, distinguishing performance from employee engagement, is that performance/citizenship is about behaviors or the results of behaviors whereas engagement is about how one feels about or experiences the job and one's intent (or motivation) to invest oneself (emotionally, cognitively, and physically) in the job (Kahn, 1990; Saks, 2006; Schaufeli, Salinova, et al., 2002). Employee engagement is not a behavior, but rather it is a state of mind leading to behavior. In direct contrast to this supposition regarding engagement as a state and separate from performance is Macey and Schneider's (2008) proposal. They suggested engagement is a process whereby *state engagement* leads to *behavioral engagement*, which they define as the combination of extra-role performance and organizational citizenship behavior. However, empirical evidence along with criticism about behavioral engagement being sometimes considered engagement and sometimes not (depending on the situation and tasks), and giving a new label to an old concept (see Griffin, Parker, & Neal, 2008; Newman & Harrison, 2008), has led the current engagement scholarly conversation away from engagement incorporating or equating with performance.

Relationship to engagement. Initial empirical studies have demonstrated the distinctiveness of engagement from job performance, as it was defined earlier. For example, Rich and colleagues (2010) showed that job engagement, as assessed using their newly developed scale designed to measure Kahn's (1990) conceptualization of engagement, is distinct from task performance (supervisory rated using Williams & Anderson's, 1991, measure) and organizational citizenship behaviors (as assessed using K. Lee & Allen's, 2002, scale). Distinctiveness was demonstrated using confirmatory factor analysis. Results showed that job engagement was correlated with performance at .35 and with citizenship behavior at .35. In my own research, confirmatory factor analyses results show the uniqueness of employee engagement as assessed using Rich et al.'s (2010) measure, from performance assessed using Van Scotter, Motowidlo, and Cross's (2000) measure of contextual performance. The correlation in one of my studies was .40.

In studies not reporting confirmatory factor analyses results, correlations between engagement and job performance are consistent with those that do. For example, in their meta-analysis, Christian, Garza, and Slaughter (2011) demonstrated the uniqueness of engagement from task performance and contextual performance, with correlations of .36 and .38, respectively. Dalal and colleagues (2012) examined the relative weights contribution of various job attitudes including job satisfaction, job involvement, and organizational commitment, and engagement for explaining the variance in task performance. Relative weights analysis, or relative importance analysis, evaluates the proportional contribution of each predictor (taking correlations into consideration) to the overall variance explained by the regression model, thus providing a relative ordering of the importance of each predictor (Azen & Budescu, 2003; J. Johnson & LeBreton, 2004; LeBreton, Hargis, Griepentrog, Oswald, & Ployart, 2007). Dalal et al. (2012) found that aside from commitment, the constructs contributed relatively equal amounts of explained variance in performance. Specifically, job satisfaction explained 16%, engagement 15%, job involvement 11%, and organizational commitment explained 4% of the variance in task performance. Their results suggest these four constructs are not redundant in their contribution to task performance, indicating some distinctiveness. These authors reported a correlation of .23 between task performance and employee engagement. What is particularly valuable about Dalal et al.'s study is that it does not just report correlations between engagement and these other constructs questioned to be the same as engagement; their dominance analysis provides some evidence that each of these constructs contributes uniquely to understanding job performance. Last, Halbesleben, Wheeler, and Shanine (2013) recently found engagement, as assessed using Schaufeli et al.'s (2002) Utrecht Work Engagement Scale (UWES) short form (a 9-item measure), was correlated with Williams and Anderson's (1991) in-role performance measure at .21 to .26, and with Williams and Anderson's citizenship behaviors directed at the organization and individuals between .23 and .42, across three samples and both self- and other-rated performance behaviors.

Unrelated to demonstrating its uniqueness from job performance, researchers have shown that the performance–engagement relationship appears consistent across rater sources, such that engagement is similarly related to self-rated performance ($r = .28$), coworker-rated performance ($r = .27$), and supervisor-rated job performance ($r = .32$), as assessed using Williams and Anderson's (1991) task performance measure (Halbesleben & Wheeler, 2008). Thus, regardless of who provides the engagement rating within a study, the correlation between job performance and engagement tends to be relatively low (thus, the two constructs are perhaps not proximally related) and about the same.

In summary, research has demonstrated engagement's distinctiveness from job performance in its various forms including task and contextual or citizenship performance, and provided evidence the two constructs are positively related. Correlations between engagement and the various forms of performance behaviors tend to be low to moderate (see Table 3.1).

Table 3.1 Relationship Between Performance and Citizenship Behavior with Engagement

Study (alphabetical order)	Construct	Correlation with Engagement
Byrne, Peters, Rechlin, Smith, and Kedharnath (2013)	Contextual performance	.40
Christian, Garza, and Slaughter (2011)	Task performance Contextual performance	.36 .38
Dalal, Baysinger, Brummel, and LeBreton (2012)	Task performance	.23
Halbesleben and Wheeler (2008)	Self-rated in-role job performance	.28
	Coworker-rated in-role job performance	.27
	Supervisor-rated in-role job performance	.32
Halbesleben, Wheeler, and Shanine (2013)	In-role job performance Citizenship behavior	.21 to .26 .23 to .42
Rich, LePine, and Crawford (2010)	Job performance Citizenship behavior	.35 .35

Job Involvement

Job involvement refers to a stable cognitive judgment about the centrality of work to one's life and identity (Lawler & Hall, 1970) and is depicted in a process whereby success at goal accomplishment leads to greater identification at work (Kanungo, 1982; Rabinowitz & Hall, 1977). Originally defined as the "internalization of values about the goodness of work or the importance of work in the worth of the person" (Lodahl & Kejner, 1965, p. 24), it refers to the centrality of work in a person's life, the importance of work, and the connection to one's core self-image. Job involvement is the "degree to which one is cognitively preoccupied with, engaged in, and concerned with one's present job" (Paullay, Alliger, & Stone-Romero, 1994, p. 225), or "a cognitive or belief state of psychological identification" (Kanungo, 1982, p. 342). Furthermore, this cognitive identification depends on the personal needs of the individual and the potential of the job to meet those needs (Kanungo, 1982). Job involvement is essentially about how one sees oneself with regard to the job, expressed as a cognitive (only) judgment of whether the job can satisfy one's needs (Kanungo, 1982). According to a meta-analysis by S. Brown (1996), this conceptualization of job involvement appears to be the most used and the clearest.

Moreover, Rabinowitz and Hall (1977) suggest that job involvement, although relatively stable, increases with success on the job; hence, greater achievement leads to more job involvement. Finally, it has been suggested employees with high intrinsic motivation report high levels of job involvement (C. Chen & Chiu, 2009; Lambert, 1991). Hackman and Lawler (1971) similarly suggested job involvement leads to internal motivation.

Relationship to engagement. Employees must be motivated to have job involvement. Indeed, motivation and job involvement are correlated with one another ($r = .55$; S. Brown, 1996), but S. Brown suggests that "motivation is likely both an antecedent and consequence of job involvement" (1996, p. 238). Hallberg and Schaufeli (2006), as well as Rich and colleagues (2010), demonstrated by using confirmatory factor analyses that job involvement and employee engagement are distinct constructs, yet rather than serve as predictors for one another, they coexist. They reported correlations of .35 and .47 between job involvement and engagement, respectively. Using Schaufeli et al.'s (2002) UWES, Kühnel, Sonnentag, and Westman (2009) found correlations of .32 and .30 with job involvement, and Steele et al. (2012) reported a correlation of .54 using the same scale for engagement. Similarly, using a composite of Schaufeli et al.'s work engagement scale and May, Gilson, and Harter's (2004) engagement measure, Dalal et al. (2012) reported correlations of .57 between engagement and job involvement. Additionally, as previously noted, Dalal and colleagues conducted a relative weights analysis to determine the relative importance of several job attitudes on task performance. They reported that employee engagement explained more variance in task performance than did job involvement (15% compared to 11%, respectively), and even more in citizenship behaviors than did task performance (25% engagement versus 6% job involvement).

In sum, correlations between engagement and job involvement tend to be moderate (see Table 3.2).

Table 3.2 Relationship Between Job Involvement and Engagement

Study (alphabetical order)	Correlation of Job Involvement with Engagement
Dalal, Baysinger, Brummel, and LeBreton (2012)	.57
Hallberg and Schaufeli (2006)	.35
Kühnel, Sonnentag, and Westman (2009)	.30 and .32
Rich, LePine, and Crawford (2010)	.47
Steele, Rupayana, Mills, Smith, Wefald, and Downey (2012)	.54

Job Satisfaction

Like job performance, job satisfaction has a long and rich history of exploration in the organizational sciences; therefore, the review here is focused only on literature that sheds light on how job satisfaction is related to or different from employee engagement. Engaged employees are satisfied with their jobs, partly because they derive meaning and accomplishment from the work (Fairhurst & May, 2006; Fairlie, 2011; Guion & Landy, 1972; May et al., 2004), which leads to a positive evaluation. Although early views of job satisfaction were primarily focused on understanding performance (Hoppock, 1935; Organ, 1977; Roethlisberger & Dickson, 1939), the definition evolved into an overall positive emotional evaluation resulting from the appraisal of one's job (Brooke, Russell, & Price, 1988; Locke, 1976; Mowday, Steers, & Porter, 1979). Job satisfaction has been described as comprising multiple facets or dimensions, such as satisfaction with pay, coworkers, supervisor, and the work itself (Dunham, Smith, & Blackburn, 1977; Locke, Smith, Kendall, Hulin, & Miller, 1964). Another characterization of job satisfaction is as a multidimensional response to the job that includes cognitive, affective, and behavioral components (Hulin & Judge, 2003), giving it a conceptual link to employee engagement as defined by Kahn (1990). Considered an evaluation held by a single individual, as opposed to an attitude experienced or determined by a group (Locke, 1976), job satisfaction is distinguishable from performance and citizenship behaviors, although the constructs are related with correlations between .20 to .40 (Bateman & Organ, 1983; Dalal et al., 2012; Judge, Thoresen, Bono, & Patton, 2001; LePine, Erez, & Johnson, 2002; Organ & Ryan, 1995; Schleicher, Watt, & Greguras, 2004).

Relationship to engagement. A number of studies have included an examination of both employee engagement and job satisfaction, with several providing correlational data only as evidence of discriminant validity. These include Saks (2006), who showed a positive moderate correlation of .52. Saks assessed engagement using his own definition or conceptualization of engagement and a job engagement measure created in that same study. Providing similar results, Mauno, Kinnunen, Mäkikangas, and Nätti (2005) reported a positive moderate correlation of .50, where engagement in their study was assessed using Schaufeli et al.'s (2002) definition and measure (the UWES). Also without confirmatory evidence of uniqueness, Vecina, Chacón, Sueiro, and Barrón (2012) reported a correlation of .60 between engagement (measured with the UWES) and task satisfaction. Similarly, Christian et al. (2011) reported a moderate correlation between engagement and job satisfaction of .53. And likewise, Dalal et al. (2012) reported similar findings with the correlation between job satisfaction and engagement at .69.

Table 3.3 Relationship Between Job Satisfaction and Engagement

Study (alphabetical order)	Construct	Correlation with Engagement
Alarcon and Lyons (2011)	Job satisfaction	.56 to .73
Byrne, Peters, Rechlin, Smith, and Kedharnath (2013)	Job satisfaction	.52
Christian, Garza, and Slaughter (2011)	Job satisfaction	.53
Dalal, Baysinger, Brummel, and LeBreton (2012)	Job satisfaction	.69
Mauno, Kinnunen, Mäkikangas, and Nätti (2005)	Job satisfaction	.50
Saks (2006)	Job satisfaction	.52
Vecina, Chacón, Sueiro, and Barrón (2012)	Task satisfaction	.60

Other studies reporting similar correlations but providing additional discriminant validity evidence in the form of confirmatory factor analyses include Alarcon and Lyons (2011), who reported correlations of .56 to .73. They compared a factor model, wherein job satisfaction was subsumed under engagement, to a model in which engagement covaried with satisfaction (not subsumed under engagement). They found the model with engagement and satisfaction as separate parallel factors (i.e., satisfaction not subsumed under engagement) fit the data best. Last, in one of my own field studies (Byrne, Peters, et al., 2013), confirmatory factor analysis confirmed the distinctiveness of engagement (assessed using Rich et al.'s, 2010, measure) from job satisfaction assessed using Warr, Cook, and Wall's (1979) multidimensional measure; the correlation between the two measures was .52.

Thus, the correlations between job and task satisfaction, and engagement tend to be moderate to high (see Table 3.3).

Organizational Commitment

Organizational commitment is considered an affective attachment to, an identification with, and an involvement in a particular organization (Mowday et al., 1979). Often referred to as simply affective commitment or just commitment, it is typically characterized by the internalization of the organization's goals and values and a strong desire to remain a member of the organization, which result in a willingness to exert extensive energy on behalf of the organization. D. Harrison, Newman, and Roth (2006) suggest that organizational commitment is an attitude (an evaluation or appraisal) with a specific target (e.g., supervisor, organization) but that it is not tied to a specific action. Commitment has also been defined as an attitudinal reaction to the work environment and leadership (Ashforth & Mael, 1989). People can commit or attach to different foci (T. Becker, 1992), such as their team, supervisor, organization, career (e.g., Okurame, 2012), or work in general, and various studies show that the foci of commitment matter (e.g., Chan, Snape, & Redman, 2011; Morin et al., 2011; Tsoumbris & Xenikou, 2010; Vandenberghe, Bentein, & Stinglhamber, 2004; Veurink & Fischer, 2011).

Others, however, have suggested that commitment is more than just an attitude but rather that it is a psychological state with behavioral linkages (Meyer & Allen, 1991). This perspective further suggests commitment has three components: affective, continuance, and normative (N. Allen & Meyer, 1990; Meyer & Allen, 1991). *Affective commitment* refers to an attachment to a particular focus (usually the organization), where the emphasis is on feeling a sense of membership and desire to remain a member. This is the form of commitment most studies consider when referring to organizational commitment or just commitment in general. Researchers are not always clear about stating "affective" commitment; when missing, it is just assumed that the type of commitment is affective rather than one of the other types. Organizational affective commitment is sometimes confused with organizational identification, possibly due to the overlap in definitions and the constructs' moderate to high correlations with each other ($r = .55$ to .78 in Harris & Cameron, 2005; $r = .67$ in Van Knippenberg & Sleebos, 2006). Organizational identification refers to a cognitive categorization process whereby employees develop a sense of self-concept or oneness with the organization. Identification relies on social identity theory (Tajfel, 1978; Tajfel & Turner, 1979), which states people categorize themselves into social groups based on their similarity to that group, and some define themselves by the characteristics of the group. Perhaps the most definitive explanation of how commitment and identification differ is commitment is considered an affective reaction and is exchanged as part of the work contract, whereas identification is about one's self-concept and depends on the saliency of the leader and one's interactions (N. Allen & Meyer, 1990; van Knippenberg & Sleebos, 2006). Although conceptually and empirically closely related, the two have been supported as being distinct (e.g., Mael & Tetrick, 1992). Commitment has also been likened to job satisfaction, but has similarly shown to be distinct (Brooke et al., 1988; Mowday et al., 1979).

Continuance commitment is about staying with the organization out of a recognition the cost of leaving is not in one's favor. Thus, the perceived cost of staying versus leaving (i.e., cost-benefit ratio) is what drives the desire to remain a member of the organization. This formative calculation is attributed to Becker's (1960) side-bets theory, which essentially says a person makes a series of judgments that ultimately determine a final decision, which is either consistent with or contradictory to other decisions and actions this person takes. A brief scenario from Becker makes the theory more clear. A few months after Rodriguez accepts a job offer he believed advanced his career, he is offered another that is truly far superior to the one he just accepted. Although very tempted to take the new offer, he realizes that, on the side, he bet his reputation for trustworthiness and integrity on not moving again for a respectable amount of time (typical timeframe society expects is about 6 months to 1 year, depending on the industry), and therefore, he is compelled to turn down the lucrative and superior job. In Rodriguez's case, the side bet is implied—general norms of society are when you take a job, you stay with it for a preliminary period. Likewise, some organizations have similar norms about accepting various positions (e.g., when you take an overseas assignment), you are expected to stay in that role for a few years to recoup the costs (e.g., shipping you overseas, job and culture ramp-up). Similarly, the "golden handcuff" rule is that by staying with the organization for X number of years, you will get a lucrative (hence, the word *golden*) financial package (e.g., stock, bonuses based on tenure, money paid into retirement accounts) that continues to grow each year you remain. However, if you leave the organization before X number of years are up, you lose the amazing package—thus, these golden handcuffs keep you in place because they are too good to let go of, and the side bet is that if you leave, you release your golden handcuffs. Thus, the side bet or trade-off might be made for you by the norms of the situation. Side bets are not necessarily financial; they can include other valuable intangibles such as seniority (along with its associated power), social networks (all your friends and power within the network), comfort with familiarity, or other intangible benefits (e.g., status). Important in Becker's theory is the recognition of the cost of discontinuing the path one has already pursued, because the theory is really about consistency of actions. Without this recognition, Becker suggests there is no commitment.

Normative commitment is the third component as identified by Meyer and Allen (1991). This form of commitment is based on personal norms and refers to a sense of obligation to remain a member of the organization. For example, Rodriguez may refuse the superior job offer not because he feels compelled by the loss of trustworthiness, but because he feels it is morally wrong to take a job and then immediately leave for another one. Normative commitment may be more evident in religiously oriented organizations or nonprofit organizations, for example, in which people join and stay because they feel obligated to those whom the organization provides services (such as a mental health facility or food bank), or perhaps they were helped by the organization at one time and they feel they need to reciprocate the support they were given. Thus, normative commitment is more about personal norms, values, and sense of obligation, than about society or external ties such as with continuance commitment (Meyer & Allen, 1991).

Meyer, Gagné, and Parfyonova (2010) proposed engagement and the three-component model of commitment (affective, normative, continuance) can be integrated using self-determination theory (Deci & Ryan, 1985) to create a continuum from disengagement (uncommitted, amotivation—absence of goal-directed activity), to contingent engagement (continuance and/or normative commitment, extrinsic motivation), to full engagement (affective and/or normative commitment, intrinsic motivation). They explain their framework by describing how the disengaged–contingent – fully engaged worker appears/behaves in terms of commitment levels. For example, the authors suggest a fully engaged worker will likely have strong affective commitment and be intrinsically motivated. The integrated framework implies commitment and engagement are distinct constructs but related and that commitment can be used to describe what is characteristic of the engagement continuum.

Relationship to engagement.   Only a handful of studies have examined the relationship between engagement and organizational commitment, but of those that have, engagement is shown as a predictor of commitment (i.e., Demerouti, Bakker, de Jonge, Janssen, & Schaufeli, 2001; Hallberg & Schaufeli, 2006; Hakanen, Schaufeli, & Ahola, 2008; Richardsen, Burke, & Martinussen, 2006; Saks, 2006). Although studies rarely indicate which form of commitment is studied, researchers are typically referring to affective commitment. When other forms of commitment are studied, they are usually explicitly called out (i.e., normative).

A number of studies using Schaufeli et al.'s (2002) measure of engagement and definition support an association between organizational commitment; however, some studies assessed only vigor ($r = .42$) and dedication ($r = .47$; Hakanen, Bakker, & Schaufeli, 2006). Also using only the vigor and dedication scales of the UWES, Hakanen, Perhoniemi, and Topinen-Tanner (2008) found engagement at Time 1 was related to commitment 3 years later, at Time 2 ($\beta = .23$). Consistent with Hakanen et al. (2006), Richardsen, Burke, and Martinussen (2006) found organizational commitment was positively correlated with employee engagement ($r = .55$), not unlike Hallberg and Schaufeli's (2006) results of .46, where employee engagement was again assessed using the UWES, but using all three dimensions (vigor, dedication, and absorption). Likewise, a number of other studies using the full UWES reported correlations of .62, .61, .57, and .66, respectively (Brunetto, Teo, Shacklock, & Farr-Wharton, 2012; De Beer, Rothman, & Pienaar, 2012; Kanste, 2011; Vecina et al., 2012). Using vigor, dedication, and absorption as separate scales, Demerouti and colleagues (2001) reported correlations of .49, .59, and .45, respectively. I specifically point out the studies using Schaufeli et al.'s (2002) UWES because researchers have criticized the overlap of items on the engagement scale with commitment, specifically the dedication scale (see Newman & Harrison, 2008). This overlap suggests that it is possible the correlations between commitment and engagement as assessed using the UWES may be partially inflated due to construct contamination.

Using his own conceptualizations of engagement, Saks (2006) found correlations of .53 and .69 between organizational commitment and job engagement and organization engagement, respectively. Using a composite measure for engagement as noted previously, Dalal et al. (2012) reported similar results with engagement and organizational commitment correlating at .60. Last, Christian et al. (2011) reported a moderate correlation between engagement and organizational commitment ($r = .59$) in their meta-analysis.

Thus, for the most part, correlations between engagement and commitment tend to be moderate to high (see Table 3.4).

Intrinsic Motivation

Intrinsic motivation refers to a drive or push that is instigated and propelled by interest and spontaneous enjoyment with and from an activity (Porter & Lawler, 1968). It is self-fulfilling in that the interest and satisfaction with the activity is rewarding, encouraging more of the same activity. Intrinsic motivation is considered a biological need for moderate arousal (Berlyne, 1966), an innate need to demonstrate mastery and competence (e.g., White, 1959), a need for personal control and self-determination (e.g., Deci, 1975), or a state wherein one does an activity for its own sake (Rheinberg, 2008). Intrinsic motivation has also been characterized as a drive that has no specific goal, achieves optimal arousal and competence, and is enjoyable (see Thierry, 1990). Very simply, intrinsic motivation refers to motivation derived from internal rewards or satisfaction, and is typically contrasted with extrinsic motivation, which is derived from an external reward or reinforcement (Thierry, 1990). A contrast of intrinsic versus extrinsic motivation was recently demonstrated using functional magnetic resonance imaging (fMRI). W. Lee, Reeve, Xue, and Xiong (2012) showed intrinsically motivated actions are determined by a portion of the brain (the insular cortex) that is related to feelings or emotions, in particular the satisfaction of needs. In contrast, extrinsically motivated or incentive-based actions caused excitation in the right posterior cingulate cortex, which is associated with value assessment and processing learned reinforcements. The implications of Lee and colleagues' findings are that intrinsic motivation has a neurological basis that is not learned or tied to external incentives, which has further implications as to whether organizational interventions will actually work to influence motivation, particularly engagement.

What makes engagement different from intrinsic motivation is engagement is goal directed, is consistent with the organization's goals, and is about one's in the work role. It is not just about being driven to continue doing something purely out of enjoyment and the reinforced enjoyment

Table 3.4 Relationship Between Organizational Commitment and Engagement

Study (alphabetical order)	Correlation of Organizational Commitment with Engagement
Brunetto, Teo, Shacklock, and Farr-Wharton (2012)	.62
Byrne, Peters, and Drake (2014), Sample 2	.51 (using Rich et al.'s 2010 scale) .66 (using UWES) .40 (using Saks' 2006 org engagement scale) .75 (using Saks' 2006 job engagement scale)
Byrne, Peters, Smith, and Nowacki and Drake (2014), Sample 3	.37 (using Rich et al.'s 2010 scale) .40 (using UWES) .42 (using Saks' 2006 org engagement scale) .30 (using Saks' 2006 job engagement scale)
Christian, Garza, and Slaughter (2011)	.59
Dalal, Baysinger, Brummel, and LeBreton (2012)	.60
De Beer, Rothman, and Pienaar (2012)	.61
Demerouti, Bakker, Janssen, De Jong, and Schaufeli (2001)	.49: vigor .59: dedication .45: absorption
Hakanen, Bakker, and Schaufeli (2006)	.42: vigor .47: dedication
Hakanen, Schaufeli, and Ahola (2008)	.23 (vigor & dedication)
Hallberg and Schaufeli (2006)	.46
Kanste (2011)	.57
Richardsen, Burke, and Martinussen (2006)	.55
Saks (2006)	.53: job engagement .69: organizational commitment
Vecina, Chacón, Sueiro, and Barrón (2012)	.66

to continue. Employee engagement is about being driven across multiple platforms of the self toward goal achievement, and one just happens to be intrinsically rewarded doing so. Thus, engagement subsumes intrinsic motivation. Engagement refers to employees making "choices about how much of their real selves they would bring into and use to inform their role performances" (Kahn & Fellows, 2013, p. 105).

Relationship to engagement. Rich et al.'s (2010) study currently appears to be one of the only available that examines the distinctiveness of employee engagement from intrinsic motivation. Other available studies focus on school engagement, which, in general, refers to students' involvement in the learning process; however, this form of engagement also suffers from having multiple unrelated definitions. Rich et al.'s confirmatory factor analyses and structural equation modeling results show intrinsic motivation and engagement (using Kahn's, 1990, definition) are only low to moderately correlated ($r = .35$), and modeled as parallel constructs (as opposed to one predicting the other). When modeled as predictors of task performance, only engagement significantly related to task performance and organizational citizenship behavior; intrinsic motivation was not related to either.

Flow

Csikszentmihalyi and Rathunde (1993) described flow as "the subjective state that people report when they are completely involved in something to the point of forgetting time, fatigue, and everything else but the activity itself" (p. 59). When one experiences flow, all attention is directed to the activity such that distractions or other random thoughts are ignored (Csikszentmihalyi & Kleiber, 1991). Flow propels action for the sake of enjoyment and the reward of the action, involves little or no conscious effort, includes an element of loss of self-consciousness, and can occur with any activity (Csikszentmihalyi, 1997; Csikszentmihalyi & Rathunde, 1993). However, it rarely occurs in everyday life (Csikszentmihalyi & Rathunde, 1993). Thus, like engagement, flow subsumes intrinsic motivation but is bigger than just intrinsic motivation alone.

Although employee engagement shares some conceptual space with flow, it is not the same as flow. The state of optimal cognitive processing, which is characteristic of engagement, resembles flow (Csikszentmihalyi, 1996); however, engagement is different from flow in that employees may be in an engaged state and perceive the activity as worth doing because it creates meaning and moves them closer to goal attainment, as opposed to doing the job or task for its own sake as with flow (Nakamura & Csikszentmihalyi, 2002). Also, unlike flow, there is no precondition of possessing a skill to become engaged. Flow requires "a balance between perceived challenges and perceived skills" (Csikszenthmihalyi, Abuhamdeh, & Nakamura, 2005, p. 601). People who are learning, but have not yet acquired a new skill, can enter a state of engagement.

Relationship to engagement. Burke (2010) reported a positive relationship between measures of engagement and flow, however, the article provides no data—thus, no statistical information can be confirmed or relayed here. To date, no other published research could be found examining relationships between employee engagement (or between job or work engagement) with flow.

Happiness

During a recent visit to Saratov, Russia (on the Volga River, not far from the Kazakhstan and Ukraine borders) I asked what employee engagement is. My hosts had never heard of the concept, but in the spirit of trying to be helpful, they suggested that perhaps it was the same as happiness. Engaged employees may display happiness at various times during work; however, engagement and happiness are different constructs. First, happiness is considered an affective construct without a cognitive component (A. Campbell, 1976). That is, happiness is experienced without first going through an intellectual process of evaluating the current state to either the past or an ideal state, like one does forming a job attitude (e.g., job satisfaction; A. Campbell, 1976). Happiness is defined as a brief and intense emotional reaction to a specific event (Clore, Schwarz, & Conway, 1994; Ekman, 1992; Russell, 1991)—a response to a trigger such as, for example, success (Fredrickson, 2001; Isen, 2000). Discrete emotions (emotions are distinct and specific) like happiness can affect one's judgment, behavior, or experience (e.g., Frijda, 1987; Lench, Flores, & Bench, 2011; Lerner & Keltner, 2000). In this way, happiness may be part of the experience of becoming engaged but is not itself the state of employee engagement. Unique to engagement is the alignment with corporate objectives and the simultaneous emotional, cognitive, and physical investment of oneself into the work role.

Relationship to engagement. There are currently no reported empirical studies examining the relationship between employee engagement and happiness, although a couple popular press publications hypothesize that the two are indeed positively related (e.g., Rampersad, 2006; Vozar, 2012).

So What Does Engagement Give Us Beyond Existing Constructs?

The preceding review can be summarized in the following way: Job performance is about behaviors directed toward fulfilling or completing a specific job task; job involvement is about how central those behaviors are to one's identity at work; job satisfaction is the positive emotional evaluation one makes about one's job; and organizational commitment is the emotional attachment one has with one's employing organization. None of these concepts embraces or conveys the investment of oneself emotionally, cognitively, or physically into one's work performance, regardless of its form.

The current definitions of engagement are insufficient at capturing what employers or consultants come to understand and refer to as engagement. That is, the currently published definitions offered by Schaufeli et al. (2002), Kahn (1990), Saks (2006), or Macey and Schneider (2008), to name a few, fail to incorporate the *zest* of engagement. They fail to capture employees' transforming their work tasks into meaningful, goal-directed, and purposeful accomplishment. For the engaged employees, work becomes something entirely different from being just a set of tasks, a job description, or a series of projects.

Employees' Reflections

In a recent engagement consulting project, I interviewed employees to understand what they think of their work, what excites or bores them, and, in general, why they come to work. The intent was to extract from their qualitative response to the question, What is engagement to them. One interview in particular stands out, although it was not the only one in which the following type of answer was shared. I interviewed a hospital janitor, who for all intents and purposes could be considered one of the lowest paid employees in the hospital. Here is how he described what he does:

> *My job is to maintain a clean and sterile environment, free of any source of bacteria or smell, so that everyone there can work in a healthy and infectious-free environment. It's critical that I do my job well because infection is a big problem at hospitals—it's well known—people come into a hospital to get better but the longer they stay, the greater their chance of getting some other illness. I take care of ensuring a healthy disease free work environment by taking away the stuff that breeds bacteria and just makes the place look unkept. I make it look clean and that makes people feel better.*

He went on to say more, but what this response conveyed to me is instead of just telling me "I take out the trash," the employee described a mental transformation of his work into something purposeful, goal directed, and meaningful than the simple task of trash removal. I interviewed other employees in the same unit, and a few described their work in this manner. Many simply gave me their task list, with a few moments of engagement sprinkled in here and there.

Can we achieve this transformation with job involvement, job satisfaction, commitment, or job performance? It seems highly unlikely given the conceptual definition of each construct and the empirical evidence supporting their nomological networks.

For some, *job crafting* (Wrzesniewski & Dutton, 2001) may come to mind after reading this example of employees' transforming work tasks into meaningful accomplishment. Job crafting refers to a process by which employees design or craft their jobs by shaping the tasks and social interactions comprising their work. Wrzesniewski and Dutton define job crafting as an action wherein "the physical and cognitive changes individuals make in the task or relational boundaries of their work" (2010, p. 179) alters employees' work identities and meanings (i.e., understanding of the purpose of work). Through job crafting, employees can change the meaningfulness or perceived significance of work (Berg, Dutton, & Wrzesniewski, 2013). The essential action of job crafting is changing one's frame or perspective of the purpose of work and/or how one interacts with others to do the work. Job crafting is complementary to job redesign—it offers a way in which employees themselves can create work that is more satisfying and fulfills their needs for positive self-image and connection with others (Wrzesniewski & Dutton, 2001). Recent research on job crafting suggests employees who job craft to modify their job resources (e.g., increase social support by interacting more with coworkers socially, restructure job tasks to increase autonomy, variety, and opportunities for development), report higher ratings of employee engagement (Tims, Bakker, & Derks, 2013). Bakker (2010) proposes job crafting is an action that engaged employees may take to sustain their engagement.

WHAT DOES ENGAGEMENT LOOK LIKE THAT MAKES IT UNIQUE?

Johan has been in his job for a while; thus, he knows it really well. Johan lives in the small community where the organization he works for is the biggest game in town. His family has worked there, and most of his friends currently work there. Thus, you could say that work is very central to Johan's life. For the most part, Johan is very satisfied with his job; his pay is OK, especially compared to his cousin's. He has decent benefits that provide for his family, and he knew when getting into the job what was expected of him. When you see Johan, he is usually happy. He has fun at work, laughing with his friends and cousins. He does, at times, become frustrated with some of the problems that pop up in his job, but he does not worry for long because he tells management about them so they can be fixed. Johan is considered a good performer because he knows the job well and he is conscientious. Johan tends to work at a steady pace and though you would say he is not tired, he is not bouncing with energy. He goes out of his way to help others, but only if he thinks it will not take much time. Johan is very committed to his job. He cannot imagine where else he would work because there are few options available in his small town. He also feels a sense of obligation to the organization; after all, his entire family has worked there, and it is a big part of the community and part of his life now.

What Johan is missing is a sense of meaningfulness and purpose in his work. If you ask Johan whether he gets absorbed in his work, lost in time, or feels a sense of passion about what he is doing and how it makes a contribution to the organization, Johan would not know what you are talking about. Johan's job is what it is, and he does not see that it could be anything else. He does not think to go beyond the actual tasks of the job, not so much in helping others but in terms of improving the quality, making the work more efficient, or combining his job with another job that makes logical sense and would save the organization money. Johan does not see that as his role, and he does not think about it in terms of making it his role. Would you say that Johan is a good worker? Yes, but you could also say that Johan is easily distracted by the antics of his friends, that his mind tends to wander a bit while is working on his tasks, and that he does not seem very excited about the work he is doing. Johan is not engaged.

In contrast, Johan's cousin Bob has the same fun that Johan has, but when he is at work he really focuses on his job. He seems enthusiastic about what he is doing and he asks questions about how to improve the quality of the product. He has sometimes made suggestions about how the company can combine jobs to make the work more efficient and increase sales. When Bob runs into a problem at work, he sticks with it and tries to solve it on his own before asking for help. Bob offers to help others to make sure that the job gets done, even if it means he has to rethink how he is going to get his own work done. At times it seems almost as though Bob is slowing work production because he is focused so much on solving a process problem, but the end result is that the new process saves time in the long run. So management is generally pretty flexible about letting Bob work out some of the problems on his own. In general, Bob is described as energetic, bouncing from project to project, and ready to go when the next task is thrust on the team. Both Bob and

Johan are good performers for the organization. The biggest difference between the two is that Bob demonstrates the characteristics of engagement. He really enjoys the role he has in the organization, and he expands the role on his own so that he can express his enthusiasm, his creative problem-solving skills, and his focus on the job. His energy creates excitement around him, and he seems to get excited by his own energy.

Conclusion

Although hard to articulate in simple terms what employee engagement is, engagement contributes to organizational behavior beyond current job attitudes and job performance, and seems more than just a static concept. Perhaps Macey and Schneider (2008) are on to something when they refer to engagement as a process as opposed to just a single trait, state, or outcome. Researchers may not agree on what exactly goes into the process (see Dalal, Brummel, Wee, & Thomas, 2008; Griffin et al., 2008; Hirschfeld & Thomas, 2008), but engagement represents some kind of transformation, production of energy, and synergistic force that creates motion in a particular direction that is aligned with the organization's goals and this is different from current constructs studied in organizational sciences.

This chapter essentially provides a review of the existing literature on how engagement is related to, yet different from existing constructs in the behavioral and organizational sciences. So how do we effectively use this information? First, it helps to know in what way and by how much engagement is related to constructs that are, for the most part, currently understood. It gives some perspective as to how engagement fits in and yet clarifies engagement is different. Second, by taking a broad, higher level perspective to understand what all this information tells us about engagement, we might conclude that engagement is "more than the sum of its parts." That is, engagement seems to include within in it some part or form of existing job constructs such as intrinsic motivation and flow, but is more than just the sum of these two constructs. Clearly, engagement shares conceptual space with existing job attitudes and is related to existing job behaviors. This may explain why both Kahn (1990) and Schaufeli et al. (2002) used so many descriptors to convey each dimension of engagement and that dimensions embracing emotions, cognition, and physiology were all necessary. Third, what this review also suggests, however, is that there is space within the engagement domain that is *not* shared by existing job attitudes and behaviors; there are still parts of engagement that have yet to be identified and that potentially explain why and how engagement is different from other concepts studied thus far. For example, engagement includes a dynamic component (a moving part), some construct yet to be named, that captures the mental processing/transformation aspect of engagement.

Walk-Away Points

- Employee engagement is a different construct than job performance and citizenship behaviors, happiness in the job, intrinsic motivation, job involvement, job satisfaction, organizational commitment, and flow. It not only shares conceptual space but also has unique space not shared with existing constructs.
- Employee engagement contributes significant added variance above and beyond a number of these different constructs in predicting outcomes such as job performance, job satisfaction, or customer service satisfaction.
- Engagement incorporates the idea of employees transforming their work into something meaningful and purposeful.

Part II

SECURING AN ENGAGED WORKFORCE

4

HOW DO WE GET EMPLOYEE ENGAGEMENT?

In the previous chapters, I explored what employee engagement is and is not, and what makes it unique from other valuable organizational and job constructs (e.g., performance, job satisfaction). The next question that follows is, What is known about how to get employees engaged. That is, how do we foster or drive employee engagement?

There is no standard, off-the-shelf approach because organizations are not all the same, industries vary, and people vary. Following is a review of research- and practice-driven approaches hypothesized or shown to relate to engagement, using either Kahn's (1990) or Schaufeli, Salanova, et al.'s (2002) definitions and models of engagement. The review that follows makes note when engagement is referred to as commitment or citizenship behaviors, or when no definition has been used. Very few, if any, evaluation studies in practice or experimental/causal-related research studies have been conducted on drivers of engagement. Most consider a driver, if they have used regression analysis or structural equation modeling, equivalent to a predictor/instigator of engagement.

Research-Based Approaches to Getting More Engagement

Theories of and Approaches to Leadership

Full range leadership. Popular press and consulting web sites assert leaders are responsible for employee engagement. Research has identified transformational leadership, in particular, as a potential focus of career and leadership development programs for fostering engagement. Using Burns's (1978) original classification of transactional versus transformational leadership, Bass (1985) advanced development on the constructs by specifying in greater detail the styles and focus of each leadership style. Transactional leaders recognize the needs of their followers alongside their own needs and convey to the followers what they need to do to meet both sets of needs. Transactional leaders do so by using contingent rewards and management by exception. Transformational leaders, in contrast, recognize both sets of needs, but instead of telling followers what to do, they arouse higher needs, activating the follower to achieve more on his or her own.

Extending Bass's work, Avolio (1999) introduced the full range model of leadership, which represents both transformational and transactional styles, but also nontransactional leadership. According to Avolio, transactions form the foundation upon which transformational leadership adds. To appreciate the full range model, both the individual and the situation must be taken into consideration, thus building on earlier contingency (i.e., leadership style depends on what the situation requires) and charismatic leadership theories. The full range model, therefore, considers all forms of leadership. Furthermore, Avolio specified four principles core to full range leadership, incorporated within the Full Range Leadership Development program. These four include (a) good leaders balance their vulnerabilities by embracing and confronting them, as opposed to avoiding or denying them; (b) relationships between leaders and followers are based on commitment and not compliance; (c) leaders with whom followers can identify and see as vulnerable are those followers will trust the most; and (d) good leaders have a clear vision of all perspectives or sides of the issue and manage those perspectives and the situation effectively. There is no empirical evidence as of yet that the full range model of leadership positively relates to employee engagement.

Transformational leadership. Transformational leaders provide an inspiring vision, aligning their followers' goals with those of the organization. They transform the workplace norms and motivate employees to achieve high levels of performance to fulfill the inspiring vision. To achieve these higher motivational levels in followers, transformational leaders must possess or display four different competencies or factors: charismatic leadership (later called individualized influence), inspirational motivation, individualized consideration, and intellectual stimulation (Burns, 1978). Individualized influence refers to the leader being a role model by displaying strong ethical principles and supporting group benefits over individual gains. Inspirational motivation refers to the leader's ability to articulate effectively and clearly with an excitement that inspires employees to achieve. Individualized consideration refers to the leader treating each employee as an individual, appreciating him or her, and recognizing his or her unique needs. Last, transformational leaders provide intellectual stimulation to encourage employees to be creative and challenge their own thinking.

Research in engagement and leadership shows transformational leadership is positively related to engagement (Aryee, Walumbwa, Zhou, & Hartnell, 2012). If one assumes employees become engaged under a transformational leader, increasing transformational leadership behaviors is the logical intervention approach. In an effort to determine to what degree an organization can increase transformational leader characteristics— is transformational leadership trainable—W. Brown and May (2010) studied 660 employees at a manufacturing unit in a large international technology firm. Their study included two parts: (1) initial baseline assessment designed to evaluate relationships between leadership behaviors (specifically transformational and transactional) and productivity and organizational outcomes, and (2) a yearlong leadership development program designed to increase transformational leadership levels among supervisors and management. Assessments were made after training to determine success in the form of improved productivity and organizational outcomes.

The intervention itself involved several steps. First, management, including the top management levels, shared the results of their initial baseline assessments regarding their management style (essentially scores on the Multifactor Leadership Questionnaire [MLQ; Bass & Avolio, 1990] and on outcomes such as follower job satisfaction and supervisor satisfaction). The purpose of sharing survey results was to increase vulnerability of the managers, encourage transparency, make a formal and public commitment to change in their own style and in the culture, and take immediate personal ownership for changes by starting with the self (demonstrating commitment and accountability). Second, managers who were not on board with the changes or willing to participate in personal leadership improvement were offered opportunities to make a "dignified lateral transfer" (Bass & Avolio, 1990, p. 528) or take a nonmanagerial position without penalty. The third step involved two days of training designed according to Avolio and Bass (1994) and Bass (1998). Goal-setting strategies were employed, and public commitment to practicing the new skills was encouraged. The fourth step lasted for 1 year, in which reminders were sent regarding personal action plans, scheduled management meetings to discuss behavioral changes and progress to date, and personal follow-up interviews with consultants hired to facilitate the overall program. The evaluation survey was offered 11.5 months later and results showed significant changes on productivity and organizational outcomes. The authors concluded that training for contingent reward and transformational leadership behaviors is doable and that it does result in positive changes within the organization.

Although their study is not about engagement per se, it does provide empirical evidence that leadership development programs designed to increase transformational leadership behaviors can be done and positive organizational outcomes result. Other research supports this assertion. For example, Parry and Sinha (2005) examined the effectiveness of Full Range Leadership Development (see Avolio, 2011; Sosik & Jung, 2010), a leadership development program based on the work of Avolio and Bass

(1991) and the full range theory of leadership (Bass, 1985). In a recent study examining the effectiveness of training for transformational leadership, Parry and Sinha conducted pre-intervention 360-degree assessment and post-intervention (3 months later) 360-degree assessments of the frequency with which participants displayed transformational leadership behaviors. The authors found all transformational leadership behaviors were displayed more frequently after training than before. They also identified that the training program was equally effective in public and private organizations, indicating there is nothing specific about the program that benefits only one sector of industry and not another. Finally, they examined whether coaching could increase the effectiveness of the training program—no significant effects were found. In other words, coaching did not accelerate or enhance the effectiveness of the training program.

Some researchers have recently looked at transformational leadership and engagement. Vincent-Höper, Muser, and Janneck (2012) examined gender differences in the effects of transformational leadership on perceived career satisfaction and engagement. They found a positive relationship between transformational leadership and engagement, and women reported higher correlations than did men.

Empowering leadership. Similar to transformational leadership, empowering leadership (i.e., leadership aimed at encouraging employees to lead and manage themselves: Conger & Kanungo, 1988) has also been empirically related to engagement (positive correlations) and may be considered another avenue for leadership development designed to enhance engagement in the workplace (Tuckey, Dollard, & Bakker, 2012). Tuckey et al. (2012) speculate that empowering leaders "directly inspired work engagement in followers" (p. 22); however, their study is correlational (a single-instance survey), and thus, no casual inferences such as these can be made. It may be empowering leaders make a difference; however, it may also be that engaged employees bring out empowerment in leaders because the employees are so engaged.

Emotional intelligence. Another strategy to increasing levels of engagement in employees may be to increase leader awareness of their effects on followers by raising their emotional intelligence. Initial research supports a positive relationship between leaders with high emotional intelligence and followers' employee engagement (e.g., Ravichandran, Arasu, & Kumar, 2011). Emotional intelligence refers to a set of interrelated skills associated with interpersonal relationships and emotional regulation. Specifically, it refers to accurate perception, appraisal, and expression of emotion, whereby one accesses and generates feelings that facilitate thought, emotional understanding, and knowledge of emotional regulation and expression (Caruso, Mayer, & Salovey, 2002; Mayer & Salovey, 1995; Salovey

& Mayer, 1989). Mayer, Caruso, and Salovey (2000) developed a measure to assess the four areas of abilities (perception, facilitation, understanding, and management of emotions) that characterize emotional intelligence.

Raising the emotional intelligence in employees themselves may be another avenue for increasing engagement. Although not designed to test this casual proposition, using a sample of 193 police offers in Australia, Brunetto, Teo, Shacklock, and Farr-Wharton (2012) found a positive relationship between the emotional intelligence of employees and their engagement. Specifically, police officers with high emotional intelligence reported high levels of employee engagement. Their study was correlational, and therefore, it is unclear if raising emotional intelligence will actually raise engagement. However, the implications of the study findings are that it should and that with a strong relationship between the two constructs (they reported a correlation of .43), one might expect the two constructs to change together.

Supportive and interpersonal leadership.   In my own research, my students and I have studied the relationship between supportive and interpersonal leadership and employee engagement. In one study (Byrne, Peters, et al. 2013), we defined supportive leadership as supervisory support combined with interpersonal and informational justice. Perceived supervisory support entails providing flexible work schedules, conveying value and importance, demonstrating appreciation and concern, and being available when employees need help (see Eisenberger, Huntington, Hutchison, & Sowa, 1986). Interpersonal fairness refers to being treated with respect and consideration, and informational justice refers to being given honest and adequate explanations for decisions (Bies & Moag, 1986). We created this multidimensional construct to represent the positive interpersonal relationships with leaders that researchers note are related to engagement (e.g., Aryee et al., 2012; Groysberg & Slind, 2012; Tuckey et al., 2012; Xu & Thomas, 2011; Zhu, Avolio, & Walumbwa, 2009). In a different study (Hansen, Byrne, & Kiersch, in press), we combined transformational leadership characteristics (e.g., vision, inspirational communication, supportive leadership, intellectual stimulation, personal recognition; Rafferty & Griffin, 2004) with informational and interpersonal justice to create the concept of interpersonal leadership characteristics. Both studies reflect the idea that the interpersonal characteristics of leaders are what employees relate to or respond to when becoming engaged at work (Aryee et al., 2012; Tuckey et al., 2012; Xu & Thomas, 2011).

In both studies that my students and I conducted, we used field samples with data collected at two time points, and we employed several of Podsakoff, MacKenzie, Lee, and Podsakoff's (2003) suggestions for minimizing common method bias (variance in scores are attributed to

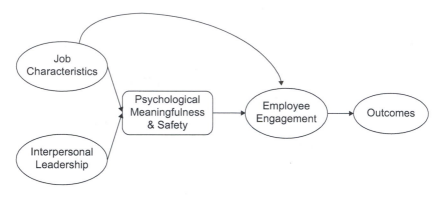

Figure 4.1 Adapted from Byrne, Peters, Rechlin, Smith, and Kedharnath (2013)

the methodology as opposed to actual differences). Both data sets were examined using structural equation modeling to simultaneous test study hypotheses and to rule out competing models. In both studies, we used measures with adequate reliability and validity evidence to support firm conclusions from the study findings. Our findings in both studies show interpersonal leadership is positively related to employee engagement. One study demonstrates a positive relationship with engagement by promoting an identification or connection with the organization, whereas the other shows leadership and job characteristics are both related to engagement through experienced psychological meaningfulness and safety (see Figure 4.1). Like most of the other studies reviewed in this chapter, these are not causal, and therefore, we can draw no firm conclusions about what promotes what. The practical implications of the research, however, are that supportive and interpersonal leadership may play a role in fostering work climates in which engagement flourishes.

Qualitative data captured during these studies revealed leader behaviors do positively affect employees.

Employees' Reflections

Some of the employees shared the following during these projects:

- *"That's what keeps me engaged . . . it's that appreciation and affirmation."*
- *"My input is valued. In this job, I like the autonomy and also the appreciation. That what I do is important—that they trust me to make important decisions and to know when to involve others versus when I can do it myself."*

- *"[T]here's a lot about fairness, I mean, there's a big thing about what's fair and what's not and the executive team is pretty much in agreement that it's important to be fair—it's one of those things where ultimately people have to be engaged. Fairness is important."*
- *"I get tons of support from my boss."*
- *"I really liked what he [CEO] had to say about employee engagement, how much he values employees, and how much he tries to balance work and life, not only for himself but his employees."*
- *"Upper management is so approachable—you can start a conversation any time . . . they take time to visit with you, talk to you and ask how your day is goin', and if there's anything they can do for me and that kind of thing. I feel really appreciated."*

Managing Stress

Job resources. In keeping with the Job Demands-Resources (JD-R) model (Bakker & Demerouti, 2008), researchers suggest that organizations increase job resources, such as social support, performance feedback, job characteristics (e.g., autonomy, skill variety, challenging work) and learning opportunities (Bakker, 2009) to increase their employees' engagement. The JD-R model (see Figure 4.2) suggests that job resources are key to enabling engagement and the presence of job demands make resources much more salient. The JD-R model combines the demand-control model (Karasek, 1979) and the effort–reward imbalance model (Siegrist, 1996) to suggest that there are two groups of job components affecting employees' stress levels: job demands and job resources. Both include physical, psychological, social, and organizational components of the job. These components are considered demands when they cost the employee, either physically or psychologically. They are considered resources when they are associated with reductions in job demands (i.e., they help achieve work goals or reduce physical or psychological costs) and/or when they stimulate growth. Job demands lead to strain, whereas job resources lead to motivation. Although the various presentations of the JD-R model are a bit vague and confusing as to exactly how the model works, it seems, in general, that the JD-R model suggests that when demands exceed resources, employees disengage; when resources exceed demands, employees engage because resources reduce the costs associated with ongoing demands.

Several researchers from the health perspective of employee engagement have used the JD-R model to explain the relationship between

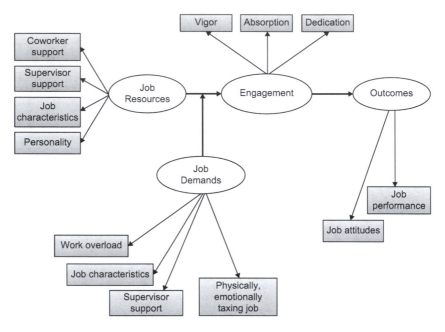

Figure 4.2 Job Demands-Resources Model (Adapted from Bakker & Demerouti, 2008)

stressors and engagement as defined by Schaufeli et al. (2002; e.g., Bakker, Demerouti, & Schaufeli, 2005; Hakanen, Bakker, & Schaufeli, 2006; Mauno, Kinnunen, & Ruokolainen, 2007; Mostert & Rothmann, 2006; Prieto, Soria, Martinez, & Schaufeli, 2008; Richardsen, Burke, & Martinussen, 2006; Rothmann & Joubert, 2007; Schaufeli & Bakker, 2004; Xanthopoulou, Bakker, Demerouti, & Schaufeli, 2007, 2009).

Similar to the JD-R model, the conservation of resources theory (Hobfoll, 1989) has been used in the stress/employee engagement research context to hypothesize that job resources buffer the negative effects of various work settings or stressors on work engagement (e.g., Bakker, Hakanen, Demerouti, & Xanthopoulou, 2007; Hakanen, Perhoniemi, & Toppinen-Tanner, 2008; Rothmann & Joubert, 2007). This research used Schaufeli et al.'s (2002) definition of engagement as a general state characterized by vigor, dedication, and absorption.

The implied intervention solution here is to help employees find ways to "buffer stress" by conserving and adding to their resources across a variety of domains, allowing them to be engaged at work. Specifically, the conservation of resources theory says that "people strive to retain, protect, and build resources and that what is threatening to them is the potential or actual loss of these valued resources" (Hobfoll, 1989, p. 516). Hobfoll (1989) defined resources as objects (e.g., home, assets), personal characteristics (e.g., stress resistant personality, strong social support system), and situations or conditions (e.g., tenure, seniority, good partnership) that are valuable to the individual. For example, skill mastery, self-esteem, financial security, employability or employment, and learning potential are considered resources that enable people to build, retain, and protect their resources. In a cross-lagged longitudinal study, Hakanen, Perhoniemi et al. (2008) found some support for the general hypotheses of the conservation of resources theory; those with resources conserved and accumulated more, whereas those prone to using resources continued to do so over time.

The results do not provide casual evidence that developing an intervention based on the principles of conservation of resources will definitely increase levels of employee engagement. Additionally, no experimental or quasi-experimental studies could be found actually testing whether changing levels of job resources affects levels of engagement. However, a recent study by Luria and Torjman (2009) may offer some potential insight into how resources support positive engagement, when using Schaufeli et al.'s (2002) conceptualization of engagement as the antipode of exhaustion. Specifically, Luria and Torjman conducted a quasi–field experiment examining the effects of various resources on coping with perceived stress (induced by a 2-day selection process), using conservation of resources as their theoretical foundation. The resources included personality in the form of core self-evaluations (e.g., locus of control, self-esteem, generalized self-efficacy, and emotional stability), physical fitness, cognition such as problem-solving ability and time management, and peer acceptance. Their results showed that those reporting high levels of core self-evaluation perceived much lower stress levels across the study compared with those reporting low scores on the core self-evaluation measure. The tasks were quite physical, and so as expected, high physical fitness contributed positively to stress coping. Cognitive ability had no effect on coping; neither did peer acceptance in this particular study. Peer rejection, in contrast, did increase perceived stress levels. The implication of this study is that positive core self-evaluations appear to play a positive role in coping with stress and, therefore, could potentially act as a resource for promoting offsetting negative conditions that take away from one's ability to become engaged.

Judge, Locke, and Durham (1997) suggest core self-evaluations are stable perspectives in which people see themselves and these reflect the "relatively stable characteristics of the person (i.e., traits)" (p. 152); core self-evaluations are, for the most part, unchangeable. Results of studies do show core self-evaluations seem to predict motivation (Erez & Judge, 2001). Given that engagement is considered a form of motivation, considering how to tap into positive core self-evaluations to ultimately affect engagement may have merit.

In contrast to the correlational studies finding positive relationships between resources and engagement, Dikkers, Jansen, de Lange, Vinkenburg, and Kooij (2010) reported job resources in the form of support (e.g., help from supervisor) and job control and job demands (e.g., enough time to get the job done, working hard) were not related to engagement over time, suggesting that engagement is stable regardless of perceived resources and job demands. The authors explained this lack of influence by suggesting that examining engagement over 18 months may not be the right time frame. That is, perhaps they should have assessed engagement more frequently on a daily or hourly basis, though such an explanation flies in the face of Schaufeli et al.'s (2002) assertion that engagement is a persistent and stable state. Dikkers et al. framed their study using Schaufeli et al.'s definition of engagement and measure. Their findings warrant experimental follow-up studies to determine for sure whether resources really do change or affect levels of engagement.

The accumulated results from most of the studies of Schaufeli, Bakker, and Demerouti, and various combinations of these authors and their colleagues, suggest job resources play a role in supporting engagement levels. Their cumulative findings also suggest that job demands are stressful and that when stressed, people report lower engagement than otherwise.

Cognitive activation.　Andreassen, Ursin, and Eriksen (2007) used cognitive activation theory of stress (Ursin & Eriksen, 2004) to explain how enjoyment of work is positively related to work engagement for those who expect it to be positive, and drive (internal motivation and inner compulsion for work) is related to job stress and burnout but only for those who expect work to be negative. Cognitive activation theory suggests those who expect positive coping demonstrate a fast cognitive activation for problem solving, whereas those with a negative expectancy for coping demonstrate a slow cognitive activation of coping responses (hence, their stress levels rise). The implied intervention solution here is towards changing expectancies for coping with stressful situations; if the expectation can be positive and toward constructive employment, the response should be engagement. No empirical study has yet tested this specific hypothesis. Additionally, the premise of cognitive activation theory is a response to stressful situations; thus, this model is really only appropriate if considering engagement from the stress literature perspective (i.e., Schaufeli et al., 2002), as opposed to the role theory perspective (i.e., Kahn, 1990).

Fostering Motivation

Job characteristics.　Interventions such as organizational culture change and job (re)design focus on changing the work environment (i.e., with the job itself or with the reporting structure) to affect employee motivation, job satisfaction, and other work outcomes. Substantial research evidence supports job redesign (see Holman, Axtell, Sprigg, Totterdell, & Wall, 2010, for a recent study). An important first step in job redesign is to conduct a job diagnoses, perhaps using the Job Diagnostic Survey (JDS; Hackman & Oldham, 1975) to determine what part of the job should be modified to address potential motivation issues. The JDS asks questions about employees' perceptions of their job and their reactions to the job itself. The survey asks about working with others, autonomy, task variety, whether the job involves completing only a small part of a larger project or completing the entire project, the importance of the job, feedback on the job, level of challenge in the job, satisfaction with the job, sense of ownership and responsibility on the job, availability of opportunity for growth or recognition, and preferences for one job over another (when the two comparative jobs presented on the survey differ on a variety of factors such as commute time, pay, level of responsibility, challenge, variety, and other job characteristics; see Hackman & Oldham, 1975, for details). The JDS is specifically designed to assess the components of job characteristics theory (see Figure 4.3), a theory that explains how job factors lead to motivation and other work outcomes. The results of the JDS provide information as to what in one's job would most positively affect motivation if changed. As mentioned, the JDS was specifically designed with the job characteristics theory in mind; therefore, those using it should be aware of its purpose and limitations.

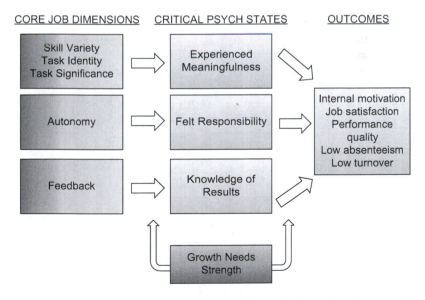

Figure 4.3 Job Characteristics Model (Adapted from Hackman & Oldham, 1976)

Luthans, Kemmerer, Paul, and Taylor (1987) conducted a quasi-experimental study implementing a job redesign solution that worked to improve satisfaction. Specifically, they conducted a 2-week intervention/study using an experimental and a control group of salespeople. The experimental group experienced a job redesign that addressed skill variety, task identity, task significance, autonomy, feedback from the job, and organization—the components of the job characteristics theory (Hackman & Oldham, 1976). The control group was given a review of company health and medical benefits. Results during and after the 2-week intervention showed that during the intervention, employees in the experimental group reported higher job satisfaction than did those in the control group. Performance, which was assessed using behavioral observations by the researchers, increased slightly during the intervention but returned to baseline levels after the intervention was over. Although Luthans et al. did not measure employee engagement, their study demonstrates modifications using job characteristics theory may have an effect on worker experiences on the job—the implications being that redesigning job characteristics may ultimately affect engagement.

In a different application of job redesign, Microsoft Corporation implemented a career model framework with an accompanying leadership development program to create the focused workforce necessary for a strategic product change (Olesen, White, & Lemmer, 2007). The first step was an assessment of the current state of the organization's managers and company culture. The second step was to develop clearly defined materials outlining management levels, job descriptions, training plans, and career paths for each level. The third step involved testing the materials and developing an online system to facilitate the career path planning that took place at annual performance evaluations. The materials, or what they called the career model, specified standards for identifying, assessing, managing, and developing employees along a particular career path. The career path can be identified by the employee, with the expectation that it is achievable, given the employee's competencies or capabilities, performance, and experience. Furthermore, the career model outlined development that was aligned with organizational goals, as well as the value propositions for the company. Full details of the model and its development can be found in Olesen and colleagues (2007). Progress over a 3-year timeframe was tracked, with specific measures in place for assessing progress and change. Although the authors do not provide empirical evidence for the success of the model in changing engagement levels, they concluded that the model did address employee engagement as part of career development and talent management. They further noted that employees recognized the organization's commitment to them and their development, which could translate into perceptions of increased support and value and feelings of significance. According to the job characteristics theory (Hackman & Oldham, 1976), efforts that develop greater significance and overall perceived value will translate into higher levels of motivation.

The job characteristics theory has received support in general, especially relating job characteristics to psychological states that then lead to motivation (see a study by Behson, Eddy, & Lorenzet, 2000). Some preliminary support in explaining variance in engagement also exists (e.g., Christian, Garza, & Slaughter, 2011), indicating the job characteristics theory holds promise for serving as input into interventions designed to promote employee engagement.

Job rotation or enrichment. Job redesign includes a number of approaches or strategies that may change certain job characteristics, affecting employees' experience of the meaningfulness of their jobs, which should lead to engagement (Kahn, 1990). Research shows that job characteristics are positively correlated with psychological meaningfulness (Becherer, Morgan, & Richard, 1982; Champoux, 1991), one of Kahn's (1990) key psychological conditions that precedes engagement. One could implement job rotation, which involves periodically rotating employees among different jobs on the same job level. Thus, employees have a chance to use different job skills, as well as learn new ones. Job enrichment, another job redesign approach, involves increasing the scope of one's immediate job by adding tasks that are directly relevant to the job itself, thereby increasing skill variety and overall interest (Walker, 1950).

Guest (1964) shares an illustrative story of job enrichment or enlargement wherein a chairman of the board asks a line employee what she would do with the job if she was the boss. The answer was "with very little extra training she could learn not only how to operate the machine but to set up her own machine (a task which the setup men performed), keep track of the inventory of different types of parts (a task of the stock men), and do her own inspection of the parts, (a job which the inspectors were doing)" (Guest, 1964, p. 3). Unfortunately, no empirical studies testing the relationship between these types of job redesign strategies and employee engagement could be found, but the answer given to the chairman of the board is illustrative of how, theoretically, an employee could be engaged by modifying the job.

Job redesign is not a panacea; it is not always effective (e.g., Frank & Hackman, 1975; Lawler, Hackman, & Kaufman, 1973), thus requiring attention to whether those in the job are ready for the change and whether the change is best for those in the job. That is, job design is appropriate some of the time but not all the time; Hackman and Lawler (1971) demonstrated an employee's need for growth (or growth need strength) factors into the relationship between job dimensions and job satisfaction.

Job crafting. Not all jobs can be designed to offer autonomy, challenge, or skill variety, thus other approaches to redesign such as job crafting (Wrzesniewski & Dutton, 2001) may be used to achieve the same overall conceptual contribution that social support or specific job resources carry. Employees can be trained in job crafting, an approach to job redesign that incorporates physical and cognitive changes employees themselves make in how they envision the task or with the relational boundaries in their work. Job crafting may or may not involve structural changes to the job; rather, it tends to emphasize how employees see what is and is not (and what can be) in the various roles they have at work. Job crafting emphasizes the role of the employee in designing or changing his or her work toward creating more meaningful work, reinforcing the concept of empowerment, and giving employees more control over their job boundaries. Berg, Dutton, and Wrzesniewski (2013) provide a rich description of job crafting along with several proven suggestions for application in the field (including references and resources). To date, no study empirically tests Wrzesniewski and Dutton's conceptualization of job crafting. Although they refer to job crafting, Bakker, Tims, and Derks (2012) use a different conceptualization of job crafting; namely, changes employees make to job demands and resources (Tims & Bakker, 2010). Bakker et al. found correlational support for their version of job crafting positively relating to engagement.

Although no research has yet examined how job crafting may play a role in fostering employee engagement, the concept holds promise as it may tap into the transformation component of engagement I defined in Chapter 2. That is, job crafting serves as a means for transforming work so it is more meaningful to the employee, and job crafting does not necessarily require changing the job tasks.

Intrinsic and extrinsic motivation. According to cognitive evaluation theory (Deci, 1975; Deci & Ryan, 1980), the precursor to self-determination theory (Deci & Ryan, 1985; Ryan & Deci, 2000), feelings of competence and autonomy underlie intrinsic motivation, which is motivation propelled by internal interest and spontaneous satisfaction from an activity. In contrast, motivation driven by an external reward or payment from an external source is called extrinsic motivation (Porter & Lawler, 1968). Research shows that challenging tasks are intrinsically motivating (e.g., Danner & Lonky, 1981), and positive feedback on tasks promotes a sense of competence (Fisher, 1978; Ryan, 1982) that fosters intrinsic motivation (Deci, Koestner, & Ryan, 1999).

Self-determination theory extends cognitive evaluation theory by describing internal and external motivation in more detail (Deci & Ryan, 1985; Ryan & Deci, 2000). The theory suggests that people are often motivated even when the task is not intrinsically interesting, either because they understand and strongly value the benefit their behavior ultimately provides or because their behavior is fully integrated into their identity, such that it is self-determined. Self-determination theory builds on the fundamental belief humans have innate tendencies toward intrinsic motivation, by identifying three needs (i.e., competence, autonomy, and relatedness) that are important for triggering and enhancing intrinsic motivation (Ryan & Deci, 2000). As long as people interpret their work environment as supporting their feelings of competence (i.e., believe they have the ability and resources necessary), giving them self-control (i.e., autonomy), and characterized by a sense of relatedness (i.e., valued and appreciated by others), they will believe their actions or behaviors are self-determined (i.e., consistent with core values and freely chosen) and be intrinsically motivated (Ryan & Deci, 2000). Thus, we can hypothesize using self-determination theory that employees become engaged because it makes them feel self-determined; that they are competent, in control, and intrinsically rewarded by the work they do (Meyer & Gagné, 2008). In support, across two studies, Gillet, Huart, Colombat, and Fouquereau (2013) demonstrated that using self-determination theory as the framework that self-determined motivation mediated the relationship between supervisory and organizational support and employee engagement.

An outgrowth of self-determination theory, the self-concordance model of motivation (Sheldon & Elliot, 1999) suggests people naturally pursue self-generated or self-integrated goals, that when attained, produce high levels of satisfaction and well-being promoting ongoing goal-striving and achievement. Self-concordant goals are intrinsic or *identified motivation*, which Sheldon and Elliot (1998) argue makes them self-integrated; that is, they are generated from within and thus are deeply valued. Identified motivation is described as acting out of personal conviction, pursing goals consistent with one's internal compass. They stress "valued" is not synonymous with "pleasant"—instead, the goals have personal meaning and individuals feel a sense of ownership of the goal. Sheldon and Elliot (1998, 1999) propose that people are driven to achieve self-concordant goals and attainment of a goal results in performance and psychological well-being. Hence, by applying the self-concordance model to employee engagement, we can hypothesize people inherently pursue self-concordant goals, and the process of achieving such goals provides a positive feeling of accomplishment and ultimately more goal-striving behavior, expressed as the motivated state of employee engagement. To date, it does not appear that anyone has tested the self-concordance model of motivation and engagement, except in school engagement literature (Vasalampi, Salmela-Aro, & Numi, 2009).

Employees with high core self-evaluations (i.e., locus of control, self-esteem, generalized self-efficacy, and emotional stability) tend to report high self-concordant work goals; they pursue goals that are internally driven, that they identify with, and that are intrinsically rewarding (Judge, Bono, Erez, & Locke, 2005). As a result, they tend to demonstrate and report high levels of goal attainment and satisfaction. One can conclude from this research that employees with high core self-evaluations may also be more likely to become engaged because of their high goal attainment. A few studies support a positive relationship between core self-evaluations and engagement (e.g., Karatepe, Keshavarz, & Nejati, 2012; Yan & Su, 2013).

Combining job characteristics with intrinsic motivation. Using self-determination theory and self-concordance model of motivation, we can speculate that changing the work environment to facilitate employees' ability to feel competent, in control (some autonomy), needs for relatedness met, and feel able to pursue a self-generated goal should lead to high levels of employee engagement. Changes to the environment can include appropriate redesign of task or job characteristics (i.e., job autonomy, feedback from the job, feedback from supervisor) to promote feelings of empowerment and intrinsic motivation (Gagné, Senécal, & Koestner, 1997), and structuring a reward and recognition system that includes feedback in addition to tangible rewards that are not contingent on task performance (Deci et al., 1999).

Although not about employee engagement, a recent study of high school students may provide some insight for full-time workers regarding job characteristics and motivation because it relates to engagement. Seeking ways to positively influence low-achieving high school students' academic trajectory, Crumpton and Gregory (2011) examined the relationship between academic relevancy and student engagement. They defined academic relevancy as whether students experience school as personally relevant and student engagement as participation in learning process as evidenced by high achievement. Their hypothesis was that students who felt school was personally meaningful to them would see the instrumentality of schoolwork and be intrinsically motivated to learn. After the authors tracked a group of low-achieving students for 1 year and controlled for their first-year engagement ratings, results showed students who saw school as personally relevant did indeed report higher levels of engagement at the end of the year. They also found a significant positive relationship between intrinsic motivation and engagement. The implications of their findings for working adults is that relevancy may be likened to task significance in the job characteristics model. That is, task significance refers to the importance of the job, whether the job means something in the bigger picture of the organization. It may also be likened to Kahn's (1990) and Hackman and Oldham's (1976) psychological condition of meaningfulness. This state refers to feeling that what one does is a meaningful contribution—it has meaning for the individual doing the work. Thus, if academic relevancy can potentially influence student engagement (which is similar to involvement and performance), it may be that helping employees find meaning at work will help influence employee engagement, or at least the aspects of engagement that tap into involvement and behaviors that result in job performance.

Creating Meaningful Work[1]

Classical theories of motivation and humanistic psychology propose people need work that is meaningful and purposeful (Alderfer, 1972; Herzberg, Mausner, & Snyderman, 1959; Maslow, 1943, 1968; Rogers, 1959, 1961b). Scholars studying meaning have proposed a search for meaning in work exists because of the weakening of religious and spiritual systems as well as with erosion in connected communities, and as such, work has become a place for belongingness from which meaning in life can be found or created (Frankl, 1967, 1978; Hall, 1996; Heil, Bennis, & Stephens, 2000; Maslow, 1998; Morin, 1995; Viljoen, 1989). Researchers note that individuals seek meaning through personal accomplishments (Frankl, 1984), by associating one's existence with something bigger or is perceived as more significant than the self (Allport, 1961) and by fulfilling purpose, value, efficacy, and self-worth (Baumeister, 1991).

Approaches to creating meaningful work (i.e., work employees consider significant and valuable; Pratt & Ashforth, 2003) may include job redesign focusing on the aspects of the job that are important to employees, such as challenging work and task significance. People ask if what they do matters in the big picture of the organization and whether it provides connection. Becherer and colleagues (1982) examined the relationship between task significance with experienced meaningfulness and found a correlation of .20. Autonomy and feedback were also positively correlated with meaningfulness ($r = .10$ and $r = .25$, respectively). These study results suggest possible approaches to job redesign that rely on components of the job characteristics theory may play a role in creating opportunities for finding meaning at work.

As another form of job design already discussed, job crafting may result in the creation of more meaningful work (Wrzesniewski, Berg, & Dutton, 2010; Wrzesniewski & Dutton, 2001). Job crafting can be done across three different domains: (a) tasks, (b) relational, and (c) cognitive. Task job crafting involves changing the actual tasks of the job by increasing or reducing the number of tasks, by changing how the tasks are completed, or by reprioritizing tasks. Relational job crafting involves changing how and when relationships and interactions are sought and invoked and with whom. New relationships may be formed whereas others may be broken or minimized to reduce interactions. Cognitive job tasking involves changing how work is perceived, framed, or understood in terms of one's identity. Employees can use one or more of these techniques to shape the meaningfulness of their jobs. To date, no empirical studies exist testing the supposition that job crafting changes employees' perceived meaningfulness, however, studies do exist for the application of job crafting (e.g., Berg, Grant, & Johnson, 2010; Wrzesniewski, Dutton, & Debebe, 2003).

Other aspects of work, such as role clarity and expected outcomes, potentially play a role in creating meaningfulness. Namely, meaningfulness and role clarity are positively correlated ($r = .49$; Nielsen, Randall, Yarker, & Brenner, 2008). According to Vroom's (1964) expectancy theory of motivation, people want to know that what they get for the work they put in is valuable to them (called valence). If the outcome of their effort is not valuable to them, they are unlikely to be motivated to direct efforts to goal accomplishment. Tests of Vroom's theory suggest that it is most predictive of intended behavior when individuals are faced with several choices, as opposed to just one (Van Eerde & Thierry, 1996). Role clarity may offer information on what one can expect of the job, thus connecting role clarity to expectancy theory.

Empirical support for a relationship between meaningful work and engagement has been shown in a qualitative study of earthquake survivors in China. Survivors reported their efforts in providing post-quake relief and reconstruction was meaningful work, which gave them energy (they explicitly reported not being exhausted by this) and made them feel engaged in the work (X. Wang, Shi, Ng, Wang, & Chan, 2011). The authors' findings are supportive of the subjective definitions of meaning, where deriving meaning from one's work is about having purpose or direction (see Park, 2010) that may result from seeing one's actions contribute to goal achievement (King, Hicks, Krull, & Del Gaiso, 2006; McGregor & Little, 1998). An implication of this research is that creating a higher order goal or purpose for which employees' work contributes may help employees find meaning or value in their work.

The conclusion from the preceding review is that meaningfulness at work appears to support employee engagement, and there may be a variety of ways to help employees derive meaning from work. Perhaps a key question for researchers to ask is whether meaningfulness is required for engagement; that is, can people in jobs in which meaning may be difficult to derive be engaged? In their chapter on dirty work, Ashforth and Kreiner (2013) would argue that they can.

Meaningful Organizations

In a recent consulting project, I worked with a nonprofit health care provider who has a very clear mission (i.e., a formal statement of the unique purpose of the organization that defines its identity within its market; Pearce, 1982)—in fact, nearly every employee interviewed mentioned the organization's mission, which was not prompted. The first part of the consulting project was to understand how the organization defined employee engagement, to identify what supports engagement, and to determine potential roadblocks to helping employees become more engaged. Some employee comments from the project are provided in the "Employees' Reflections"

Employees' Reflections

When asked what gets them out of bed and into work, interviewees produced statements such as the following:

- "[B]eing connected to the mission of the organization."
- "I really like work for this organization; it has a good mission; a mission I believe in. I get why . . . why we need to be the way we are. The mission itself if really important to me."
- "Being able to support the mission is important to me. Not only that it exists and I agree with it, but being able to actively promote the mission by making sure our financials are clean, we get clean audits, we're in good financial standing, and that, at least in a financial way, we are well respected for our practice is important to me."
- "I really do have a lot of connection to the work that we do here, and the mission of this organization. It is meaningful."
- "[T]he mission does seem to really drive conversation and decision-making such as I've witnessed so far. And again that unity, I don't know, in my experience, derives from clarity in leadership, a clear vision from leadership, so clearly that's being conveyed here. So, I think it's quite impressive actually."
- "[I]t's just in the way we talk about our work and identify with this mission of the organization. It gives me a lot of information about where are we as an organization because it's all going to come back to engagement and the feeling of being engaged or not."
- "I've read things about leadership and being a part of a mission-oriented organization and some of it is just what I believe and what I come to with myself which is knowing why you're working where you're working. I feel it's important to have a purpose behind my work I feel like it's important to be aligned in your purpose."

Suh, Houston, Barney, and Kwon (2011) examined organization mission fulfillment (OMF) and employee mission engagement (EME) in a large nonprofit health care organization. They defined OMF as the degree to which the actions and messages of an organization are congruent with its stated mission, and operationalized it (i.e., measured it) as mission strength—that the respondent agrees the organizational decisions are consistent with the mission statement and the culture sustains the mission. EME was defined as "a psychological state in which an employee desires to exert effort and devote careful attention to ensure the fulfillment of a mission that he or she perceives as significant or meaningful" (Suh, et al., 2011, p. 78). The construct was operationalized as working hard to ensure the mission is carried out and the extent to which one is motivated by the mission. Unfortunately, the authors' three-item measure of EME did not quite capture their definition, and it is not a measure of employee engagement; therefore, we can draw no conclusions from the study about employee engagement. However, the results of the study are nonetheless informative because (a) this appears to be one of the only studies focused on organizational missions and (b) the results indicate OMF and EME are positively correlated. Because transformational leadership incorporates the idea that the leader provides an inspiring vision, perhaps future research could tie transformational leadership to Suh et al.'s OMF and EME and examine their relationship to engaging employees.

People seek work that is meaningful out of a desire to have a good working life (Brown et al., 2001; Csikszentmihalyi, 1990). Meaningful work is valued, provides connection to others, and allows one to feel a part of something bigger than the self (Baumeister, 1991; Baumeister & Vohs, 2002). Thus, organizations that can provide a superordinate goal to which employees can connect and feel joined with others in achieving may result in employees finding meaning at work and ultimately engagement (Chalofsky & Krishna, 2009; Kahn, 1990; Rosso, Dekas, & Wrzesniewski, 2010). A meaningful organization with a strong mission to which an employee can relate can offer organizational and leadership purpose, as well as the opportunity for personal purpose through goal and value alignment. Last, it may be a strong and clear mission ties into concepts relevant in expectancy theory, in that what employees are working for is clearly defined in the mission.

Table 4.1 provides a comprehensive list of possible interventions or solutions for engagement, their theoretical foundation, and what kind of supportive evidence they have for their use in promoting engagement.

Table 4.1 Interventions for Promoting Employee Engagement

Suggested Intervention	Theoretical Foundation	Examples of Empirical and/or Practical Support
Change expectancy for coping and self-efficacy for coping	Cognitive Activation Theory (Ursin & Eriksen, 2004)	None for engagement; see Meurs & Perrewé (2011) for use in occupational stress and potential application with Schaufeli, Salanova, González-Romá, and Bakker (2002) approach
Conserve or obtain resources to buffer stress; build resource capability	Conservation of Resources Theory (Hobfoll, 1989)	Two-wave three-year longitudinal: Hakanen, Perhoniemi, & Toppinen-Tanner (2008)
Empowering leaders	Empowering Leadership (Conger & Kanungo, 1988)	Correlational support: Tuckey, Bakker, & Dollard (2012)
Full Range Leadership Development, Transformational leadership training	Full Range theory of Leadership (Avolio & Bass, 1991) Transformational leadership theory (Bass, 1985)	Experimental design: Howell & Frost (1989) and Kirkpatrick & Locke (1996) both looked at charismatic leadership Quasi-experimental support: Barling, Weber, & Kelloway (1996); Brown & May (2010); Dvir, Eden, Avolio, & Shamir (2002); Parry & Sinha (2005) Practice support by Avolio & Bass (1994)
Increase Emotional Intelligence	Mayer & Salovey (1995)	Correlational support: Ravichandran, Arasu, & Kumar (2011) Longitudinal experiment: Cherniss, Grimm, & Liautaud (2010)
Increase job resources	Job Demands-Resources Model (Bakker & Demerouti, 2008)	Correlational support: Hakanen & Roodt (2010)
Increase Work-related Intrinsic Motivation	Self-determination Theory (Deci & Ryan, 1985)	Correlational support for related concepts, not engagement per se: Gagné Senécal, & Koestner (1997)
Job Redesign	Job Characteristics Theory (Hackman & Oldham, 1976)	Meta-analytic support for the job characteristics theory: Behson, Eddy, & Lorenzet (2000)
Meaningful Organization	Meaningfulness (Baumeister, 1991)	Paper on how to develop a mission statement: Cochran, David, & Gibson (2008) Chapter on creating meaningful work: Pratt, Pradies, & Lepisto (2013)

What Might These Interventions Look Like
for Engaging an Employee?

Lena has been working for a few years at a job that pays minimum wage. She works for a supermarket chain where her job varies between stacking the shelves, greeting customers at the door, servicing the cash register, and moving inventory around the store. Her organization has recently been promoting the idea of employee engagement, a concept that she understands means she needs to be more involved at work and come across as more enthusiastic or excited about the work. She's not sure if that's what they mean by engagement, but that's what it seems to her.

In Lena's last performance evaluation, her boss talked about what the organization expects of her now that she has been there for a while. He talked about her taking charge of deciding when she performs her various duties such as when she should be greeting at the door versus when she should be moving or stocking inventory. He provided her access to the overall scheduling system so that she could determine when she is most needed at which position. Lena told him she was not sure if she could handle the stress of figuring out where she should be and when. He told her that she has actually already been managing her schedule when she has come to him and suggested that she switch positions because she noted that people needed help and when she has offered to work extra hours because a larger than expected shipment arrived. They talked about it a little bit, and Lena realized that indeed she has been managing her own stress levels by asking for help when she needs it or by identifying when she needs time off because she has been working extra hours. It just never occurred to her that that was what she was doing. Her boss also asked her what she thinks her work really means to the organization and to herself. He asked her to create an individual mission statement that would reflect what she thinks is important in the work that she does for the store. Finally, her boss asked for feedback on whether he has been providing appropriate direction, conveying excitement about the stores overall goals, and what he can do to help her develop her work skills so that she can move to the next levels in the organization.

What Lena experienced in her performance appraisal was her boss developing her self-efficacy for coping and managing her own stress. Her boss also used aspects of job characteristics theory to give Lena more autonomy and the opportunity to feel more task identity by understanding how she can fit in and contribute to the bigger picture of managing the store by allowing her to rearrange her schedule of tasks. Last, her boss made efforts to work on developing his own transformational leadership style by helping her to determine how to create more meaningful work for herself and by asking for feedback on whether he is displaying characteristics of transformational leadership such as inspirational motivation and individualized consideration.

Practice-Based Approaches to Getting More Engagement

When considering nonacademic or practice-driven solutions, most indirectly incorporate the essential components of Kahn's (1990) model, relying heavily on the principles of the job characteristics theory (Hackman & Oldham, 1976). For example, a publication on the Society of Human Resource Management's (SHRM) website reports results of a survey (no date for the survey provided) that rates employees' responses as to which corporate practices (i.e., appear to be mostly benefits and/or compensation) were effective in keeping them engaged (not defined). Most were about job characteristics such as challenge, autonomy, and skill variety, along with growth opportunity (e.g., promotions, training) and feedback (e.g., performance reviews), and Kahn's psychological conditions of meaningfulness and safety (e.g., encouraged to share ideas; see SHRM Foundation, n.d.).

Another example is found in Zappos, rated in the top 25 of *Fortune* Magazine's "100 Best Companies to Work For." Zappos is an online shoe and clothing store, recently acquired by Amazon.com, another online store that sells a much broader variety of products. Zappos uses a number of strategies for hiring and promoting an engaged workforce as reported by Perschel (2010). Though no empirical support for the strategies is provided, they appear consistent with the principles of the job characteristics theory and seeking person–organization fit. Specifically, their strategies include (a) hire people whose values match those of the organization (i.e., this may be considered similar to hiring based on person–organization fit); (b) train new hires on the culture and core values, clarifying expectations for engagement; (c) challenge and grow employees' skills (i.e., similar to challenging work and skill variety core job dimensions of job characteristics theory); (d) empower employees and give them autonomy to implement their best judgment (i.e., similar to autonomy of job characteristics theory); (e) create a culture for free expression (i.e., this may be considered creating a culture for Kahn's, 1990, state of psychological safety); and (g) provide feedback in the form of rewards for behaviors consistent with the organization's goals and values (i.e., similar to feedback in job characteristics theory).

Originally aimed at addressing issues of turnover, strategies to improve job fit may have the side benefit of facilitating engagement. Specifically, Moreland (2013) recommended one approach similar to Perschel (2010), namely, hiring people whose skills and education match the position requirements and continuing education to maintain the match as job requirements change. Although she did not call it job analysis, Moreland recommended assessments to determine specific competencies necessary for success on the job and then make those requirements for knowledge, skills, and ability clear during recruitment and selection. Ongoing assessments of employees are recommended throughout their tenure to reevaluate fit as job requirements change and as employees develop. Again, no empirical evidence is provided in support of these recommendations. However, if we assume that job fit, like person–organization fit, represents a match between the employee's knowledge, skills, abilities, and values with those of the organization, and such a match promotes experienced psychological meaningfulness, employees experiencing fit will be engaged.

Other practitioners suggest that the way to foster employee engagement is by focusing on career development and career planning (e.g., Wozniak, 2013) because "engagement is a byproduct" (Wozniak, 2013, p. 44). Wozniak (2013) defined engagement as emotional involvement and commitment to the organization. By understanding how they have an impact on the overall organization (one could interpret this as task significance from job characteristics theory), Wozniak suggests that employees will become emotionally involved and committed.

Stevens (2013) proposed that if you match employees' wants for a worthwhile and inspiring job (one could interpret this as meaningfulness and challenge) with organizations' wants for high performing employees, you get the "basis for employee engagement" (p. 91). She defined engagement as a combination of a psychological contract, satisfaction, and motivation. Stevens suggested the way to promote engagement is to create a supportive and nurturing work environment by having learning opportunities, an open-door management policy (i.e., employees can meet with manager at any time), shared ownership in projects and the organization overall, task significance, and an "inspiring leader" (Stevens, 2013, p. 92). Furthermore, she suggested that organizations can build engagement by recruiting those who most likely fit the culture (i.e., one could interpret this as person–organization fit), by having a socialization process, opportunities for career development, reward and recognition programs, by conveying value via surveys (i.e., assessing pay and benefit satisfaction, opportunity for input), flexible work schedules, and building trust. Although none of these suggestions is harmful, there is no evidence any are related to employee engagement.

In a similar fashion, Lavigna (2013) advocated the following for improving employee engagement, which he defined as "a heightened employee connection to work, the organization, the mission or co-workers" (p. 11): publicly advocate for government and public service, provide strong and stable leadership, support employee development, articulate goals and values of the organization, emphasize the organization's vision, involve employees in decision making, encourage risk-taking, encourage higher levels of education, accommodate unique employee needs, weed out "bad fits" (p. 12), set clear performance expectations, and treat employees fairly. Again, although the recommendations may not be harmful to the organization or its employees, there is no evidence (except for fairness) to support these suggestions foster (or are even related to) employee engagement. It may be possible one or more of these various approaches indirectly affects employees' engagement levels.

A. Harrison (2012) provided no definition of engagement, but provided five tips for improving engagement, which she reports is lacking in more than 70% of U.S. workers (she refers to results from a Kenexa, 2009, study). Harrison (2012) recommended that the organization must (a) evaluate team members and resources to ensure that "the right people on your team and the right resources in your artillery" (p. 10); (b) make sure that organizational values are clearly communicated to employees so they can "live them" (p. 10); (c) be open to feedback from employees; (d) "live the brand" (p. 10), which means employees must be "brand ambassadors" (p. 10); and (e) make sure that communication messages within the organization are clear and say what you want (i.e., do not focus so much on how it is said, but what is said). The language of the article is exciting (e.g., artillery, ambassador, live the brand) but lacks substance (i.e., what exactly is engagement, and what does it mean to live the brand or be a brand ambassador?) and evidence that the suggestions have anything to do with employee engagement—assuming you know what Harrison means by engagement.

Many practice-based approaches to fostering engagement seem to touch on one or more of the principles of job characteristics theory; however, not all do. There is one practice approach that takes a personal, reflective perspective for fostering "resolution, passion, and energy," resulting in being more "proactive and self-assured" leading to faster and more clear thinking, which together allows you to "express your personal intentions, identity, ideals, values, and driving force"—all implied as the definition of engagement (Rampersad, 2006, p. 18). Employee engagement is not formally defined. The intention of the article is to convey how to create the right social and contextual environment that can foster one's engagement. Specifically, Rampersad introduces the "personal balanced scorecard" (2006, p. 18), which comprises four dimensions assessed using seven questions. The dimensions include internal (physical and mental health), external (relations with others), knowledge and learning (knowledge, skills, and abilities), and financial stability. The seven questions include (a) Who am I? (b) Where am I going? (c) What type of relationship would I like to have with others? (d) Which factors make me unique? (e) Which results do I want to achieve? (f) How can I measure my personal results? and (h) How do I want to achieve the results? (see Rampersad, 2006, for details). The answers create an awareness of the self in the form of a personal balanced scorecard, from which an action plan can be written and tracked. Rampersad suggests that permanent and long-term changes can be achieved by following his plan, with the implications being that positive engagement follows.

The list of publications similar to these reviewed earlier is long and continues. Although most recommendations are provided by people with years of experience in human resources or in-depth experiences within a particular organization, none provides evidence the recommendations are related to engagement and most fail to provide a definition of engagement. Nearly all include at least one component of the job characteristics model (e.g., task significance, challenging work, autonomy), refer to resources of some kind, or mention meaningful work.

In my capacity as a trusted advisor and technical expert in psychometrics for a medium-sized organization (about 12,000 employees) in the United States, I was asked to review a number of vendor solutions for assessing and developing employee engagement. Keeping the names of the vendors confidential, I can share the following observations: Instead of measuring employee engagement, the vendors' solutions assessed organizational affective commitment, satisfaction, organizational citizenship behaviors, and climate factors associated with employee engagement. For example, their surveys measure supervisory support, coworker relations, and general resources, not unlike those resources noted as examples in the JD-R and conservation of resources models (e.g., flextime, benefits, training). During presentations, when I asked about whether they assess engagement itself versus what is considered a driver of engagement (i.e., climate factors that are thought to relate to engagement), the vendors each acknowledged that their instruments do not actually measure employee engagement but rather that they measure aspects of work they believe predict or drive engagement. None defines engagement using definitions proposed in the academic literature, such as Kahn's (1990) and Schaufeli et al.'s (2002), nor do they use any other published definition or model for that matter (e.g., Saks, 2006). None (at that time) offered validity evidence for their solutions in changing scores on "engagement" as they defined the construct. An important limitation in my anecdotal evidence here is I was only asked to review a small number of solutions—there are hundreds available (at least according to searches on the Internet), and it is possible some have roots in the research literature and/or provide substantial validity evidence.

In summary, there are a number of research- and practice-based approaches to fostering employee engagement, yet none to date has been shown to do just that—to foster or increase employee engagement.

Reflections from Byrne's Qualitative Work

The approaches to fostering engagement reviewed above are based in either theory or practice, yet none are based on what employees themselves have said might foster their engagement. In 2010, I worked with a health care organization that asked me to identify what engagement looks like in the organization and what prevents engagement for the employees. Using a qualitative methodology, my team and I interviewed 32 individual employees. The research team also facilitated four focus groups of four to eight people each across the four branch locations. The questions we asked were scripted and included items such as "What about your job do you like least?" "What prevents you from getting into your job?" and "What would it take for you to work your fullest capacity—to give all of yourself (mind, soul, and body) into this job?"

In 2011, I conducted another similar project, working with another health care organization that asked me to identify for them what engagement looks like and what prevents engagement for the employees. Again using a qualitative methodology, my team and I interviewed 48 individuals and conducted four focus groups ranging from four to eight participants each, held at the organization's different locations. The questions were scripted so all interviews and focus groups were asked the same questions. Example questions include "Can you tell me about a situation at work (within the last month) in which you would say you felt unengaged?" "What does being unengaged at work mean?" "What does it look and feel like?" and "What made you feel that you couldn't become engaged?"

Table 4.2 shows the themes extracted from both studies that reflect potential drivers or factors that encourage engagement. Although these drivers have not been confirmed in a larger sample that might provide generalizability information, they came from employees themselves (and a reasonably large number for qualitative work), which suggests they carry some weight in determining what moves employees to become engaged.

Table 4.2 Qualitative Findings on Drivers of Engagement

Theme	Examples
Meaningfulness	Meaning of work itself Meaning of the mission or vision of the organization Fulfilling work Making a difference
Alignment	Head and heart alignment Goal alignment within organization Value and skill match between self and the organization (P-O fit)
Relationships	Great colleagues and coworkers Mentors and being able to mentor others Supervisory support Organizational support Mutual respect Trust
Communication	Clarity of goals and vision for the organization Clear job and role expectations Small power distance
Job itself	Challenging work Opportunity to participate in work-related activities that are not directly tied to the job (e.g., volunteer within the organization) Fun or can have fun while doing it Involvement in innovation, creativity, and developing new things or solutions Skill and task variety
Personal (i.e., valuable)	Developmental opportunities Learning environment Voice; being asked for input and using the input Being asked to speak up when you see ways to improve the organization Regular and timely feedback that provides validation of the self and how to become validated (when the feedback is constructive toward improvement) Benefits that allow for downtime when it's needed
Good leadership	Skilled, effective, and authentic

What to Do About Engagement?

Given most approaches reviewed above have only correlational support, at best, for relating to employee engagement, what should an organization and researchers do about employee engagement?

First, evaluation studies are sorely needed. If organizations and academic researchers can partner to evaluate interventions, these findings will go a long way towards offering insight into whether and how engagement can be promoted. Experiments within organizations can be hard to coordinate, but quasi-experiments and longitudinal studies are feasible with enough cooperation between both parties.

Second, if researchers expand the scope of their investigations into engagement beyond the primary and overwhelmingly dominant goal of advancing theory, these studies could make a broader contribution that reciprocally influences theoretical thinking about engagement. That is, after reading several peer-reviewed journals, one could argue a majority of the research in the academic realm is so focused on theory that the practice of the field seems a very distant cousin at best. Because of business trade-offs, pure practice-based papers often leave out the scientific rigor necessary for drawing causal conclusions (e.g., experimentation, controls for common method variance, reliable and public-domain measures), making them impossible to use in meta-analyses (because they tend not to report full correlation tables, effect sizes, and complete measurement information) or for researchers evaluating the full merits of the study. Thus, a meeting in the middle is necessary.

There are enough studies on engagement that Table 4.1 of suggested interventions is still useful in guiding researchers and practitioners as to what to do about engagement. Contributions to understanding what drives engagement can be made by conducting experimental studies to accurately assess the antecedents of engagement. For example, although correlational studies show a relationship between engagement and leadership, job characteristics, and job resources, and most suggest via theory that these are predictors of engagement, few, if any, causal studies support this assumed direction of relationships. If engagement is a state of motivation, we can assume employees become engaged on their own given the right conditions and work factors. Thus, climate factors such as norms, expectations, company policies, and organizational culture in general will likely influence the probability of employees finding the right conditions to become engaged (e.g., Byrne, Palmer, Smith, & Weidert, 2011).

Individual differences may influence engagement levels; hence, researchers should consider a person–situation interactionism framework. For example, some have suggested that a proactive personality (i.e., stable tendency to, under one's own initiative, change one's work environment for meaningful improvements; Bateman & Crant, 1993) may be an individual difference construct worth studying with engagement (e.g., Bakker, Tims, & Derks, 2012). Preliminary findings show a positive relationship between engagement and proactive personality (Dikkers et al., 2009). Others have initiated studies examining the Big Five and engagement (i.e., conscientiousness, neuroticism, extraversion, agreeableness, openness to experience; see Inceoglu & Warr, 2011; Liao, Yang, Wang, Drown, & Shi, 2013).

Practitioners may consider a number of these strategies knowing that even though correlation does not mean causation, it does mean covary—thus, as one construct goes up, so does the other and most likely the relationships are actually reciprocal. For example, it is quite possible engaged employees attract leaders who feel comfortable with a transformational or authentic leadership style, because those types of leaders are at their best leading engaged employees. Similarly, it is possible that employees who are engaged are able to find and obtain resources that enable them to be even more engaged, allowing them to attract and effectively use more of their resources.

Conclusion

Much research is needed to understand what drives engagement, and what truly results from it and not from tangential increases or changes in mood, ability, skill, or general attitude toward work and leadership. Collaboration between the research and practice community is needed to more fully realize the gains from both research and practice. Last, it may be that a perfect set of interventions eludes us because "there are no guarantees about when individual workers will fully engage. There are some workers who may never become engaged, and others who will do so easily and often" (Kahn & Fellows, 2013, p. 111).

Walk-Away Points

- Several approaches for promoting employee engagement exist, some with theoretical backing and others without. Leadership as a driver for engagement is popular; however, surprisingly few studies demonstrate that leadership is related to engagement, and virtually none shows that it increases engagement.
- Meaningful work and meaningful organizations show promise in fostering engagement.
- Very few, if any, research- and practice-related suggestions for how to increase levels of engagement in employees have empirical, causal support indicating that applying the techniques or changes suggested will actually result in changes in engagement.
- When employees are asked what promotes their engagement, they respond with a variety of drivers that may be grouped into seven categories including alignment, communication, and personal factors.

NOTE

1. See Dik, Byrne, and Steger (2013). This book contains several chapters from notable experts about how to create meaning and purpose at work.

5

WHAT PREVENTS EMPLOYEE ENGAGEMENT?

Many consulting or practice writings refer to engagement by describing the costs of disengaged employees to corporate industry. However, none of these writings describes or defines what disengagement or unengaged workers look like or what exactly they mean by disengaged workers. Their focus is on engagement as an outcome (Wefald & Downey, 2009), which they define as the opposite of disengagement.

What Is Disengagement?

Kahn (1990) defined personal disengagement as the "uncoupling of selves from work roles; in disengagement, people withdraw and defend themselves physically, cognitively, or emotionally during role performances" (p. 694). He noted that when people disengage they withdraw, becoming passive in their roles. He likened disengagement to robotic or automatic behaviors, or displaying effortless performance. He further suggested that people who are disengaged hide their identity, thoughts, and feelings while at work. These people perform their roles in a thoughtless script, as opposed to interpreting their role in becoming involved or connected with what they are to accomplish. They may push their tasks onto others or, when in a managerial role, may excessively delegate to their employees. They withdraw from challenging or questioning others and do as they are told. Ideas are kept to the self and creativity is diminished. Similarly, Fineman (1983), in his exploration of the meaning of work by examining individuals recently unemployed, also determined disengagement is a psychological distancing and withdrawal from work. Disengagement was marked by the passage of time with little thought to the job tasks but being sufficiently present to do the job.

Burnout: Is It the Same Thing as Disengagement?

The descriptions of disengagement offered by Kahn (1990) and Fineman (1983) appear similar to those of job burnout. Job burnout refers to "the response to chronic emotional and interpersonal stressors on the job and is defined here by the three dimensions of exhaustion, cynicism, and sense of inefficacy" (Maslach, 2003, p. 189). Thus, burnout is a response to an overwhelming or chronic stressor. Exhaustion leads employees to distance themselves emotionally and cognitively from their work. Cynicism is characterized by a negative and callous response to coworkers and to the job itself, and is highly correlated with exhaustion. Feelings of inefficacy are feelings of ineffectiveness and inability to accomplish one's goals or job tasks. It has been found to develop not only in parallel with exhaustion and cynicism, but also as a consequence of these other two dimensions of burnout (Maslach, 2003). Exhaustion and cynicism are found to develop because of work overload and social conflict. Inefficacy, in contrast, appears to be a result of lack of resources to complete the job.

Maslach (2003) emphasized that burnout is a social construct—the interpersonal framework in which burnout develops is a key component of understanding burnout. It is not just an individual's response to stress, but it is also a reaction to the interchange between the individual and others' in his or her workplace and the general work situation itself. Although some research has demonstrated a connection between burnout and a few demographic variables (e.g., single vs. married, younger vs. older; Maslach, Schaufeli, & Leiter, 2001), most findings lean toward situational context rather than demographic or dispositional factors. For example, excessively or chronically challenging jobs, imbalance of resources versus demands, and consistent personal and role conflict consistently show up in the situations most likely to elicit burnout (Schaufeli & Enzmann, 1998). Maslach (2003) suggested that burnout represents a misfit between the person and his or her work environment—the job exceeds the individual's capacity in some form.

Although research must be launched to examine the potential similarities and differences between disengagement and burnout, conceptually there appear to be a few key differences. First, job burnout is a stress response—a personal reaction to the work environment and its dynamics. Disengagement is referred to as a decoupling of the self from the job, of which burnout may be a behavioral display of disengagement. Thus, disengagement may predict burnout. Second, burnout refers to a complete exhaustion level at which one cannot perform the job task and at which one becomes negative and cynical toward others and the job. In contrast, disengagement does not necessarily include physical exhaustion—individuals complete their work but with an emotional detachment that removes their sense of identity with the work and the organization. Perhaps a more clear delineation between burnout and disengagement can be found within the studies my students and I have conducted (reviewed in Chapter 4 and in what follows).

Byrne's Qualitative Field Research on What Is Disengagement

As noted in Chapter 4, I previously worked with a health care organization who asked me to identify what engagement looks like in the organization and what prevents engagement for the employees. As part of the project, interviewees identified what disengagement felt like and looked like, and what prevented them from becoming engaged. Similarly, and described in more detail in Chapter 4, I worked with another health organization, also to identify what engagement looks like and what prevents engagement for the employees.

Table 5.1 lists themes extracted from the responses from both studies of what disengagement is.

Table 5.1 Themes Extracted From Qualitative Work—What Is Disengagement

Theme	Examples
Hiding	Flying under the radar
	Psychological, emotional, and cognitive distancing oneself from others at work
	Escape from the work stuff that is draining, such as the politics and personal conflicts
Counterproductive	Resisting change but not being able to say why
	Complaining and becoming argumentative
	Doing sloppy work; not feeling motivated to try to make the work of good quality (do what it takes to just get by, but nothing more)
Negative emotions	Feeling disconnected from the organization
	Feeling disconnected from the system and from others in the system
	Feeling a lack of control over the work, the work environment, and things you should be able to control to do your job well
	Feeling a lack of curiosity when you used to have a lot of curiosity that drove your energy
	Feeling trapped, like you can't get out of the bad situation and it's not the work that's pushing you away; you want to do the work but can't
	Feeling rejected, like a failure, unable to achieve success after constant trial and error
	Lack of feeling of ownership
	Feeling helpless to change what isn't working around me; learned helplessness
	Low morale
	Not meeting one's own bar for success; disappointment in the self that continues on and can't seem to find a way or get the help needed to jump over one's own bar

(Continued)

Table 5.1 (Continued)

Theme	Examples
Withdrawal	Dislike the job itself—not interested in the work or the objective
	Not wanting to do the work anymore even though it's what you say and intuitively know you enjoy
	Making excuses for not performing responsibilities
	Refusing to partake in organizational initiatives
	Passivity
Time factor	Not an overnight thing—seemed to happened after a succession of ongoing events, issues, lack of support, etc.

Some of the examples within these themes are similar to those noted by Kahn (1990), such as distancing of oneself and disconnecting from the organization or others. Likewise, some are similar to those used for describing burnout (Maslach, 2003). The interviewees suggested feeling emotionally exhausted led to their becoming disengaged. Specifically, employees talked about how emotionally draining the work itself could be, even though they loved what they did, and they referred to how having to collaborate and gain consensus on every single decision (even small) became exhausting. Additionally, though they were exhausted, they did not withdraw from the work but rather reduced their contribution. A number of examples we extracted that were different from burnout and from Kahn's work include doing sloppy work and complaining, which we categorized as counterproductive.

An interview we had with another individual outside the scope of these two studies gave us some insight into potentially key differences between burnout and engagement.

Employees' Reflections

When I think about whether I'm truly disengaged, I think that perhaps I'm burned out—but not actually disengaged. I don't think I'm disengaged because I have a ton of work opportunities that I'm excited about, lots of work to do that I typically enjoy, am excited about moving my personal success forward, I've started some new projects that I can control and work on independently, and I have focus—though I do get tired and distracted. I feel emotionally excited about what I do and I seem to have enough energy to do it when I get into it. I wake up and go to work, though I tire easily from the excessive interaction and stupid things that people around

---

> *me say and do. If I could just be in my own space and do my own thing, I think I would be seen as very engaged. I feel burned out because I'm wanting to be away from these people—I am cynical about their ability to change and all of a sudden become good leaders, and I am more tired than I used to be. I feel like having to deal with that outside noise takes me away from doing what I really want to do—which is engage in my work.*

What Inhibits or Prevents Engagement?

My research suggests a variety of organizational and individual factors inhibit or prevent employees from becoming engaged. Tables 5.2 and 5.3 list themes of what inhibits engagement, extracted from both studies.

The results from my qualitative research suggest both individual and organizational factors get in the way of employees becoming engaged. Specifically, organizational factors refer to those over which the organization seems to have the most influence or control, such as the amount of work individuals do on a daily or weekly basis, the amount of management they receive (or the lack thereof), whether individuals behavior or decisions are appropriately scrutinized or people are held accountable for their decisions, and the establishment and reinforcement of norms that might suggest speaking up in the interest of helping your organization is considered resistance to organizational policies or change (Van Dyne & LePine, 1998).

Individual factors were those individuals could control or interpret on their own based on their own personal situations. For example, whether family problems (e.g., sick family members) result in an inability to focus at work is an individualized response (Lazarus, 1991; Lazarus & Folkman, 1984). Some people compartmentalize their home and work lives such that when they are at work, they do not focus attention on what is happening at home because they feel they have taken care of the home needs so they can go to work (e.g., J. Howard, Rechnitzer, & Cunningham, 1975). Others are unable to take a compartmentalized approach, and so they maintain passive or constant thinking about worries at home. Lack of progress toward goal achievement could be either an individual or an organizational factor, depending on what is preventing the progress. However, how one interprets lack of progress and the response to it is really individualized (Linnenbrink & Pintrich, 2010). Some people may feel the lack of progress is solely attributed to the organization and just a part of working—they focus on what they can make progress. For others, the lack of progress on one task inhibits their ability to feel engaged in their work in general (Ouweneel, Schaufeli, & Le Blanc, 2013). They

Table 5.2 Qualitative Findings on Organizational Inhibitors to Engagement

Theme	Examples
Resources	Lack of support Resource constraints such as people, time, and equipment Technology that inhibits one's ability to do the job effectively Lack of work–life balance
Interpersonal	Overly chatty coworkers, subordinates, bosses, or other work colleagues who mean well but you can't deter them because the norm prevents you from stopping excessive time-wasting like this (i.e., a lack of ability to control your work environment) Hostile or emotionally abusive work environment (secretive, manipulative, emotionally punishing) Lack of demonstration of caring about individual development, growth in the job and/or to be able to do other jobs; demonstration of lack of commitment to employees Lack of professionalism amongst coworkers and/or supervisor, and little ability to fix Feeling lack of trust from others that you can do the job
Leadership	Being micromanaged Poor and ineffective management and leadership Negative organizational politics Lack of accountability Inequity High or excessive workload—prevents goal achievement Lack of voice or ability to provide input to positively change the system or job so that it is more efficient; demonstrates a lack of trust Too much focus on the bottom line, not enough on process A norm that suggests or implies speaking up about concerns implies lack of support for the organization – thus suggestions meant for improving the work environment are seen as resistance to change or disagreement with management Constant change that creates transition confusion and lack of clarity over roles and objectives Poor communication, nondirect communication (e.g., beating around the bush and not addressing the "real" issues); miscommunication, and lack of communication (information vacuum)
Other	Mundane work

feel stuck, and they cannot focus on other tasks because the one task is not getting done.

Emotional exhaustion, as defined in the responses from our interviewees, was not a general or a global emotional exhaustion or burnout to which the term generally refer. That is, individuals referred to how

Table 5.3 Qualitative Findings on Individual Inhibitors to Engagement

Theme	*Examples*
Significance	Feeling undervalued, not recognized
	Feeling taken advantage of, taken for granted
Fit	Work that is not a match for one's skills, knowledge, and ability (lack of fit)
	Lack of agreement or alignment between the head and the heart (what makes sense intellectually, versus what feels right)
	Lack of necessary skills for self or others
Non-work related	Family problems such as sick family members
	Inability to focus on work due to non-work interferences
	Non-work related factors that require attention but take time and thus compete with work (e.g., life maintenance, home care, pet care, needy family members)
Communication	Relational issues (conflicts, personality clashes)
	Very long learning curve or when feedback on performance has a long delay cycle
	Emotional exhaustion from the work itself and by having to excessively cooperate with others to gain consensus or agreement on every decision
Stress	Physical constraints such as injury or chronic pain
	Lack of progress towards goal achievement—inability to complete job or accomplish work goals, or inability to do the job to a high quality because of excessive workload or deadlines

emotionally taxing the work was itself, in particular within the health care institution. The job itself required a lot of them emotionally, and because they loved the work and believed what they were doing was important, they were unable to invest of themselves in a balanced or managed fashion. Thus, every day and every case (i.e., client) was emotionally draining. Interviewees explained that when you do this day in and day out, the emotional drain regarding that work in particular takes its toll. Additionally, excessive need for cooperation or gaining consensus or agreement on every decision, though perhaps originally intended to keep everyone involved as part of creating a positive work environment became negative, preventing people from goal accomplishment. Individuals had to use a lot of emotional energy to negotiate, communicate, and understand the perspective of many others within the organization before any action or decision could be made. This energy expenditure was perceived as negative, especially when it was about very small decisions that could easily have been made by one person without detrimental effects to others. It was clear from these interviews that the exhaustion was targeted at the specifics of the job—people did not talk about being exhausted about all aspects of the job or all the time, they did not seek to distance themselves from others, nor did they talk about becoming cynical. Thus, they did not describe being burned out, just emotional exhaustion at various times.

Following up on the second qualitative study I conducted, I asked participants questions about injustice, job demands, and supervisor or coworker incivility. The injustice questions were those developed to specifically ask about injustice (i.e., violation of social, moral, and fairness norms; Bies, 1987; M. Fine, 1983), as opposed to justice (e.g., fairness perceptions at work). Job demands included pressure to complete tasks; pressure to get a lot done; role ambiguity; poor physical working conditions such as poor lighting, noisy or distracting sounds, uncomfortable or cramped office design; and resource inadequacies. Participants rated how often their job included or required the items/actions. Finally, incivility items (see Cortina, Magley, Williams, & Langhout, 2001) asked for ratings on how often participants had been put into the situation by their supervisor or coworker and included "put you down make demeaning remarks about you and/or to you," and "made unwanted attempts to draw you into a discussion of personal matters." Results of the analysis showed supervisor incivility and injustice were both negatively related to employee engagement. Thus, the more incivility or injustice an employee perceived, the lower his or her reported engagement levels. Research has shown that responses to incivility or injustice at work include withdrawal behaviors, detachment, and avoidance behaviors (Cortina & Magley, 2009; L. Howard & Cordes, 2010), and such behaviors and reactions appear to be associated with disengagement as noted in our qualitative studies.

In summary, the themes extracted from the qualitative studies on inhibitors to engagement cumulatively suggest that both factors or aspects of the organization and within the individual's life play a role in preventing or inhibiting engagement. Some were job demand and job resource related, suggesting the job demands-resources (JD-R) model (Bakker & Demerouti, 2008) may serve to help explain what inhibits engagement. Thus far, the model has been used to explain engagement, but perhaps its greater utility is in examining when employees are or will become disengaged. Leadership has frequently been pushed as a means for fostering engagement, but the results from my qualitative work suggest leaders also play a key role in inhibiting engagement. Thus, a lack of leadership or a bad leader is actually harmful and should be addressed quickly. Notable here is that themes for engagement inhibitors did not match drivers of engagement—thus, job characteristics, a frequently noted driver of engagement was not mentioned in the negative (i.e., a lack of job characteristics creates disengagement), whereas the lack of job characteristics were noted in the themes for creating disengagement.

Theoretically Derived Inhibitors/Roadblocks

Very little research to date has examined what is disengagement and what inhibits or prevents employees from becoming engaged. An examination of the research and theory leads us to the following possible theoretically derived inhibitors or roadblocks to engagement shown in Table 5.4.

Table 5.4 Theoretically Based Inhibitors to Engagement

Inhibitor	*Foundational Theory or References*
Control, lack of autonomy, feedback suggests incompetence regardless of competence level, and inability to relate to others	Self-determination theory (Deci & Ryan, 1985) Job characteristics theory (Hackman & Oldham, 1976)
Distrust	Theory of Collective Distrust; Kramer (1994)
Inequity	Organizational justice (Bies & Moag, 1986; Deutsch, 1985)
Lack of clear mission or vision provides meaningful goals and purpose to the work	Meaningful work; Baumeister (1991)
Lack of job or organizational fit; work value congruence	Person-job or person-organization fit; Bretz, Ash, & Dreher (1989); Chatman (1991); Meglino, Ravlin, & Adkins (1989) Attraction-Selection-Attrition (ASA) model; Schneider (1987)
Negative organizational politics	Ferris, Frink, Beehr, and Gilmore (1995); Ferris, Russ, and Fandt (1989)
Organizational change	Interdependence theory (Kelley, 1984); Michela and Vena (2012)
Reduction and loss of job resources	Job demands-resources model (Bakker & Demerouti, 2008); Conservation of Resources Theory (Hobfoll, 1989)
Threats to psychological availability (e.g., distraction from non-work related concerns, illness)	Kahn's (1990) Engagement Model
Threats to psychological meaningfulness (e.g., inability to determine purpose of work, lack of fit with organizational vision, job does not relate to goal of the team)	Kahn's (1990) Engagement Model
Threats to psychological safety (e.g., untrustworthy supervisor, workplace gossip, work concerns taken out of context and used against oneself)	Kahn's (1990) Engagement Model

According to Kahn

Kahn's (1990) work leads us to the following possible inhibitors of engagement. First, the three psychological states—psychological safety, psychological availability, and psychological meaningfulness—lead to employee engagement. Thus, anything that takes away from individuals' ability to feel psychologically safe and psychologically available or to get a sense of psychological meaningfulness from the job should inhibit their ability to become engaged.

Threats to psychological safety. Working in an environment that lacks trust in employees, fosters criticism, and promotes discrimination against individuals who may approach work differently will produce a work environment that threatens psychological safety. Employees who convey an unpopular opinion but one offered in the spirit of improving the work environment (e.g., voice behaviors; Van Dyne & LePine, 1998) will feel psychologically unsafe in an organization that stifles or fails to encourage such positive and constructive criticisms. The presence of excessive negative organizational politics will also inhibit psychological safety, because organizational politics are intentional actions that promote and protect some individuals at the expense of others or the organization (R. Allen, Madison, Porter, Renwick, & Mayes, 1979; Ferris & Kacmar, 1992). Additionally, organizational policies that appear to discriminate against individuals of multicultural races or differing personal relationship preferences may inhibit perceptions of psychological safety. Supervisors who are untrained in positive coaching can also contribute to a negative psychological safety climate by giving inappropriate or poorly communicated feedback. For example, when employees make mistakes or behave in ways the organization does not sanction, supervisors who are unskilled may fail to understand why employees make mistakes or how these mistakes may be avoided in the future, and unable to give the necessary feedback that preserves employee self-esteem while fostering improvement. Employees who are treated inappropriately are unlikely to ask for help when they need it or may even retaliate against supervisors who are perceived as punishing (Hershcovis et al., 2007; Treviño & Brown, 2005).

Threats to psychological availability. For employees to feel psychologically available they must be able to focus in the moment at work. This means being able to feel that their family is cared for as needed, that any financial stresses can be addressed appropriately, and that they feel physically able to perform on the job or perform as needed. Thus, workplaces should have policies in place that are family-friendly and support medical conditions, that help employees who find themselves in financially tough situations, and enable support from supervisors and colleagues when illness or injury ensues for the employee. For example, policies such as flextime (e.g., being able to come to and leave work between a range of hours as opposed to a specific single time, such as arriving between 7–10 a.m. and leaving between 4–7 p.m.) may allow individuals who need more time in the morning to get to work (e.g., individuals with family responsibilities or who live far from work and deal with horrible commutes) or who have nonwork obligations in the early afternoon or evening to meet them (e.g., picking up kids from day care). Employees who feel their job is at risk may also be inhibited from feeling psychologically available on the job. That is, if they are constantly worried about their job security, they will not feel able to focus on the job because they would be worried about messing up or doing something that puts the job at risk. Another way to inhibit psychological availability is to constantly ask employees about outside non-work-related issues as opposed to giving employees freedom to discuss when desired. For example, although they have good intentions, coworkers who constantly ask about a chronically ill family member or a recent financial disaster will create an environment that prevents psychological availability for the employee who is truly trying to be focused on work while at work. Additionally, constantly receiving phone calls or e-mails from non-work-related entities will also minimize psychological availability. One could argue constant use of social media sites such as Facebook or Twitter reduces psychological availability; however, if frequent visits to these sites relieves anxiety over how a family member or close friend is doing, one could argue contrarily that social media facilitates their feelings of availability.

Threats to psychological meaningfulness. Psychological meaningfulness is achieved when an employee feels his or her investment in the job role is rewarded by the positive feelings and energy the job creates and the sense of personal value from doing the job. Psychological meaningfulness is not always something a leader must give to an employee; employees do not always need outside recognition to feel their work is meaningful or to be assigned a job society considers "meaningful" (e.g., health care worker or firefighter; see Ashforth & Kreiner, 2013, on finding meaning in dirty work). Employees who feel that the work itself makes a meaningful contribution to society, to something bigger than themselves, or inherently pays them back emotionally, physically, and cognitively will feel psychological meaningfulness (Kahn, 1990). For example, the employees of the second health organization I studied felt the work they did, regardless of whether it was recognized by the organization, was meaningful because it made a difference in the lives of those patients who needed help. Taking away employees' ability to complete the job, restricting their use of skills to complete a variety of tasks on the job, or taking away their ability to make their work feel like a meaningful contribution will inhibit their ability to perceive psychological meaningfulness in their work role and thereby will inhibit engagement.

Psychological withdrawal. Kahn (1990) suggested disengagement was when an employee withdraws him or herself from the work role, detaching from identification with the organization, and fulfilling tasks in an automated or robotic manner. Although Kahn did not specify what leads to disengagement, we can hypothesize from the literature on withdrawal and identity creation within organizations what may lead to disengagement. Research on psychological withdrawal suggests employees distance themselves when their relationships within the organization are threatened (e.g., Michela & Vena, 2012). For example, during organizational change when employees are unclear on how the change affects them, they will enter in a self-protective function that involves psychological distancing. Psychological distancing is achieved through devaluing the organization and reducing organizational identification. Uncertainty from change or mergers triggers distancing in the form of loss of affective commitment and satisfaction (Michela & Vena, 2012). Perceptions of inequity in relationships also result in withdrawal (Taris, van Horn, Schaufeli, & Schreurs, 2004). Researchers have further noted that various forms of withdrawal exist, such as psychological withdrawal, lateness, absenteeism, and turnover (Beehr & Gupta, 1978). Thus, psychological withdrawal is not the only kind of withdrawal employees may experience that results in this disengagement. In the sociology literature, alienation or powerlessness within the specific organizational setting results in social isolation (Shepard, 1972), which may also contribute to disengagement as it may affect employees' psychological availability (Kahn, 1990).

It appears that the results from my qualitative studies provide initial support for using Kahn's (1990) model to explain inhibitors to engagement. Many of the examples from the interviews could be construed as threats to psychological availability, meaningfulness, and safety, and those threats were what employees said caused or were directly related to their disengagement and/or reduced engagement at work.

According to the JD-R Model

Maslach and Leiter (1997), and Maslach, Leiter, and Schaufeli (2001), suggested disengagement results when one's energy turns into exhaustion, involvement becomes cynicism, and efficacy becomes ineffectiveness, essentially the three dimensions of burnout. Thus, according to

Maslach and colleagues, disengagement is the same as burnout. This definition became the foundation of Schaufeli, Salanova et al.'s (2002) definition, which is most often used with the JD-R model (Bakker & Demerouti, 2008).

Threats to job resources. If we use the JD-R model to hypothesize potential antecedents to disengagement, we would be likely to propose a lack of resources and excessive demands should result in disengagement. Thus, if an organization withdraws support or does not provide organizational support, does not have policies and procedures that provide for family care, has management who provides no feedback, and fails to provide learning or developmental experiences for employees, employees should perceive a job-resources vacuum. The model implies that job demands have to be in excess of job resources to see a lack of engagement, but it is not clear quite how job resources and job demands work together. We can hypothesize that if there are not enough resources to offset demands, demands at some point will become too overwhelming making it hard for employees to become engaged—because the perception of job resources are necessary for engagement (Bakker & Demerouti, 2008).

A similar model to the JD-R model, the conservation of resources (COR) theory (Hobfoll, 1989), suggests people seek to obtain, foster, and conserve resources (e.g., personal, social, material) that are of core value to themselves, and the aggressive loss of these resources results in burnout and other stress related outcomes. Thus, threats to one's ability to foster and retain core resources will result in burnout or disengagement (Schaufeli et al., 2002). For example, traumatic stress or conditions of rapid loss of resources challenge one's ability to retain and foster resources, whereas job-related demands result in slow resource loss (Hobfoll & Shirom, 2001), which may not lead to burnout if individuals have enough reservoirs of other resources to cope with this slow drain.

Threats of high demands. The presence of excessive demands without resources to offset those demands will result in burnout. For example, if the organization creates work assignments that have high emotional, mental, or physical pressures and demands, and in general pushes employees to their limit, according to the JD-R model, disengagement will follow. High demands that tax employees' ability to cope and recover either physically or emotionally will drain their reserves. The JD-R model is fairly simple in that it proposes that burning out employees will lead to disengagement. Another aspect of the model is personal resources, such as personality characteristics or traits that lend themselves to resiliency, and recovery and coping from stressful situations.

Just as the results from my qualitative studies served as initial evidence in support of a lack of components from Kahn's (1990) model (i.e., lack of psychological availability), they too serve to support the JD-R model for predicting disengagement. As noted previously, it may be the JD-R model is more effective at predicting disengagement than engagement, a supposition that has yet to be tested empirically.

Other Models of Engagement

Saks's model of engagement. Saks (2006) proposed that employee engagement (i.e., "the degree to which an individual is attentive and absorbed in the performance of their roles," p. 602) depends on one's role (Rothbard, 2001), and as such, employees develop both job and organizational engagement. Relying on social exchange theory (Blau, 1964), Saks argued that employees choose to become engaged in response to developing an exchange relationship with their organization. In return for the economic and socioemotional resources given to them by the organization, employees give varying levels of job and organizational engagement (Saks, 2006). Though his model is unclear as to which form of engagement is targeted in exchange for what from the organization, and social exchange relationships are exclusive of the economical exchanges (see Blau, 1964), the results of Saks's correlational study are that job characteristics (e.g., autonomy, task identity, skill variety, task significance, feedback from others, and feedback from the job) were predictors of job engagement and that organizational support was a predictor of both job and organizational engagement (although a stronger predictor or organizational than job engagement). Support from the supervisor, rewards and recognition, and fairness were not significant predictors of either form of engagement. Job and organizational engagement were measured using scale items developed by Saks. Moderate to high correlations were reported between the two forms of engagement and between job and organizational engagement with attitudes such as organizational commitment and job satisfaction (e.g., correlations ranged from .52 to .69), hinting at the possibility of either construct contamination or common method bias (surveys of all study variables were completed in a single sitting).

Psychometric concerns aside, Saks's (2006) study offers some potential suggestions for inhibitors to engagement, namely, the lack of autonomy, feedback, task identity and significance, or skill variety may inhibit an employee's ability to become engagement. These job characteristics are those of the job characteristics theory (Hackman & Oldham, 1976) that lead to internal motivation and were hypothesized as part of Kahn's (1990) model of engagement, as well. Likewise, a lack of support from the organization, in particular, may inhibit engagement. Lack of support from the immediate supervisor, according to Saks's results, should not matter because supervisory support was not significantly related to either form of engagement. Another possible hypothesis from Saks's model may be anything that threatens the social exchange relationship with the organization should result in disengagement. That is, issues with trust, lack of reciprocity, or psychological contract breaches may result in a weakening of the social exchange relationship, resulting in at least a reduction of engagement, if not actual disengagement (e.g., Agarwal & Bhargava, 2013).

Trust issues and lack of support from the organization were noted in the qualitative results shared previously, suggesting there could be merit to using Saks's (2006) model, or in particular his use of social exchange theory, to hypothesize when disengagement may occur. None of the interviewees, however, noted that issues might be more clearly indicative of a breach in a social exchange relationship, indicating my findings are not as supportive of the use of Saks's model as they are of the other models for proposing inhibitors and causes of disengagement.

Macey and Schneider's model of engagement. Macey and Schneider (2008) suggest there are three forms of engagement: trait, state, and behavioral. Trait engagement cannot be changed by the organization or person as it is a dispositional characteristic. Thus, engaged employees are proactive, positive, conscientious, or autoletic, and those without such personality traits are not likely to become engaged. Scoring high in these personality traits, however, leads to feelings of energy and absorption, which Macey and Schneider say compose state engagement. Thus, when engaged, employees are satisfied, involved, and committed to their workplace. As a consequence of their feelings of energy and positive attitudes, they demonstrate behavioral engagement in the form of extra-role behaviors, personal initiative, and they adapt to the job. According to this model, we could hypothesize inhibitors to engagement include personality characteristics that tend to reflect negative affectivity or mental disorders that prevent an otherwise positive disposition from emerging (e.g., clinical depression). State engagement may be inhibited by excessive demands that drain energy or reduce positive feelings at work such as excessive conflict or by having to juggle too many competing tasks that inhibit involvement in any single project or task. Additionally, Macey and Schneider proposed that job characteristics or work attributes moderate the relationship between trait and state engagement. Therefore, work environments that inhibit employees' autonomy and are monotonous or overly simple may inhibit even the right personalities from becoming engaged (perhaps just experiencing very low engagement). Poor leadership that fails to empower employees may stifle the normally positive employee; Macey and Schneider also hypothesized transformational leadership as a moderator to the state engagement—behavioral engagement pathway. Last, if employees are placed in work conditions or in organizations with norms that fail to allow them to exhibit extra-role behaviors or personal initiative, their level of behavioral engagement will be inhibited or reduced.

Some examples and themes extracted from my qualitative studies appear to provide initial support for using Macey and Schneider's (2008) model to hypothesize disengagement. For example, excessive demands, conflicts, poor leadership, excessively controlling work environments, and monotonous work were reported as inhibitors in the qualitative studies, and they appear here as possible inhibitors.

Other Inhibitors From Related Research

Inability to balance work and life demands. My qualitative studies revealed a number of inhibitors to engagement for which some research support exists. For example, consequences of micromanagement include inhibited performance, stifled innovation, and strained communication between employees and supervisors (e.g., Francaro, 2007). The inability to achieve perceived work–life balance can have negative consequences on employees' ability to invest themselves in work (Hobson, Delunas, & Kesic, 2001). However, employees do not always work because the job is a career or fulfills them; they work as a means to supporting their non-work-related activities where they fulfill their goals and life ambitions (S. Friedman, Christensen, & DeGroot, 1998). Ways to encourage disengagement for these individuals is to fail to recognize the value and importance of their life outside of work and to be unwilling to find a balanced integration of work and life that takes advantage of the gains one gets from non-work-related activity (see S. Friedman et al., 1998, for good examples of how balance is achieved). Work can be fulfilling or meaningful for those who see it as a means to an end, when the end is a better non-work-related life. Thus, recognizing different value systems and appreciating that meaning and engagement may be in the eye of the beholder has merit.

Threats to competence, autonomy, and relatedness. Self-determination theory (Deci & Ryan, 1985; Ryan & Deci, 2000) proposes employees' intrinsic motivation is triggered to fulfill feelings of competence and autonomy. Self-determination theory suggests that people are motivated, even when tasks are not intrinsically interesting, because they know their behavior will provide or meet their needs for competence, autonomy, and relatedness. Thus, anything that inhibits employees' efforts to feel competent on the job or to enjoy autonomy or control that fulfills intrinsic motivational needs will inhibit their ability to become engaged. For example, a work environment that seems overly controlling or rigid or that seems to stifle employees' needs to relate to others will create a negative work climate for engagement.

Poor leadership. Researchers have shown that leadership is positively related to engagement (e.g., Aryee, Walumbwa, Zhou, & Hartnell, 2012; Tuckey, Dollard, & Bakker, 2012), and therefore, poor leadership or lack of leadership is likely to inhibit or prevent employees' from becoming engaged. Leaders who demonstrate high levels of emotional intelligence have been associated with employees' reporting high engagement (e.g., Ravichandran, Arasu, & Kumar, 2011); thus, leaders without this social intelligence are likely to inhibit engagement in their followers. Lastly, in my own research, interpersonal and supportive leadership has been positively associated with high levels of engagement; therefore, leaders who fail to provide the caring, relationship oriented, and work-related supportive behaviors of interpersonal and supportive leaders may inhibit employees' ability to perceive the psychological conditions or identification that is necessary for becoming engaged.

Lack of organizational purpose. Research surrounding meaningful organizations suggests employees who work for organizations that do not consider employees' need for meaning in their work will inhibit their employees' ability to become engaged (A. Brown et al., 2001; Chalofsky & Krishna, 2009; Kahn, 1990). Thus, failing to provide a clear superordinate goal, a clear mission, or a vision or failing to create clear order and purpose to the goals of the organization may result in employees struggling to become engaged; their need to understand what makes their work meaningful will be inhibited by their lack of clear purpose.

Distrust. The lack of trust within organizations inhibits becoming engaged. Specifically, trust within organizations allows employees to be vulnerable to the actions of the organization (Kramer, 1994). Employees who trust the organization believe it will make decisions in their best interest (Kramer, 1999). Distrust—the lack of confidence in others and their actions or intentions—can be triggered by situational cues that hint of hidden agendas or unfaithful intentions (G. Fine & Holyfield, 1996). Cues can be as simple as being considered a part of one group, such that those in other groups are automatically viewed as different, untrustworthy, and in some way less than those in one's own group (see social categorization; Sherif, 1963; Tajfel, 1978; Tajfel, Billig, Bundy, & Flament, 1971). Based on a review of the literature, Kramer (1999) hypothesized that unmet expectations, healthy suspicion of organizations, computer monitoring and surveillance, unintended consequences of regulations meant to be positive (e.g., trucker's log book was to promote compliance with driving hours laws but resulted in either truckers' driving while too tired and having two log books—one for inspection and one for actual hours driven), and psychological contract breach can all result in distrust.

Stifled innovation and broken promises. Organizational climates that stifle innovation and creativity, as well as jobs where tasks become monotonous and predictable lead to disengagement (Fineman, 1983). Employees feel trapped by their work as opposed to energized by it, leading them to psychologically, if not physically, withdraw. Broken promises, unmet expectations, and failure to see a productive end to one's job effort (e.g., working hard on a project to have it cancelled and dismantled) all lead to disengagement (S. Fineman, 1983).

Workaholism equals too much engagement? I cover the idea of too much engagement and workaholism in Chapter 10 in more detail, but it warrants some mention here regarding discussing disengagement. It has been suggested too much engagement leads to disengagement (Macey, Schneider, Barbera, & Young, 2009), or essentially burnout. That is, employees who are given too much challenge at work, too much autonomy, too much support for engagement, and their work is too meaningful will become disengaged, distancing themselves from work. Macey and colleagues (2009) base this assertion on the idea engagement is like other constructs that when too much is present it results in an overload of the psychological system.

Although no empirical work has yet explored whether there is such a thing as too much engagement, the literature on passion and workaholism may shed light on what Macey et al. (2009) were suggesting. Andreassen, Ursin, and Eriksen (2007) examined two components of workaholism—drive and enjoyment of work—and found positive relationships between one aspect of engagement (i.e., absorption) and enjoyment of work. Enjoyment of work was characterized as being motivated to work for sheer enjoyment and satisfaction. Thus, this research suggests that high absorption at work is related to workaholism. In contrast, when examining passion as a two-dimensional construct comprising obsessive (e.g., inability to control one's need to work) and harmonic passion (e.g., appreciate work more when learning new things), consistent with Vallerand and Houlfort (2003), and engagement, Forest, Mageau, Sarrazin, and Morin (2011) determined that harmonious passion was consistent with positive well-being, autotelic experience, and concentration at work. Obsessive passion was associated with low levels of well-being. Obsessive passion was not associated with flow or affective commitment, both of which are often sometimes aspects of engagement (Saks, 2006; Schaufeli et al., 2002). Workaholism refers to self-imposed demands that are compulsive and neglectful of other areas of life (Burke, 2009), similar to Vallerand and Houlfort's (2003) definition of obsessive passion. However, working compulsively is positively associated with engagement ($r = .27$; Schaufeli, Taris, & Bakker, 2006). In summary, the research is inconclusive about whether too much engagement results in burnout or in disengagement.

Lack of person–organization fit. In my qualitative studies described previously, lack of job and organizational fit was mentioned as an inhibitor to engagement. Although person–organization or person–job fit have not been studied with employee engagement, based on the comments from our interviews, I suspect that lack of fit leaves employees struggling to connect with others in the organization. This lack of connection most likely contributes to a mismatch with support or aligned purpose. When a lack of congruence between employees' values and those of their supervisor or organization exists, negative consequences such as low commitment and low job satisfaction result (Bretz, Ash, & Dreher, 1989; Cable & Judge, 1996; Gregory, Albritton, & Osmonbekov, 2010). When employees perceive a mismatch or lack of fit or congruence between their personalities and organizational attributes, they are less likely than those perceiving a match to feel they belong in that organization (Cable & Judge, 1994; Chatman, 1989; Meglino, Ravlin, & Adkins, 1989). Substantial research in recruitment and selection demonstrates that fit matters in terms of prospective employees' choices for places to work and initial attitudes once on the job (e.g., McCulloch & Turban, 2007; Nikolaou, 2003; Pfieffelmann, Wagner, & Libkuman, 2010; Resick, Baltes, & Shantz, 2007; Saks & Ashforth, 2002). Therefore, additional study of person–organization fit is warranted to determine to what degree a lack of fit inhibits feelings of belongingness that ultimately tie into feelings of disengagement.

WHAT DOES INHIBITED ENGAGEMENT LOOK LIKE?

Maxim has been an assistant professor for about 4 years. He has, of lately, been contemplating whether he should find another job. He still likes the job, but he thinks it may be a bad fit—that this is not the right career for him or maybe not the right university. On one hand, he feels that the work he is doing is very valuable—that he is making a difference for his students, especially when their parents tell him at graduation how he changed their kids' lives. On the other hand, he struggles to find his work meaningful beyond that; after all, how many people actually read and not just cite his articles?

Maxim feels under constant scrutiny as to whether he is producing enough publications, getting good enough teacher ratings, and involved in the same level of service as his colleagues around him. He feels that he cannot ask for help from the faculty in his department; he is afraid that if he shares his struggles with any of them, they will hold it against him when he comes up for tenure and promotion. In his mid-tenure review, he was told he is doing OK but that he needs to produce more and get better teacher ratings; this feedback made him feel like a failure besides not telling him how to produce more or teach better. He also heard some of the professors who he thought liked him brought up concerns he felt were unsupported and unfair. It seems as though there is definitely a club at work, to which he does not belong. He has very little seniority, and he is constantly reminded of that when decisions are made. He has interjected his suggestions into discussions, but his opinions are often ignored; he feels as though he is invisible at times. As a result, he has started avoiding the faculty in his department by scheduling office hours during the regular faculty meeting. He likes his colleagues, but he feels they exclude him from decision making and from hallway conversations, so he avoids them. He figures that if he detaches from work a bit and distances himself from his colleagues, he will not feel so hurt by their actions. Sadly, his department head has done nothing to reach out to him or hold the faculty accountable for his success. After all, they hired him and at that time believed he would be successful; should they not be helping him, making him feel valuable, and that he belongs?

He has little connection with the university, mainly because no one has reached out to him to offer guidance or support. No one has offered to show him the best way to get materials from the library, which local restaurant has the best food, or where the quietest coffee shop is on campus—when he is at work, he feels alone most of the time. Unfortunately, Maxim also feels alone at home—he works all the time including weekends. He has two small children, but he does not feel that he actually sees them much because he is always tucked away in his home office, working.

Conclusion

Little is known about disengagement; thus, the preceding propositions are mostly theoretical with some related research suggesting that they may be plausible. We can infer from research on engagement and on likely inhibitors of engagement what may lead to disengagement, assuming disengagement is either the opposite of engagement, a supposition that needs empirical testing. Kahn (1990) proposed that engagement is a moment-to-moment phenomenon; thus, it may be possible that people vacillate between intense engagement and disengagement (perhaps in this case, disengagement is just low or nonengagement) all day long, but when averaged over the course of a day, those people may report general high levels of engagement. Or, moments of disengagement simply may not register in their memories, since it could be disengagement is just not as salient to them as is moments of engagement. Empirical research is necessary to understand what is disengagement and what it is relative to engagement.

Walk-Away Points

- Inhibitors to engagement in the workplace include factors within the organization's control and within the employees' control; some are situational, some are employee disposition, and some are interactions between situation and employee; fit matters.
- By focusing on what creates engagement, we may be able to avoid disengagement; however, even with all the support, the right situational characteristics, the ideal circumstances, and the best of leadership, some people still may not be engaged.
- Employees who are asked to become engaged or to be more engaged than they are now are essentially being asked to share their intensity, enthusiasm, persistence, and adaptability when they may not be willing or able to do so. Thus, knowing inhibitors does not translate into automatic success in achieving 100% engagement from all employees at all times.
- Research into disengagement can be advanced by combining theories into a mega-theory of disengagement.

6

HOW DO WE ASSESS EMPLOYEE ENGAGEMENT AND CHOOSE A GOOD MEASURE?

A number of years ago, I was invited to a vendor selection meeting by a client of mine. My role was to be the expert in psychometrics (i.e., field of psychological measurement), there to evaluate the quality of the measures and solutions offered by each vendor. Of the four consulting firms that presented, not one was able to provide answers to some basic measurement questions about its engagement surveys and packaged solutions. The irony of the situation is that all the vendors were informed by the client that an expert in psychological measurement would be sitting in on the meeting to evaluate solutions and to help choose one for the client, yet none were prepared with the information for which the vendors' should have known I would ask. Not only were their definitions of engagement not about engagement, but they also had no evidence their measures assessed their chosen definition, nor how well. The client would have chosen one of these solutions thinking an engagement measure and a solution for fostering engagement in the culture was soon to be deployed, yet none of these measures and solutions would ultimately provide information about levels of employee engagement or how to change them.

The client's lack of detailed knowledge of psychological measurement or organizational design is not atypical, nor is it a criticism of this particular client, or of clients in general. We cannot all be experts in everything at all times. Although I cannot share an entire process of organizational development and design aimed at engagement in one chapter, I can share how to ask a few of the basic and fundamental questions that guide the development of a solution and selection of a good measure of engagement. For example, two fundamentals questions that should be asked include (a) Does the measure consistently and accurately assess engagement every time it is used? and (b) Does it actually assess engagement as it claims it does? Without the answers to these questions, it is difficult to choose the right engagement instrument. How can interventions be designed, conclusions be drawn about research or investigative results, or recommendations be provided about what to do with engagement without knowing if engagement is what was measured? Furthermore, with survey in hand, another basic question should be, How is this survey best used to affect culture change or help establish the desired culture? The answers to these questions can put the researcher or practitioner on a good path toward an engagement solution that actually gets at employee engagement.

Asking and answering the first two questions above (e.g., consistently accurate, measure what is claimed) require some basic understanding of psychological measurement. This chapter will help. I first discuss how to evaluate a psychological measure of employee engagement and then discuss other approaches to assessing engagement, approaches that do not involve an already established instrument or survey. Following that, I review some basics about using surveys to effect culture change. Lastly, I review the available measures of engagement that can be reviewed without purchasing a proprietary instrument or violating company copyright agreements.

Although this chapter may seem fundamental to those trained in psychological measurement, this is not just a review of basic measurement terms. How that knowledge is used in practice is not always taught in graduate school programs, and if it is taught, science versus practice trade-offs typically are not. For those trained a while ago, sometimes a refresher on the basics is just what is needed; thus, this chapter should prove helpful. Why include a chapter about measurement in a book such as this? Because we so often leave information about psychological measurement to complex measurement books only those knowledgeable in the area know to read or buy, we create an artificial separation between understanding what engagement is and how it is measured. It is as if the measurement happens somewhere else, other than with the construct. Measuring engagement accurately is critical for successful interventions and advancement of the scientific and practice approaches—we must treat the topic in parallel with engagement recognizing an artificial separation causes more harm than good.

Some Basics About Measurement

There are no doubt a large number of books and articles available that review psychometrics in great detail, but not everyone needs to understand measurement theory or technique to that extent. Armed with a basic understanding of a few fundamentals in psychological measurement can go a long ways toward placing the researcher or practitioner in a more informed position when selecting a good engagement survey. The basics can be grouped into two large categories: (a) the validity of inferences, conclusions, or decisions made with the survey and (b) the reliability of the survey scores.

Validity refers to the evidence available that supports the interpretation of the scores from the survey or measurement instrument, in this case, the interpretation of the scores from an engagement survey. Thus, the fundamental question validity answers is whether there is sufficient evidence to say the interpretation one wants to make from the engagement scores is an acceptable interpretation—we have evidence these scores can accurately be interpreted in this way. Validity is about how the scores will be used—what conclusions are made from the scores (American Education Research Association [AERA], American Psychological Association [APA], & National Council on Measurement in Education [NCME], 1999). There are various sources of validity evidence rather than different types (Binning & Barrett, 1989). Each source of evidence speaks to the overall validity evidence available for evaluating the quality of decisions or conclusions one can make about test scores (AERA, APA, & NCME, 1999). To evaluate the validity evidence for a measure, one has to start with a definition of employee engagement. I have reviewed a few definitions from the research community and have offered my own in Chapter 2. An organization can also develop its own definition, as one of my clients in health care is currently doing. Although a few aspects of existing definitions appeal to them, they want to create a new one that more closely reflects the nature of their work, in particular, their focus on patient care, and to incorporate the language of their organizational culture.

Face Validity: What the Items Look Like They Measure

When considering an existing measurement instrument to assess engagement, one should look at the items and evaluate the measure's face validity. Face validity refers to whether the measurement instrument, typically a survey in the case of engagement, *looks* like it assesses what it claims. Do the questions look like they ask about employee engagement? With definition in hand, looking at the items of a measure provides perspective on how members of the organization will view the items when responding and whether they will question the overall intent of the measure. For example, an item on the Utrecht Work Engagement Scale (UWES; Schaufeli & Bakker, 2003) says "At my work, I feel bursting with energy." Engagement is about demonstrating high energy on the job, and thus, this question appears to fit the concept being measured. Another question, however, that asks about whether coworkers are dedicated to producing quality work (a question similar to one that appears on the Gallup Organization Q[12], which Gallup purports measures engagement; see Buckingham & Coffman, 1999; Gebauer, Lowman, & Gordon, 2008) seems off track from the construct of interest—respondents may naturally wonder how that question is directly about their own engagement level.

Face validity is not sufficient for deciding if a measurement instrument is a good one because some items that are good at assessing the underlying meaning of a construct do not always look as though they are getting at the construct—for example, they do not say, "I am engaged." Valuable questions may assess levels of engagement by asking indirect questions such as "I am energetic in my work tasks" (from the UWES; Schaufeli & Bakker, 2003; Schaufeli et al., 2002) or questions that assess underlying components of engagement such as "At work, I concentrate on my job" from the Job Engagement Scale (JES) authored by Rich, LePine, and Crawford (2010). Although not sufficient by itself, face validity contributes to how the measurement instrument is received by participants and respondents and, therefore, should not be ignored. It provides information about how individuals may view the items and respond, which does affect how the scores should be interpreted. That is, if respondents feel that they are being asked about topics they consider personal when they were told they would be surveyed about their engagement levels, they may be hesitant to complete the survey and respond inappropriately (e.g., choosing a neutral response or not responding at all) just to hide their personal thoughts from the test giver. Face validity is a subjective judgment about the items of the scale—it is a guess about how the respondents may view and complete the measure, and is not an evaluation of how well the items assess the construct.

Construct Validity: Evidence That the Measure Assesses its Purported Construct

Construct validity, in general, refers to whether there is empirical evidence the measurement instrument assesses the construct it was intended to assess (AERA, APA, & NCME, 1999). Construct validity evidence says this measure assesses employees' engagement level and not commitment, involvement, job satisfaction, or any other construct that is not engagement. Validity is not an either–or quality and is not based on a single study. Validity evidence is constantly accumulating in support of either a measurement instrument's ability to assess its construct or another construct it appears to be measuring instead (Guion & Gibson, 1988). Specific validity evidence that contributes to evaluating whether a measurement instrument is a good one to use includes internal structural, convergent, divergent, and criterion-related validity evidence (Cronbach & Meehl, 1955). The focus is on looking for cumulative evidence that suggests the measure is assessing what it claims and that it does this well (Cascio, 1998).

Internal structural construct validity. Internal structural or factorial construct validity evidence refers to information that confirms the conceptual structure of the measurement instrument as proposed by theory. It provides evidence the relationships among test items fit the theoretical construct. Specifically, if the theory suggests that three components compose employee engagement—physical energy, emotional expression, and cognitive processing—the factorial construct validity evidence for the measurement instrument should confirm the assessment of three individual components or dimensions. Typically, this evidence comes in the form of confirmatory factor analysis. Confirmatory factor analysis is a statistical technique that provides information about how well items within a measure correlate with each other, or do not, as they are expected a priori (B. Thompson, 2004). Based on the theory, the researcher inputs into the statistical tool how items are supposed to relate to one another and not relate to one another. The confirmatory factor analysis then determines how closely the data represent the structure the researcher inputted (B. Thompson, 2004). Current dominant theoretical perspectives of employee engagement are that three components compose the construct, though exactly what those three are varies by theory (see Kahn, 1990; Schaufeli, Salanova, et al., 2002). Thus, each measurement instrument assessing employee engagement as defined by Kahn (1990) and by Schaufeli et al. (2002) should have within it items assessing these three components. The theoretical frameworks also suggest these three components may be correlated, but should not be identical. Items within the measurement instrument that assess energy level should be correlated with the items assessing the emotional aspect of employee engagement, but not be so highly correlated they are considered identical for assessing the same construct. Additionally, if the researcher inputs into the software package that items within each subscale of the measurement instrument should relate most strongly to one another as opposed to relating more highly with other items within other subscales, the results of the confirmatory factor analysis should support this structure. Finally, confirmatory factor analysis is often used to provide not only factorial construct validity evidence but also convergent and divergent validity evidence (Cronbach & Meehl, 1955).

Convergent validity evidence. Convergent validity evidence is accumulated when one is able to show that assessments of constructs theoretically expected to relate to, or correlate with, the construct of interest actually do. So, for example, convergent validity evidence for a measure of commitment would be that measures of loyalty are positively and moderately correlated. In the case of engagement, convergent validity evidence would be in the form of measures of high energy levels, enthusiasm for the job, motivation, and cognitive focus correlating moderately with the measure of engagement. If the correlations are too high (e.g., $r = .70$ or more), one should be concerned that the measure of employee engagement is too similar to measures of other constructs that should be theoretically related, but not be identical, to engagement.

Divergent or discriminant validity evidence. Divergent or discriminant validity evidence is shown when constructs that are theoretically expected to differ from or not relate to the construct of interest, do not. For employee engagement, constructs such as intelligence or loyalty and demographic variables such as biological sex should show low or nonsignificant correlations with employee engagement. Divergent validity evidence is important in distinguishing whether or not employee engagement is different from other similar constructs in the workplace, such as intrinsic motivation. It is also important to know whether the measure one is using to assess employee engagement does not itself assess constructs expected to be different from employee engagement, such as loyalty. If validity evidence demonstrates that the engagement measure assesses loyalty as well as employee engagement, the measure is not a clean assessment of engagement, or we say that it is confounded or contaminated by other constructs.

Combined, convergent and divergent validity evidence for a measure of employee engagement demonstrates the measure assesses employee engagement and not other similar constructs or constructs it should not be measuring. Thus, when obtaining scores on a measure of employee engagement that has supportive convergent and divergent validity evidence, one can be assured that the results do actually inform the organization of levels of employee engagement and not something else.

Criterion-related validity evidence. Criterion-related validity evidence provides information about what (i.e., attitudes or behaviors) employee engagement is expected to predict in the workplace. That is, what criteria or outcomes do scores on this measure of employee engagement relate to and by how much? For example, employee engagement is expected to predict job performance in the workplace (Bakker & Demerouti, 2008; Britt, 1999; Kahn, 1990). Thus far, the two most popular measures of employee engagement, the UWES and the JES, are both positively related to job performance in the form of contextual performance and self-reported performance behaviors. I could find no research reporting experimental data that would provide evidence confirming that engagement actually predicts job performance. Existing research suggests a strong positive correlation between employee engagement and job performance; however, the direction of influence is unknown without experimental data. Because motivation results in effort in a particular direction (Kanfer, 1990), which in the workplace generally means job performance, and theoretical models of engagement suggest engagement is a motivational state (e.g., Kahn, 1990), it follows that employee engagement should precede job performance and not the other way around. However, it is quite possible employees who perform well on the job are enthused by positive feedback they receive on their performance, building their self-efficacy (e.g., Karl, O'Leary-Kelly, & Martocchio, 1993) and their sense of meaningful contribution, thereby becoming even more engaged; thus, most likely the relationship between employee engagement and job performance is reciprocal, which is expected if engagement is indeed a motivational construct (e.g., see Skinner & Belmont's, 1993, study of student engagement's reciprocal relationship with performance in the classroom). Another example of a criterion with which employee engagement should relate is well-being. The job demands-resource (JD-R) model (Bakker & Demerouti, 2008) suggests that engaged employees should report positive well-being, and research supports this assertion (e.g., Mostert & Rothmann, 2006).

Criterion-related validity requires attention to both the validity evidence for the measure of interest and the measures of the criteria variables (Cascio, 1998). One challenge with obtaining criterion-related validity is attributed to first having a measure of the construct of interest, in this case employee engagement, with substantial construct validity evidence in the form of convergent and divergent evidence. Second, the criterion must also be measured using an instrument that has construct validity evidence of its own. To know the responses obtained with the measure of interest are truly related to the criterion of interest, one must know the two measures assess unique and different constructs. For example, if the criterion is job satisfaction, the measure of employee engagement must assess engagement and not job satisfaction; the measure of job satisfaction must assess satisfaction, not commitment. Another example from the engagement literature is that engagement is often referred to as the financial loss resulting from unengaged workers. A measure of unengaged workers should exist, and a way of measuring financial loss must be available to make this claim. To date, there is no known measure of disengagement, and assuming it is simply the opposite or low end of the engagement scale is using a measure that has no validity evidence.

Reliability: Does the Measure Assess the Same Construct Every Time?

Another important criterion for the measurement quality of the instrument is the reliability of the data obtained using that instrument (Nunnally & Bernstein, 1994). The reliability of data says that every time the measurement instrument is used under the same conditions using the same sample, the same results should be obtained (assuming some stability in the construct of interest). Thus, if I ask participants or respondents to complete a measure of employee engagement today, when I ask them to complete the same measure 1 month from now, I should obtain the same responses. This assumes that the construct of employee engagement is stable enough that levels of engagement will not dramatically change between now and then. If the construct varies from day to day, perhaps the two times to offer the measure should not be 1 month apart but rather 1 hour apart. Reliability is a necessary condition for validity—it is difficult if not impossible to accumulate validity evidence if the scores obtained using the same measure are constantly changing within the same sample. Furthermore, poor reliability can attenuate relationships (Reinhardt, 1996) between engagement scores and its criteria, which may suggest no relationship exists when one actually does.

The reliability of data obtained using a measure can be assessed using a variety of statistical techniques such as test-retest, which is the method I have described here of giving the same measure twice to the same sample. Reliability is sample dependent (Pedhazur & Schmelkin, 1991); it can only be obtained from a set of test scores, not from the test itself (Gronlund & Linn, 1990; Vacha-Haase, 1998). Therefore, like validity evidence, reliability is not a property of a scale or measurement instrument itself.

A frequently used analogy for the reliability of data is the use of a ruler. When a ruler is used to measure a desk, every time that ruler is used, the same results should be obtained. If the desk is 3 meters long, every time the same desk is measured using that same ruler, the length assessed should be 3 meters. Of course, no one is perfect, and each time the ruler is used, the reported result may vary slightly from the previous instance. Instead of exactly 3 meters, the second reading may be 3.1 meters or 2.95 meters. This minor fluctuation in measurement—the inability to be perfect every time is called *error of measurement*. The range of error of measurement should be very small (e.g., + or −.05), and likewise for a measure of employee engagement. Because of the various forms of systematic error that enter into assessing psychological constructs, such as remembering the specific items on the measurement instrument from the first time it was taken to the second time (meaning that people just respond the same way the second time as the first because they remember their previous response), different approaches to estimating the reliability of data other than test-retest (administering the same instrument twice to the same group of people) are available to deal with the different kinds of error of measurement.

Because this is not a textbook on psychological measurement, I will not go into additional details here on all the different approaches for obtaining reliability estimates. There is, however, one other method besides test-retest worth mentioning because it is probably the most often reported method and not always the most appropriate. Specifically, that method is internal consistency, and it produces a reliability estimate called the coefficient alpha, also called the alpha coefficient (Cronbach, 1951). Unlike test-retest, deriving coefficient alpha requires only one test administration. Alpha coefficient is an estimate of the degree to which each item within the scale is correlated with every other item within the same scale for a particular sample. A high correlation coefficient suggests the items are all measuring the same thing because they are all highly related to one another. Alpha coefficient is influenced by the number of items in a scale and by their average correlations; a low alpha (<.50) may suggest the test is too short or the items are not similar enough to one another to capture the same construct (Nunnally & Bernstein, 1994). A low alpha may also suggest the measure is not unidimensional; it assesses more than one single construct. The assessment of internal consistency only makes sense for constructs with a single dimension. Using the current definitions of employee engagement as comprising at least three dimensions (e.g., Britt, 1999; Kahn, 1990; Macey & Schneider, 2008; Schaufeli et al., 2002), engagement is a multidimensional construct and requires a scale that assesses its dimensions. Therefore, a single alpha coefficient estimate may not be appropriate because items that assess one dimension of the construct may not be very highly correlated with items that assess another dimension. Each dimension or subscale of engagement should report a high alpha coefficient estimate because each dimension should be assessing a single subcomponent of engagement. Because the dimensions are supposed to be related and reflect overlap with the other dimensions of the measure, the dimensions should demonstrate reasonably high correlations, suggesting that it is likely high alpha coefficients can be obtained. Indeed, researchers have reported high alpha coefficient estimates in their studies when using the JES or the UWES (e.g., Andreassen, Ursin, & Eriksen, 2007; Rich et al., 2010).

There are no set standards for what a "good" reliability estimate of the data should be, but many have used above .7 for research and above .9 for decision making, based on the works of Nunnally and Bernstein (1994).

The Consequences of Using a Measure Without These Pieces of Evidence

Using a measurement instrument without evidence that it actually measures what it says, in this case employee engagement, can result in a few consequences that have varying ramifications depending on why engagement was measured in the first place. Let me be clear here: Those who move forward with surveys assessing employee engagement and have not been armed with some knowledge about psychological measurement may not know whether the instruments they are using assess engagement. The assumption is when the vendor provides a given scale; it is a good one. Or, in some cases, choosing a measure without validity evidence may be driven by financials and practicality. There simply are times and situations in which one must move ahead with what is in hand and, knowing the limitation of not having the necessary evidence, be ready to evaluate, explain, and make trade-offs.

Individuals in organizations assess engagement and then use the numerical results to make research decisions or financial decisions about where to invest and how much to fix or improve engagement. Before learning about the value of validity evidence, some of my clients previously put money into award-and-benefit systems, held their leaders accountable for their employees' engagement scores by managing amount of pay raises or promotion opportunities based on those scores, threatening to let go of those with the lowest scores or who do not improve them after two measurement cycles, and attacking the usual sources of job satisfaction such as pay, benefits, and extras such as picnics and T-shirts, thinking these efforts will ensure higher engagement scores. Although some of these efforts may affect the intended audience, the effect is not always the desired one and not toward increasing engagement.

Organizations often issue the same measure every 6 months to 1 year, obtaining trending data on whether their organizational interventions are working. When organizations use measures of job satisfaction and commitment, rather than engagement, they implement interventions that are designed to affect these constructs as opposed to engagement. However, job satisfaction and commitment are affected by the economy (e.g., Green, 2010; Maguire, 1983; Pryce-Jones, 2011), among other factors such as pay (Locke, 1976), and, therefore, may or may not change much because of actions on the part of the organization. Gallup Organization's *State of the American Workplace* (2013a) report suggests that between 2008 and 2010, efforts by organizations to improve employee engagement have not been working. Because Gallup's measure of engagement actually assesses satisfaction and not engagement as defined in the research literature (see the later discussion), these reports are actually about the efforts organizations have been making to change job satisfaction and commitment. Gallup's report may well be stating that organizations are not changing their employees' satisfaction levels, which is valuable when focusing on satisfaction. Additionally, one could take the report to suggest that some of the same factors that influence job satisfaction and that may potentially influence engagement as well are not improving. However, important here is employee engagement can change and remain high even when external factors associated with the economy are low (Kahn, 1990; Mauno, Kinnunen, & Ruokolainen, 2007; Schaufeli et al., 2002), factors that may independently affect job satisfaction but not engagement (see Chapter 3, in which I discuss how engagement is not the same as job satisfaction). The key point is that tracking the wrong indicator or basing staffing or leadership decisions on erroneous information may be misleading for researchers and practitioners alike.

For the researcher, the use a measure without validity information can be detrimental. The accuracy of the nomological network (Cronbach & Meehl, 1955) relies on knowing the relationships identified and connected in the network are backed by solid evidence—evidence that can be replicated and supported in other studies. Because science and practice are intertwined, each reciprocally affecting the other; the paths taken in science and the conclusions drawn find their way into practice and ultimately have financial and real-people consequences.

How to Use This Information for
Selecting a Measure of Engagement

The preceding information may seem basic to some (especially those who are aware that what I described is just one approach to measurement) and a little overwhelming for others. The take-away points are that (a) one wants the accumulated evidence the data obtained using a measurement instrument of employee engagement to demonstrate high reliability from sample to sample, and, hopefully, in samples that mimic the one of interest (e.g., health care, high tech, blue-collar labor), and (b) one wants substantial validity evidence for the measure including forms of convergent and divergent validity evidence, as well as criterion-related validity evidence, if the goal is to "predict" some criterion such as performance, well-being, or job satisfaction.

Those writing or offering the measurement instrument should provide accumulated evidence of consistent reliability of scores and sufficient validity evidence to evaluate the quality of the engagement measure. Most vendors providing engagement solutions may not necessarily volunteer the information up front, but when asked, they should be able to provide it quite easily and without constraint or extra cost. Many who are not in the test construction business and instead in the management solution business may not be familiar with the basics of theory and techniques in psychological measurement, even though they are providing a measurement instrument to assess employee engagement. Their organization may not have the skilled personnel to collect data such as the construct validity evidence necessary for demonstrating their measure assesses engagement and not commitment and scores from their measure correlate with scores on measures of well-being or performance. Thus, to assume that everyone has the information and can readily provide it may be a faulty assumption.

What if validity information is not available? There are some measures and their uses for which validity evidence is simply not available in a format noted earlier (e.g., construct, convergent) or unobtainable because the measures are proprietary and the vendors have not published their data. First, if none of the validity information can be obtained, try to find information about how the items were written or chosen for the measure (such as the story behind the creation of the survey). This information could provide some sense as to how well the items were constructed, whether they were developed based on a theoretical model of engagement, and whether thought was put into how to distinguish these items and the overall scale from measures assessing other similar but different constructs. Second, track down information about how and whether the items have been used in an instrument elsewhere and what variables or constructs might have been correlated with the measure containing those or similar items. Correlations offer information about convergent and divergent validity evidence. Third, a number of my clients like using questions that they feel better represents their work environment than those already available in public domain. The costs of some proprietary measures can be prohibitive, so developing their own measure seems like a good next move, as does modifying existing measures to fit the organizational norms. By developing items, construct validity evidence begins at the design stage—writing items based on a theoretical framework, having subject matter experts review the items, collecting data to modify and improve the scale, and collecting convergent and divergent validity evidence before putting the measure into practice or surveying the entire organization.

When not given the opportunity to conduct preliminary qualitative studies to assess the culture and language of the organization, I have drawn from existing measures of engagement and related constructs to write items that have higher face validity for the organization and indirectly get at the theoretically proposed definitions (e.g., Kahn, 1990; Schaufeli, Bakker, & Salanova, 2006). I look into the scholarly literature for research on similar constructs and examine their scale items to determine how to assess engagement as separate from these scales. I include measures of other constructs that may seem similar to engagement, such as job involvement and passion, and during analyses, I run tests to assess the uniqueness of the items I claim to the organization are measuring engagement. I perform a pilot test for a number of reasons including but not limited to collecting initial data to evaluate the quality of the home-made scale. I conduct exploratory and confirmatory factor analyses on all the study variables and, as a consequence, modify items as needed. The collection of the full sample occurs because I know I have some pre-liminary evidence in support of the measure. There are other approaches to collecting validity evidence and interested readers can consult sources such as *Alternative Validation Strategies: Developing New and Leveraging Existing Validity Evidence* edited by McPhail (2007).

My main goal in these situations is to be able to say, with confidence and data to back me up, that I have measured engagement and its associated constructs as best as possible, so the conclusions drawn are about engagement and actions taken as a result of the scores are going to be about engagement and not about something else that kind of looks like, smells like, and feels like engagement but is not. Organizations with whom I work seek results obtained using scientifically rigorous methods and results that they can argue and defend when asked why one intervention was chosen over another. Applications for various awards, such as the Malcolm Baldrige National Quality Award (http:// www.nist.gov/baldrige/), require evidence of high-quality studies using well-developed measures within the organization. However engagement is defined, the goal of using scientifically rigorous methods to assess engagement and its antecedents and consequences is a worthy one— find ways to confirm what you want to measure is what is measured and measured well.

Available Measures of Engagement

The Utrecht Work Engagement Scale

By far, the most popular measure of employee engagement in the academic literature is based on Schaufeli at al.'s (2002) definition of engagement that started out as Maslach and Leiter's (1997) definition of engagement: the direct opposite of burnout. The Utrecht Work Engagement Scale (UWES) was developed to assess the three dimensions of Schaufeli et al.'s definition: vigor, dedication, and absorption. The UWES has a history tying it to the stress literature, and specifically, the burnout literature. Grounded in positive psychology, Maslach and Leiter noted that people who were not burned out seemed engagement. Thus, the initial perspective was that engagement was the opposite of burnout and could be assessed using the Maslach Burnout Inventory (MBI; Maslach & Jackson, 1981); low scores on the MBI's three dimensions (exhaustion, cynicism, inefficacy) translated into high scores on the three engagement components (vigor, dedication, absorption, respectively). However, Schaufeli and Bakker (2003) determined they could not adequately measure employee engagement using the MBI burnout inventory because (a) engagement may not be the exact opposite of burnout (no perfect negative correlation) and a direct opposite of inefficacy did not seem to fit conceptually with the idea of work engagement and (b) understanding the relationship between engagement and burnout was confounded by using the same questionnaire to measure both constructs. Therefore, they modified the definition and measurement instrument, moving it away from its direct connection with burnout (although still refer to it as the antipode of burnout), suggesting that the two constructs, though related, are conceptually unique and experienced differently (Schaufeli & Bakker, 2003). Their new definition of engagement comprised the three dimensions, vigor, dedication, and absorption, and engagement is a persistent affective-cognitive state of mind. Further, they noted their three dimensions reflect their characterization of engagement as high levels of strong work identification, energy, and happiness and as feeling enthusiastic and proud of one's work.

The UWES is a self-report questionnaire that assesses vigor with six items, dedication with five items, and absorption with six items. Respondents rate the frequency with which the items are experienced. Although the UWES test manual (Schaufeli & Bakker, 2003) reports confirmatory factor analyses results demonstrate a better fit to a three-factor structure than a one-factor structure, their reported fit statistics are nearly identical for the 9-item version, and unacceptable for the 15-item and the 17-item version (fit indices are all below standard acceptable values; Hu & Bentler, 1999). There is no statistical test of difference in fit (e.g., chi-square difference test), and no item or scale factor loadings provided.

The test manual reports on the development of the UWES. The selection of opposites of the dimensions of burnout are not explained in this manual, thus for this scale it is unknown whether the conversion was theoretical or based on what seemed to be the opposite construct. As Maslach and Jackson (1984) explain, the three-part definition of burnout was not derived from theory, and as such, neither is the engagement definition espoused by Schaufeli, Salanova, et al. (2002). Because of the lack of strong conceptual foundation to the dimensions of engagement, and the lack of a prior theory that explains why these three new dimensions should be distinct, an exploratory factor analysis is justified, yet none is provided in the manual. The few researchers who have used the UWES and conducted exploratory analyses report the three dimensions are not distinct (e.g., Sonnentag, 2003; Storm & Rothmann, 2003). My own research is consistent with these findings—exploratory factor analyses result in a single factor of engagement with significant cross-loadings of items, as opposed to three distinct dimensions. Others have also reported varying results using both the 17-item and 9-item versions of the scale (Wefald, Mills, Smith, & Downey, 2012).

The confirmatory factor analyses provided in just a handful of studies of the UWES lack the details necessary to adequately evaluate the measure to its full merit (see Cole, Walter, Bedeian, & O'Boyle, 2012, and Wefald et al., 2012, for exceptions). That is, with no adequate fit indices, no statistical difference test, no item loadings and cross-loadings, and no factor correlations, it is challenging to determine the true psychometric strength of the measure. The UWES has been used in many studies; however, very few have actually conducted a confirmatory factor analysis to demonstrate the factorial structure or the construct validity of the measure.

Despite the lack of psychometric information, the authors of the UWES can boast of its popularity in a number of countries and in a significant number of studies. Summarizing findings from studies using the UWES is a little difficult because not all studies employing the measure use all three dimension scales or assess engagement as a single score. In general, the UWES and/or one or more of its dimensions are negatively related to role ambiguity (Prieto, Soria, Martinez, & Schaufeli, 2008) and psychosomatic complaints (e.g., headaches; Hallberg & Schaufeli, 2006; Schaufeli, Taris, & van Rhenen, 2008) and positively related to supervisory support (Bakker, Hakanen, Demerouti, & Xanthopoulou, 2007), organizational commitment (Hakanen, Bakker, & Schaufeli, 2006; Richardsen, Burke, & Martinussen, 2006), and self-reported in-role and extra-role job performance, and innovativeness (Schaufeli, Martínez, Marques Pinto, Salanova, & Bakker, 2002).

Recently, Cole, Walter, Bedeian, and O'Boyle (2012) conducted a thorough review and meta-analytic examination of the UWES versus the MBI and concluded from the data that there is more than acceptable overlap between the scales and that their relations with other constructs are such that they cannot be considered unique constructs or unique measurement instruments. The authors' findings raise some questions about previous studies using the UWES to assess employee engagement, especially with stress-related outcomes (i.e., one expects relationships because the UWES essentially measures a degree of burnout). Although Cole et al.'s study is only one, it is a meta-analysis, which considers the findings of many studies combined; thus, their results should not be dismissed just because the UWES has been popular thus far. Researchers wishing to continue to use the UWES for their examination of employee engagement should provide psychometric details of the UWES for their sample and should be aware that at least one study suggests that it is essentially measuring the same as the MBI. The implication of Cole et al.'s study, as well as Wefald et al.'s (2012), is that researchers may need to devote new attention to solidifying the psychometric properties of the measure.

The Job Engagement Scale

The second measure of employee engagement in the academic literature is the JES produced by Rich, LePine, and Crawford (2010), designed to assess Kahn's (1990) definition of engagement. This measure assesses three dimensions of engagement Kahn proposed: affective, cognitive, and physical self-expression. The measure is relatively new; therefore, few studies using this measure have been published as of yet.

The measure was originally developed because none existed assessing Kahn's (1990) seminal conceptualization of engagement, and the UWES incorporates items that assess the antecedents of engagement as proposed by Kahn (e.g., items on challenge and meaningfulness). Thus, if one wishes to assess Kahn's perspective on engagement, the UWES is not the right measure to use. Based on an extensive review of the literature on the assessment of the dimensions of Kahn's engagement, Rich et al. developed a measure of 18 items, 6 per dimension. The scale was pilot-tested and submitted to exploratory factor analysis. Items were subsequently modified when needed and a cross-validation study was performed using a different sample. Substantial model testing in the form of confirmatory factor analyses with various model configurations supported a second-order structure, with the three dimensions as first-order factors. An additional sample was recruited for the 2010 study, and again, confirmatory factor analyses supported the second-order structure (details are provided by Rich et al., 2010).

Exploratory and confirmatory factor analysis evidence was provided by Rich et al. (2010) for this scale, demonstrating the three dimensions' distinctiveness and only moderate correlations with each other. Additionally, Rich et al. provided validity evidence for the distinctiveness of engagement from a number of other theoretical antecedents, consequences, and related constructs. However, given the newness of this measure, the jury is still out on the validity of its use across a variety of samples.

Job and Organizational Engagement

Another measure of employee engagement, also used in the academic literature, was developed by Saks in 2006. His measures of employee engagement assesses job (five items) and organizational engagement (six items) as two separate scales. At first glance, these scales seem to borrow somewhat from a number of constructs. For example, items assess the extent to which individuals are all consumed by their job, they lose track of time (absorption, flow), and their involvement as an organizational member is the most exciting and is exhilarating (involvement, identification). Both scales include an item stating "I am highly engaged in this [job or organization]" (Saks, 2006, p. 617). Saks provided evidence that these scales were moderately correlated with each other ($r = .62$) but were considered separate (he offers an overview of factorial results to indicated separateness of scales from each other, but no detailed listing of factor loadings).

Saks proposed employees offer job and organizational engagement as part of a social exchange relationship (Blau, 1964) with the organization. His regression results suggest that job engagement is related to job characteristics, job satisfaction, organizational commitment, citizenship behaviors beneficial to the organization, and organizational support, whereas organizational engagement is related to organizational support (more strongly than to job engagement), procedural justice, job satisfaction, organizational commitment, and citizenship behavior beneficial to both individuals and the organization. Thus, both scales are similarly related to other constructs, with just a few exceptions.

A couple of my clients believe employees are engaged in their job and/or their organization. They intuitively like the idea of engagement in one's specific job in which the focus is on completing tasks, as well as engagement in the organization, which implies a kind of investment in the organization's goals. Organizational leaders and human resource managers emphasize the need for engagement to be aligned with meeting organizational goals; thus, having employees very energized and focused on task completion that is not in the direction the organization wants to go is inefficient and undesirable. Interestingly, although the idea of organizational engagement is appealing in some practitioner and organizational circles, a search through the Web of Science online database reveals few, if any, at the time of this writing, have used Saks's (2006) model or scales in the research literature. It may be that further analysis of Saks's scales or integrating the items into either the JES or the UWES may be a good next step for ensuring the idea of engagement in the job or engagement in the organization can be developed and used by others.

Nonacademic Engagement Scales

Other scales exist, such as the Gallup Organization's Q^{12}, but because of the proprietary nature of these scales, they are not used in the research literature except by individuals associated with the consulting organization or who have signed an agreement to use proprietary measures (e.g., Harter, Schmidt, & Hayes, 2002; Luthans & Peterson, 2002; Macey, Schneider, Barbera, & Young, 2009; Medlin & Green, 2009; Zhu, Avolio, & Walumbwa, 2009). Consulting firms such as Towers-Watson, Kenexa, Gallup Organization, Valtera (now owned by Corporate Executive Board), and the Hay Group, to name a few, all boast their own measures of employee engagement, but the proprietary nature of these surveys makes it difficult, if not impossible, for researchers to confirm the scale's ability to assess employee engagement. Likewise, the definition used by these consulting firms is, for the most part, unknown unless they provide a glimpse of their model on their websites, or if known, is quite different from Kahn's (1990) and Schaufeli, Salanova, et al.'s (2002) definitions. It is important to state here that the goal may not always be to assess employee engagement itself, by itself, or to assess the academic versions of the construct, but rather the goal may be to assess the work environment that potentially fosters engagement and the outcomes that result. For example, as previously mentioned, some vendors I reviewed admitted their measures did not assess engagement but assessed predictors or drives. If this is the goal, a number of vendor solutions, to the best of my knowledge based on minimal review, are definitely worthy of consideration given what we currently know about what predicts engagement. Importantly, organizations want to know what they can change in the organization to increase their employees' behavior that facilitates meeting organizational goals. Thus, not only is it important to measure employee engagement, but it is also important to measure aspects of the work environment that may relate to engagement. It may also be the case that once clear definitions are available for scrutiny, the proprietary measures may perform very well in assessing engagement.

For example, although the Q^{12} is considered proprietary, items from the Q^{12} have been published in public-domain research papers (Harter et al., 2002) with the copyright note the items are not to be reprinted or reproduced without permission. Therefore, the items will not be produced here, but anyone can go look at them in Harter and colleagues' published paper. Harter et al. note employee engagement is defined as involvement in and satisfaction at work. They further note the Q^{12} demonstrates high convergent validity with measures of overall job satisfaction. However, a visual review of the items reveals that even though they do not ask about employee engagement, they appear to ask about aspects of the work environment that potentially foster engagement. For example, the survey items ask about the clarity of role expectations, job resources, feedback, supportive supervisors and coworkers, and job characteristics such as task significance. All these concepts have been studied as antecedents to employee engagement; thus, the Q^{12} may be considered a very quick and surface snapshot of work dimensions considered positively related to engagement. In many situations, such a snapshot is quite valuable; however, they should be followed up with more intensive efforts to pinpoint how and where to devote intervention time and effort.

Comparing Scales

Table 6.1 compares and contrasts available measures and their validity evidence, allowing one to choose the scale that best fits the needs and has the available evidence to support its use. In the table, I include engagement measures I have had access in the public domain, ranked in order of most frequently used to least frequently used. The Q^{12} is reported last because it is a proprietary measure, but the items have been shared in at least one public domain article (Harter et al., 2002) and at least one book (Buckingham & Coffman, 1999), and it is a very popular measure with organizations who hire for engagement solutions.

Table 6.1 Validity Evidence for Available Measures of Employee Engagement

Measure	Authors and Notes	Fundamentals	Validity Evidence
Utrecht Work Engagement Scale (UWES)	Schaufeli, Salanova, González-Romá, & Bakker (2002)	3 dimensions (vigor, dedication, absorption) each producing a separate score that can be combined together to create a single score; based on definition of engagement being opposite of burnout	Factorial validity evidence: Exploratory and confirmatory factor analyses (both the 17 and 9 item versions of the UWES): 3 dimensions not clearly distinct from each other—sometimes 1, 2, or 3 dimensions emerge depending on sample (Wefald, Mills, Smith, & Downey, 2012). Some find the three dimensions distinct after they remove some offending items (varies by study) and a second-order structure fits best (e.g., Liao, Yang, Wang, Drown, & Shi, 2012). Convergent & divergent validity evidence: Correlates with self-efficacy, need for achievement, positive affectivity, job satisfaction, organizational support; lacks sufficient divergent validity evidence across 3 samples (Wefald et al., 2012). High correlations with organizational commitment and job involvement, task significance and variety, and conscientiousness, but not so high engagement is considered the same as these constructs (Christian et al., 2011). UWES may be considered the same as Maslach Burnout Inventory (Cole et al., 2012).

Engagement Scale	May, Gilson, & Harter (2004)	Based on Kahn (1990) designed to measure physical, cognitive, and emotional engagement.	Factorial validity evidence: Evidence failed to support the three dimensions as unique, thus authors used an overall scale score using only those items demonstrating internal consistency reliability and some balance across the three dimensions. No information available for scale item construction, or evidence of distinctiveness from other constructs in the study (i.e., no factorial validity evidence). Convergent & divergent validity evidence: Correlations reported are positive between engagement and meaningfulness, job enrichment, and supervisor relations, and negative with outside activities such as volunteering in the community (May et al., 2004). Engagement using May et al.'s (2004) scale was also correlated with knowledge-sharing (Chen, Zhang, & Vogel, 2011).
Job Engagement Scale (JES)	Rich, LePine, & Crawford (2010)	3 dimensions (physical, cognitive, affective) combined to create a single scale score—dimensions cannot be used as independent scales; based on Kahn's definition of engagement as expression of physical, cognitive, affective self when fully invested into the job role	Factorial validity evidence: Exploratory and confirmatory factor analyses indicating 3 dimensions are distinct from each other and form a second-order factor (Rich et al., 2010). Convergent & divergent validity evidence: Correlates with task performance, organizational citizenship behavior, and perceived organizational support (Rich et al., 2010). Also correlated with perceived supervisory support, organizational commitment, and psychological meaningfulness (Byrne, Peters, & Drake, 2014). Byrne, Peters, & Drake show JES not correlated with sex but is with age.

(*Continued*)

Table 6.1 Continued

Measure	Authors and Notes	Fundamentals	Validity Evidence
Job engagement and organizational engagement	Saks (2006)	2 independent scales—one focused on engagement in the job and the other focused on engagement towards the organization; based on engagement being considered	Factorial validity evidence: None provided. Convergent & divergent validity evidence: Both job and organizational engagement were equally correlated with organizational support, supervisory support, job satisfaction, citizenship behavior, and commitment (Saks, 2006).
Self-engagement (self-engagement is defined as "being personally responsible for and committed to one's performance", Britt & Bliese, 2003, p. 247)	Britt (1999) Measure of self-engagement as defined by Britt; not the same as employee or work engagement	Based on an integration of Kahn (1990), Kanungo's (1982) job involvement, Lodahl & Kejner's (1965) self-efficacy/job involvement concept, and commitment. Calls the combination of these three concepts the Triangle Model.	Factorial validity evidence: None provided. Convergent & divergent validity evidence: Correlates with perceived control and job training (Britt, 1999), and negatively correlated with work stress and psychological distress (Britt & Bliese, 2003). Does not correlate with citizenship behavior (Britt, McKibben, Greene-Shortridge, Odle-Dusseau, & Herleman, 2012) even though many other studies show engagement is positively correlated with citizenship behavior (e.g., Christian, Garza, & Slaughter, 2011; Rich et al., 2010).

| Q$_{12}$ (items shown in Harter, Schmidt, & Hayes, 2002, but are noted as copyrighted) | Gallup Organization —reported in Harter, Schmidt & Hayes (2002) Measure of satisfaction with aspects of work that others have shown are related to engagement, but Gallup claims it measures engagement. | Based on criterion-keyed method of scale development where items are chosen based on whether they are endorsed by those who considered their manager to be excellent and not endorsed by those who considered their manager to be weak. | Factorial validity evidence: None is available. Convergent & divergent validity evidence: Positively associated with customer satisfaction and turnover intentions (Harter et al., 2002). Correlations between satisfaction and engagement with other constructs were identical to one another (Harter et al., 2002) indicating these two constructs are probably not distinct. |

My Own Research on Engagement Scales

Recently, my colleagues and I conducted a study of the UWES and the JES using three different samples of working adults (Byrne, Peters, & Drake, 2014). We found that the two measures are different enough from each other that they are not assessing the exact same construct. That is, they do not relate to the same variables in the same way, and in some cases, they do not relate to the same variables at all. Thus, when evaluating their nomological networks (Cronbach & Meehl, 1955), we see that they do not occupy exactly the same space in a single network.

Visual comparison of the UWES versus the JES. Neither the JES nor the UWES assess engagement as a moment-to-moment phenomenon, a conceptualization of engagement Kahn (1990) put forth. Questions on both the JES and the UWES are phrased as a statement about how one is or about one's perspective in general (e.g., "At work, I am absorbed in my job" and "In my job, I feel strong and vigorous" respectively), even though the JES is modeled after Kahn's moment-to-moment conceptualization of engagement and the UWES is modeled after Schaufeli, Salanova, et al.'s (2002) conceptualization of engagement as a persistent and stable state. Thus, one might expect items on the JES to be phrased perhaps in this manner: "At this moment, I am devoting a lot of energy to the tasks of my job." For the UWES, one might expect items to be phrased as "In general, I am enthusiastic about my job."

The UWES uses a different rating scale than the JES, which may contribute to assessing a slightly different perception of the construct. Specifically, the UWES uses a frequency scale ranging from "Never" to "Every day," in which people rate how often they feel what is described in the item. The JES uses an agreement scale ranging from "Strongly disagree" to "Strongly agree."

Statistical results. Although each measure is described as having three distinct factors, they do not appear as such across our three samples. There is some overlap of items across factors within scales. There are also a few items that cross-load between the UWES and the JES. Another finding from the study is the UWES relates to stress outcomes, job and organizational commitment, and organizational support more strongly than does the JES. The JES, in contrast, relates to psychological meaning, supervisory support, and coworker commitment more strongly than does the UWES.

Not currently incorporated in the three-study paper is a comparison of the UWES, the JES, and Saks's (2006) measures of engagement. We assessed both job and organizational engagement as measured by Saks, alongside the UWES and the JES, in one of the field samples. We found the UWES was related to Saks's organizational engagement scale, whereas the JES was not. The JES was more strongly related to Saks's job engagement than it was to the UWES.

Conclusion About Measures of Engagement

The disadvantage of any of the scales noted earlier is they all assume engagement is the same for every organization and engagement is a single construct definition (when one is provided). Given the literature on organizational climate, the predictors of employee engagement in terms of leadership styles, support, characteristics of the job, and individual sense of meaning and purpose in the job, it is unlikely a single scale that assesses engagement can work well in every organization. Organizational cultures differ, as do country cultures. It may be that some industry characteristic requires a different kind of assessment of employee engagement, and perhaps even a different definition of engagement. My own qualitative research findings in different health care organizations suggest engagement is not conceptualized identically from organization to organization, even though there may be some similarities.

Perhaps a quick snapshot of engagement using standard scales such as the UWES or the JES may give a high-level view of engagement, enough to move the organization forward. However, to design specific interventions that address concerns within the organization that are preventing employees from becoming engaged may require a custom measure that effectively assesses employee engagement in that particular organization.

State of Measurement of Engagement

So where are we with the measurement of employee engagement? Not very far, but that means there is a lot of room for improvement. There are two existing scales in the academic literature; however, they may not be ideal. Specifically, neither captures the moment-to-moment engagement of Kahn's model. Each scale seems to relate to different outcomes more strongly than the other, which suggests they are different in some way. Thus, they both say that they assess engagement; however, because they are not interchangeable, which one do we use and when? They both claim to have three separate dimensions; however, the dimensions do not appear distinct in every sample; hence, is the nature or the composition of the multidimensional construct of engagement variable, or is it the measures are currently written to be sample dependent? Last, neither reflects some of the key components of engagement as have been put forward by practitioners, which include passion and goal alignment with the organization.

Another disadvantage of the standardized measures that are available is they are all questions used in surveys. In two of the healthcare industry field studies I conducted and reviewed in Chapters 4 and 5, I used the JES to assess employee engagement. My results showed that physical and cognitive engagement cross-loaded and were very highly correlated with each other. I concluded that because the jobs were more cognitive than physically oriented, employees may have interpreted the items asking about physical engagement as a cognitive awareness of their energy use. For example, items such as "I devote a lot of energy to my job" and "I work with intensity on my job" could both be answered in reference to energy and intensity of thinking—not necessarily of the physical activity of the body. In Chapter 2, I note a new definition of employee engagement wherein I suggest rather than physically engaged, people are physiologically engaged. None of the existing measures incorporates the possibility of physiological arousal without a physical outburst.

Furthermore, one could speculate to accurately assess physical engagement, a different method than a questionnaire-based survey is needed. In an earlier study, not yet discussed in this book, one of my students and I attempted to assess physical engagement using physiological measures; specifically, galvanic skin response and heart rate. This was a lab study in which we attempted to create or foster engagement within participants; we were unsuccessful. What is important about sharing this attempt to examine physical engagement is it may not be unreasonable to assume a physiological measure is the best way to assess that which is supposed to be physiologically arousing. Additionally, when employee engagement is described within the practice environment, it is nearly always described as a behavioral observation; that is, we can see when an employee is engaged and when not. I have argued earlier that, consistent with current research literature, employee engagement is a motivational state and the effects of engagement may be observed in *some* employees, but perhaps not all. This may be particularly relevant in some occupations versus others. Thus, one could potentially include an observational measure to assess the consequences or effects of employee engagement, but not use it as the only source of data. This observational data would serve as non-self-report data that could be used in conjunction with other data on engagement obtained via surveys and physiological measures. Perhaps a corroboration of a variety of methods as suggested here is required to accurately assess a construct that has an affective, cognitive, and physical/physiological dimension.

With such a need for more research in developing accurate and adequate measures of employee engagement, what should an organization that wants to assess employee engagement do today? There are at least a few approaches organizations can take. First, organizations can use the existing scales that are available in the academic literature, or a proprietary measure offered through hiring a consulting firm. Look for measures that have sufficient validity evidence and can be used reliably, allowing for comparison across units. By using measures that have evidence of actually assessing employee engagement and not other constructs such as organizational commitment, job involvement, or other antecedents or consequences of engagement (such as support or performance), the organization can be sure it is getting an assessment of engagement.

Second, organizations can hire smaller consulting firms and independent consultants who have experience creating customized assessments for employee engagement or researchers to create custom measures. It is possible that large consulting firms can provide a certain amount of customization to their existing measures, sometimes with a price; however, these firms often provide benchmarking data that make customization of the actual engagement items impossible. The same scrutiny should apply—be sure that the custom assessment is based on the use of rigorous scientific methods and gets at engagement, not just its antecedents or expected consequences.

Last Word on Measuring Engagement

The purpose of research is to advance our understanding and continuously improve by questioning previous findings and building anew. Thus, if the Cole et al. (2012) study causes researchers to revisit the UWES and Schaufeli et al.'s (2002) definition of engagement to determine how both can be improved to more accurately define and assess employee engagement and not burnout or the antecedents and consequences of engagement, then the research will have served its purpose. Furthermore, examining and studying the JES across more settings and in different countries is another good action to take, as it may also have weaknesses that show up with extensive use and be visible with meta-analytic techniques. Both measures may benefit from collaboration with organizational researchers or practitioners interested in a more complete definition that reflects engagement as described in practice. It may be that some aspect of a practitioner scale is valuable to add into a scholarly scale, or vice versa, which cannot occur unless the two are in conversation. Because science informs practice and practice informs science, more close conversation is necessary.

Last, the assessment of employee engagement appears to be separate from the assessment of student engagement or clinical engagement. Student engagement refers to the level of effort, sustained concentration or focus, persistence over time, enjoyment, and intention to finish school tasks that students feel and display in school and outside of school working on educational tasks (e.g., homework; Brophy, Rohrkemper, Rashid, & Goldberger, 1983). Student engagement refers to behavioral and emotional components of student involvement and level of motivation in learning (Skinner & Belmont, 1993). Thus, at some level, employee engagement and student engagement tap similar constructs—cognitive, emotional, and behavioral motivation. The employee engagement and student engagement literatures, thus far, have been treated separately, but perhaps there is something to be gained by considering the commonalities.

Walk-Away Points

- Good measures produce reliability of scores and have validity evidence in support of their use.
- A number of employee engagement scales are available; however, based on the available evidence at the time of this writing, none is outstanding.
- A big opportunity exists for researchers to develop good measures of engagement with the collaboration of practitioners, to keep measures grounded in science and yet be usable for practice.
- Measures for cross-cultural use are sorely needed (see Chapter 9 for more on international studies).

Part III

COMPETITIVE ADVANTAGE

7

HOW DO WE IMPROVE EMPLOYEE ENGAGEMENT FOR COMPETITIVE ADVANTAGE?

Ulrich and Lake (1991) argued that "building better products or services, pricing goods or services lower than the competition, or incorporating technological innovations into research and manufacturing operations must today be supplemented by organizational capability—the firm's ability to manage people to gain competitive advantage" (p. 77). One can think of competitive advantage as the "ability to generate above normal returns relative to competitors" and the "social version of survival of the fittest" (Ployhart, 2012, p. 62).

To be competitive, today's businesses must be flexible, shifting their product lines quickly and generating new market demand before their current market declines. New technology (importantly, the Internet) and open trading across geographical borders have pushed customer-focused solutions to the surface and widened the range of providers such that innovation (and not just product, but also process) is essential for survival (Teece, 2010). For organizations to respond to the market competition, they must have employees who are flexible and capable of adapting to change in support of the organization's mission; thus, organizations are increasingly focusing on human resources (human capital), not just their technological advances (Jin, Hopkins, & Wittmer, 2010). Recruiting talented individuals is essential for sustainable competitive market advantage, and to do so, organizations must present a positive corporate image that will meet the needs of talented individuals who are new to the workforce, as well as appeal to their sense of "fit" in the organization (Rau & Hyland, 2006). Furthermore, competition in the world market requires innovation—the intentional development or creation of novel ideas, idea promotion, and realization or application of these new and novel ideas that benefit the group and/or organization (Amabile, Conti, Coon, Lazenby, & Herron, 1996; Janssen, 2000; Kanter, 1988; Scott & Bruce, 1994).

Many suggest for companies to be innovative, competitive, and sustainable, they must have an engaged workforce (e.g., Byrne, Palmer, Smith, & Weidert, 2011; Macey et al., 2009; Ncube & Jerie, 2012; Rich,

LePine, & Crawford, 2010). The hypothesis here is that engaged employees are more willing and able to change as needed by the organization, than employees who are not engaged. Although no study has yet been conducted to test this specific hypothesis, a recent study reported positive correlations between employee engagement and willingness to support an organizational change intervention ($r = .37$, $p < .01$; van den Heuvel, Demerouti, Schreurs, Bakker, & Schaufeli, 2009). Initial research has linked employee engagement to innovative work behaviors (e.g., Agarwal, Datta, Blake-Beard, & Bhargava, 2012; Bhatnagar, 2012; Chughtai & Buckley, 2011), adding to the conclusion that engagement is essential for competitive advantage. The hypothesis that for organizations to compete in the world market they must have engaged employees is also supported by the research reviewed in previous chapters; engagement is positively correlated with job performance, task performance, and citizenship behavior (or extra-role behaviors). For organizations to compete, they must produce, and this holds true around the globe.

Research to date suggests employees become engaged with (a) the right amount of resources; (b) an ability to manage work stressors; (c) trust to feel safe to fully invest themselves in the work task; (d) an interpersonal leader creating connection and a meaningful vision; (e) ability to create and find meaning in the work; (f) support and connection with others at work, allowing them to focus on the job and align themselves with the organization's values; and (g) job– and person–organization fit (e.g., Aryee, Walumbwa, Zhou, & Hartnell, 2012; Bakker & Demerouti, 2008; Berg, Dutton, & Wrzesniewski, 2013; Biswas & Bhatnagar, 2013; Z. Chen, Zhang, & Vogel, 2011; Christian, Garza, & Slaughter, 2011; Kahn, 1990; May, Gilson, & Harter, 2004; Zhu, Avolio, & Walumbwa, 2009).

One way to provide these seven components to employees is to have an organization with an organizational culture that supports these components, as well as employees who proactively seek ways to become and stay engaged. Although the previous chapters refer to drivers and inhibitors of engagement, this chapter pulls them together, along with other factors not previously discussed (e.g., selection), to create the right climate for engaging employees and keeping them engaged.

An Organizational Culture for Engagement

Organizational culture refers to the combination of norms, behaviors, practices, and expectations of the organization by which employees come to understand and experience their workplace (Ostroff, Kinicki, & Muhammad, 2013; Ostroff, Kinicki, & Tamkins, 2003; Schein, 1990, 2000). Employees' experience of organizational culture tells them what to believe about the workplace, how to behave at work, what they will be rewarded for, the organization's values, and to what extent they become connected to the organization and its members (Jones & James, 1979; Rentsch, 1990, Schneider, 1990). Organizations that establish a culture for engagement maximize the probability that their employees will be engaged at work because they have provided the resources and fostered the relationships that are believed to trigger engagement. In the following, I review a number of factors that can be manipulated to create a culture for engagement.

Resources. Leaders and immediate managers are in a good position to provide resources, such as training, scheduling flexibility, help in the form of experts or more employees devoted to a project, or guidance on how to remove roadblocks preventing task completion (Eisenberger, Huntington, Hutchison, & Sowa, 1986; Graen & Uhl-Bien, 1995). Initial research into transformational leaders' effect on follower engagement suggests transformational leaders, those who lead by aligning subordinates' goals with those of the organization through an inspiring vision (Bass, 1985), promote employees' feelings of self-efficacy (Lester, Hannah, Harms, Vogelgesang, & Avolio, 2011), which results in them feeling they have what they need to do the job and do it well. Thus, promoting self-efficacy may also be considered a type of resource (Bakker & Demerouti, 2008) a leader can provide. Resources can come from other sources, however, such as coworkers who offer support (Byrne, Dik, & Chiaburu, 2008; Chiaburu, 2010; Sloan, 2012), or the job itself through job control or autonomy, access, opportunities for development, and job or skill variety (Crawford, LePine, & Rich, 2010).

In a recent study, my coauthors and I (Byrne, Peters, Rechlin, Smith, & Kedharnath, 2013) proposed that resources could be divided into a few different types, two of which are those available on the job, such as autonomy and skill or task variety, and those from the leader, such as fairness and support. Our results indicated that these forms of resources differentially related to engagement through their relationship with psychological meaningfulness and safety (which were both differentially related to engagement) and that engagement subsequently positively predicted job performance and negatively predicted turnover intentions. These findings suggest that resources are not perceived as all having the same value, can come from various sources, and do relate to the key conditions Kahn (1990) suggested are required for engagement.

Sufficient resources are implicated in the development of a culture for creativity, a precursor to innovation according to Amabile and colleagues (1996). Resources come in the form of an organizational culture that encourages creativity by providing fairness, rewards and recognition, a safe environment for sharing new ideas and obtaining constructive judgment, and leaders who develop a shared vision employees can support with their new ideas. Supervisors who are good role models by demonstrating support for the group, valuing individual contributions, and showing confident in others' ability to develop new ideas are also considered a necessary resource for promoting employee creativity. Likewise, access to funds, materials, information, and necessary equipment are essential support for promoting creativity (Amabile et al., 1996). Though preliminary research shows a positive relationship between engagement and innovation (Bhatnagar, 2012; Chugtai & Buckley, 2011), no studies to date have examined employee engagement and creativity or engagement and the organizational culture recommended for promoting creativity.

Managing work stressors. Some employees demonstrate the ability to cope with stress and work overload more effectively than do others. For example, those with high resistance to stress or dispositional optimism (Baltes, Zhdanova, & Clark, 2011; Collins, 2007; Holahan & Moos, 1985; Maas & Spinath, 2012; Carver & Scheier, 1998) tend to fare better. However, aspects of the job, coworkers, and leaders' efforts can make managing excessive job demands and workload easier. For example, employees with job autonomy, work schedule flexibility, job control, and voice have the ability to accommodate personal stressors such as family needs at home by rescheduling their work obligations and by pushing back when the workload or other negative aspects of the work environment are unreasonable (Baugher & Roberts, 2004). Providing employees the facilities to balance their work demands enables them to manage their stress and become engaged at work (Richardsen, Burke, & Martinussen, 2006). Additionally, lacking the appropriate skills to do the job becomes a workload management problem (Freeney & Tiernan, 2009); hence, skill development can be a resource. A large number of publications exist for managing stress at work including Quick, Murphy, and Hurrell (1992) and Rossi, Perrewé, and Sauter (2006); thus, readers are encouraged to consult these and other published resources for more information on stress management.

Besides individually oriented approaches in stress management, however, managing work stress can also come in the form of a culture in which support for one another and from management is the norm and in which those with a high tolerance for stress or hardiness are selected into jobs where stress is the norm (because they can handle the stress, whereas others cannot). For example, military personnel selected for special forces should score higher on tests for stress resistance or psychological hardiness (Arendasy, Sommer, & Hergovich, 2007; Bartone, Roland, Picano, & Williams, 2008). For jobs in which stress fluctuates or is not the key characteristic of the job (e.g., chronically high stressful conditions), it may not be as critical to select for psychological hardiness regarding achieving engagement.

Trust. Substantial evidence shows trust in the supervisor or leadership makes a big difference in employees' perception of work and their ability to perform on the job (Sousa-Lima, Michel, & Caetano, 2013). Trust also plays an important role in creating a climate for psychological safety (i.e., Aryee, Budhwar, & Chen, 2002). The nature of the employee-organization exchange is based on social exchange theory (Blau, 1964), which suggests employees are obligated to reciprocate to an organization or leader who offers something of value, such as support. The social exchange relationship is predicated on trust, in which the organization trusts the employee to reciprocate and the employee trusts the organization to continue in this relationship once obligations are fulfilled. Trust is a necessary condition for vulnerability, in which employees and the representatives of the organization demonstrate a belief in each other's dependability, reliability, and competency and an emotional feeling of mutual caring (McAllister, 1985). The condition of trust translates into feeling safe to express one's competency on the job without negative consequences when the message is critical, a key aspect of perceived psychological safety (Kahn, 1990). Trust follows in climates of justice or fairness (e.g., Aryee et al., 2002; Byrne, Pitts, Wilson, & Steiner, 2012; Korsgaard, Schweiger, & Sapienza, 1995), and leaders have control over fairness procedures and outcomes (e.g., Bies & Moag, 1986; Byrne & Cropanzano, 2001). Researchers have recently found a direct relationship between trust in the supervisor or leader and employee engagement, as well as an indirect relationship between authentic leadership and engagement via trust (D. Wang & Hsieh, 2013). People work harder and tend to respect a leader they consider competent (Justis, 1975), and as a result, they tend to trust the leader (Tan & Tan, 2000). Additionally, employees who trust their organization believe its leaders are competent and will take the organization in a direction that is beneficial (Tan & Tan, 2000). Thus, trust in both their leader and their organization is essential for employees to feel a fit and a willingness to be vulnerable to invest in their job roles.

Interpersonal leadership. Leadership characteristics that are interpersonal in nature seem to be most related to employee engagement (Aryee, Walumbwa, Zhou, & Hartnell, 2012; Hansen, Byrne, & Kiersch, in press; Tuckey, Dollard, & Bakker, 2012). Interpersonal leaders can promote positive well-being in employees (Arnold, Turner, Barling, Kelloway, & McKee, 2007), which serves to increase perceptions of psychological availability (Kahn, 1990). Transformational leaders, in particular, tend to demonstrate interpersonal characteristics that positively relate to engagement, such as personally recognizing employees' efforts, conveying caring and an appreciation for employees, and connecting employees' goals with those of the organization, thereby increasing their feelings of value and significance (Bass, 1985; Rafferty & Griffin, 2004; Walumbwa,

131

Avolio, & Zhu, 2008). Transformational leaders inspire their followers to seek and create meaning at work by aligning their goals with those of the organization (Bass, 1985; Yukl, 2010). Similarly, authentic leaders, those who are characterized by acting consistent with their internal beliefs and remaining true to themselves including sharing vulnerabilities (Avolio, Gardner, Walumbwa, Luthans, & May, 2004), promote trust and engagement in their followers (Hassan & Ahmed, 2011). The willingness to be vulnerable and encourage open criticism in the spirit of improvement sets up the authentic leader to create a climate for psychological safety, paving the way for engagement (Kahn, 1990). Walumbwa, Christensen, and Muchiri (2013) suggest that transformational leaders can promote engagement by influencing their followers' perceptions of meaningful work. They recommend a number of strategies including developing their employees' self-efficacy, and job redesign and describing work in ideological terms.

Finding and creating meaning. Employees who perceive a fit between themselves and their jobs or organizations are more likely to find meaning in their work (Shamir, 1991). Shamir (1991) proposed a self-concept-based theory of motivation to explain why people seek meaning and ultimately become engaged at work. He suggested that people need to self-express in a way that is consistent with their self-concept, to maintain and enhance their self-esteem, and to increase the congruency of their self-concept and behavior. Doing so gives them a sense of meaning—they are behaving and expressing themselves in a consistent and corresponding manner with their self-concept. Taking this perspective suggests that employee engagement comes from within the employee, and therefore is not under the leader or manager's full control, and can be encouraged through job factors, social factors, organizational culture, and other actions that enable and help employees align their behavior with their self-concept.

Based on the self-concept theory (Shamir, 1991), self-concept-job fit refers to a congruence between individuals feelings of their self-perception as derived from their work performance and their ideal self. Their performance on the job creates a self-perception on how they are doing; what their knowledge, skills, and abilities are in performing the job; and if this self-perception matches or is consistent with their identity or self-concept of how they should be able to perform on the job, they have self-concept-job fit (Scroggins & Benson, 2007). A lack of congruence is a lack of self-concept–job fit. When individuals feel that they have self-concept–job fit, they have meaning at work—their working is meaningful; those who lack fit seek ways to create fit. Scroggins (2008) found self-concept–job fit was positively related to meaningful work, which in turn was related to job performance, and was negatively related to turnover intentions. Scroggins suggested self-concept–job fit can be developed via career planning and progression activities, and job redesign (Oldham & Hackman, 1980).

A relatively new approach to a form of job redesign is job crafting, which refers to the process of redefining and reframing the way a job is designed to personally fit and work for the individual employee (Wrzesniewski & Dutton, 2001). By conceptualizing one's work tasks differently than they are now, and changing the boundary conditions of the job—that is, changing the tasks a bit, modifying how much time is spent on the various tasks, changing how one relates with others on the job, or changing how one sees the job tasks themselves—one can essentially craft the job to be more meaningful to the self (Wrzesniewski & Dutton, 2001). By empowering the employee to job craft, the employee can create his or her own meaningful work structure within the boundaries of organizational demands (the authors are not advocating employees change the core deliverable or requirement of the job, e.g., become an accountant when their job is customer service; Berg, Dutton, & Wrzesniewski, 2013).

Connection with others. Friendship at work involves a voluntary and amiable relationship between two employees, which includes support for each other's social and emotional goals (Song & Olshfski, 2008). Humans have a "powerful, fundamental, and extremely pervasive" need for belongingness and relational bonds (Baumeister & Leary, 1995, p. 497). As such, friendship at work fulfills individuals' needs for belongingness and relatedness, thus promoting individual health and well-being (Reis, Sheldon, Gable, Roscoe, & Ryan, 2000). Additionally, friendship offers individuals a sense of security and positive social validation (i.e., via reciprocity), thereby facilitating development of each individual's positive self-concept (Bukowski, Motzoi, & Meyer, 2009). Friendship may also potentially foster engagement through Kahn's (1990) critical states (e.g., friendship in the workplace could promote perceived psychological safety). Friendship is a fundamental aspect of human life that gives meaning to life (Bukowski et al., 2009) and it appears friendship can enhance engagement. The Gallup Organization includes an item on their Q^{12} asking about having a best friend at work (see Buckingham & Coffman, 1999; Gebauer, Lowman, & Gordon, 2008; Harter et al., 2002). This item, most likely, works to predict employee outcomes because it captures to some extent this powerful need for belongingness.

Friends, coworkers, and others of close proximity in the workplace fulfill another important function—that of creating a social reality. Social information processing theory (Salancik & Pfeffer, 1978) suggests that employees draw on past behavior and what others around them think to form their own attitudes, behaviors, and beliefs to adapt to their current situation, as well as to create the reality of their own past behavior and situations. Thus, they are constantly adapting and absorbing from the information in the social environment. Social information processing theory applied to engagement suggests that employees may alter their perception of the meaningfulness of their work, and ultimately their engagement, through processing the information and social environment around them—their friends at work.

Connections with others work well when colleagues and leaders operate from a base of civility. Civility refers to the interpersonal behaviors that demonstrate respect for others (Andersson & Pearson, 1999). A lack of civility or incivility (i.e., disrespectful and rude behaviors that are milder forms of mistreatment as compared to aggression, bullying, or other negative behaviors that inflict psychological harm) is related to employee stress outcomes including anxiety, lost productivity, and even worse, retaliation (Bies & Tripp, 2005; Skarlicki & Folger, 1997; Yamada, 2000). Those who are on the receiving end of incivility report greater psychological distress than those who are not (Cortina, Magley, Williams, & Langhout, 2001). We can hypothesize that a culture of incivility inhibits the development of engagement, because employees who are surrounded by incivility may spend tremendous energy coping with the stress these conflicting and negative interactions create. It is also possible that employees who find friendship with those who are civil can experience engagement (i.e., the civility helps buffer the incivility).

Incivility threatens inclusion. Recent theorizing in inclusivity and diversity suggests inclusion is grounded in the balance or tension between belongingness and uniqueness, in which one feels a strong sense of belongingness and fit, yet is also appreciated and valued for his or her uniqueness (although this may be a particularly Western culture perspective; Shore, Randel, Chung, Dean, Ehrhart, & Singh, 2011). When defined this way, inclusivity refers to being accepted for oneself and being given the opportunity to express one's true self without fear of exclusion or isolation (i.e., psychological safety). Psychological safety is essential for engagement (Kahn, 1990). Furthermore, the need to feel unique, acknowledged for one's individual contribution and individuality seems particularly relevant for experiencing psychological meaningfulness—that what one does is meaningful in and of itself; meaning is not just derived from the recognition the organization can give but from the feeling what one is doing is making an important contribution and the gain relative to the cost of effort is worthwhile (Kahn, 1990). Finally, not having to fight assimilation (being treated as an insider when you conform and downplay your uniqueness), exclusion (your uniqueness is not valued so you are an outsider, but others are valued for their uniqueness and treated as insiders), or differentiation (treated as an outsider but uniqueness is valued; Shore et al., 2011) allows one to spend energy and attention on the job task, freeing up cognitive and emotional loads for experiencing psychological availability (Kahn, 1990). Thus, inclusivity, being treated as an insider and encouraged to retain your uniqueness (Shore et al., 2011), may be a key organizational culture component that contributes to experienced psychological conditions necessary for engagement. A current limitation of this perspective of inclusivity is the emphasis on the individual, which is a perspective firmly based in the Western culture (I review different cultures in Chapter 9); therefore, this particular approach may not be as applicable to Eastern cultures where individualism is not the central value.

Congruence between person and organization or job. Person–organization fit (P-O fit) may be a good example of a construct that reflects employees' perceptions of some of the right conditions for engagement. Specifically, P-O fit refers to the degree to which an employee's skills, needs, values, and personality are congruent with those required for the job (Chatman, 1989; Kristof-Brown, Zimmerman, & Johnson, 2005). When employees perceive strong P-O fit, they report high levels of engagement (β = .48; Biswas & Bhatnagar, 2013). Importantly, relatively to perceived organizational support, fit contributes more to explaining the variance in engagement.

P-O fit can be taken into consideration when selecting and hiring employees, which may address popular writings suggesting employers hire engaged employees (C. Wright, 2012). In support, some have suggested fit with the organization or job is and can be used in making selection decisions (e.g., Cable & Judge, 1997; Sekiguchi & Huber, 2011). Research shows those with congruence between their values and needs with the organization or with their jobs are less likely to quit, tend to report higher job satisfaction, demonstrate higher levels of organizational commitment, and perform at a higher level than those with low fit (Kristof-Brown et al., 2005; Lauver & Kristof-Brown, 2001). Furthermore, various forms of fit have been identified, such as person–group, person–supervisor, and person–job (Kristof-Brown et al., 2005), all demonstrating slightly different relationships with employees' attitudes and behaviors. For example, person–job fit was more strongly related to job satisfaction than were other fits, and organizational commitment most strongly related to person–organization fit. These results suggest that ensuring a good congruence between employees and the organization at the time of hire and then ensuring a good fit between employees and their supervisor and team (or coworkers) may make a difference in the extent to which employees are able to develop and find meaningfulness in their work (Scroggins, 2008).

Likewise, employees who perceive alignment between their job tasks and the organization's strategic goals or priorities report higher levels of work engagement than do those who do not perceive alignment, and those higher levels were maintained over a 1- to 3-year period (Biggs, Brough, & Barbour, 2013). Based on their review of the literature, Jin et al. (2010) suggested that "organizations with superior human capital resources that are aligned with the overall organizational strategy will outperform their competition and have long-term success" (p. 941). The authors additionally offered that such competitive advantage is achieved because employees' skills and knowledge directly relate to productivity,

135

employees with such skill and knowledge are scarce, the tacit knowledge developed by employees working in and with the organization make them imitable, and the combination of employees skills, abilities, and background experience with the organization make them non-substitutable.

Table 7.1 summarizes the various actions organizations can take to address factors of culture that have been empirically associated with promoting employee engagement.

Table 7.1 Actions Organizations Can Take to Create Culture for Engagement

Factor	*Actions*
Resources	• Training, scheduling flexibility, mentors or expert employees, organizational support • Transformational or interpersonal leaders who emphasize both vision and employee relations • Access to necessary information, equipment or materials for creativity and job task completion
Managing work stressors	• Scheduling flexibility, workload distribution strategies, job control, voice to suggest process improvements, appropriate autonomy • Supervisory support • Job fit for stress-tolerant or hardy personalities
Trust	• Leadership trust • Transparent and frequent communication • Climate of justice or fairness
Leadership	• Interpersonal and/or transformational • High accountability • Trustworthy • Empowerment
Meaning	• Career planning • Organizational mission or vision • Job crafting
Connection	• Create climate that promotes and encourages friendship • Matrix structures that require cross team collaborations • Zero-tolerance for incivility or discrimination • Employee ownership through open-book management or stock options
Congruence	• Fit with the organization and the job values and skills

What Does a Culture for Engagement
Potentially Look Like?

Jaspreet chose to work for Gingo-Bird, a retailer that manufactures
and sells all products related to birds. She loves birds and was drawn
to apply for their opening when she heard Gingo-Bird is a fun place
to work. A friend of Jaspreet's works for Gingo-Bird and talked often
about how even though the organization is large and spread across a
number of European locations, the employees feel connected because
of the regular company gatherings, the local meetings and gatherings,
and the opportunities to find mentors across the organization. Part of
the job benefits are going to the company meetings held in different
countries (France, Germany, Belgium, and the Netherlands). Being an
animal lover, Jaspreet liked the organization's mission "Protect, Promote, And Pamper Birds of All Feather." She also liked that reports
about the company suggested that it "walk the talk" (does as it says it
will do). Annual reports from the organization posted online showed
their financials were solid, despite volatility in the overseas markets,
and their leadership team highly regarded. They adopted an open-
book management practice from the United States (see Case, 1995;
Stack, 1994), and employee ownership programs made Jaspreet
feel that the organization was transparent in its policies and wanted
employees to own and have input into how the organization should
be run. Another aspect of the organization's statistics that appealed
to Jaspreet were its reports on diversity—the company boasted high
percentages of individuals from various ethnic and religious back-
grounds, a wide range of age groups, individuals from several European and Asian cultures, and a relatively even balance of men and
women on both the board and in leadership levels.

Since she was hired, Jaspreet has had some family issues and needed
to take time off. Her boss and teammates were supportive and worked
with her to develop a schedule that supported her needs, yet also
ensured the work was completed, and no one felt taken for granted.
Jaspreet was able to shift her responsibilities to allow for more flextime, yet this also gave her the chance to continue contributing to the
new ideas the team was developing for bird-games, which allowed
them to compete for company rewards in best ideas. Team members
attended classes when first hired to learn how to have healthy debates
without turning the discussions into disrespectful competition. They
learned how to agree to disagree and how to discuss sensitive topics
as needed. When asked to participate in a longitudinal diary study of
engagement, Jaspreet's ratings trend high.

Selecting for Engagement for Competitive Advantage

A logical question that should be asked is whether organizations can select for engagement, assuming competitive advantage for organizations can actually be achieved with engaged employees. That is, are some people predisposed to engagement such that one could select for this characteristic, ensuring an engaged workforce? I noted earlier how P-O fit may be a helpful factor in selection, but P-O fit is not a predisposition.

According to Kahn (1990), engagement is not a stable trait or characteristic of an individual; it is a moment-to-moment experience that naturally fluctuates depending on the work context, individual him or herself (ability to be present or not; Kahn, 1992), and other factors of the work and job role itself. In contrast, Schaufeli, Salanova, et al. (2002) define engagement as a stable and persistent state; however, engagement is still nonetheless a state. Macey and Schneider (2008) offer perhaps the only definition thus far that incorporates the concept of engagement as a trait, hence a stable individual difference characteristic that could be selected for in job application situations. The authors define trait engagement as a positive orientation towards work indicated by proactive personality (e.g., tendency to influence or take charge of one's work environment), conscientiousness, trait positive affect, and autotelic personality (e.g., tendency to participate in activities for their own sake). Their argument is that people who score high on these traits are more likely to become engaged.

Macey and colleagues (2009) propose employees with proactive or conscientious personality characteristics are likely to be positive and productive, resulting in engagement. As noted in Chapter 4, research has shown positive correlations between engagement and proactive personality (Dikkers, Jansen, de Lange, Vinkenburg, & Kooij, 2009). Furthermore, Dikkers and colleagues (2009) found that proactive personality was positively related to higher scores in dedication and absorption 18 months after their initial assessment. Causation cannot be inferred because the two data points were self-report surveys with no intermediary intervention and no controls to isolate whether it was indeed the proactive personality that caused the increase in engagement. Nonetheless, these findings suggest the two constructs are related.

Correlations between engagement and conscientiousness ($r = .14$, $p < .05$) are not that high according to Liao, Yang, Want, Drown, and Shi (2013). Liao et al. examined person–situation interactions on engagement, namely, the effects of personality (i.e., neuroticism, agreeableness, conscientiousness, openness, and extraversion) on the relationship between quality of team-member relations (team-member exchange) and engagement (Schaufeli, Salanova, et al., 2002) in a sample of 235 Chinese employees. Agreeableness had the highest correlation with engagement at $r = .22$, $p < .01$. Over a 3-month period, they found employees with high extraversion, low neuroticism, and low conscientiousness were more engaged when they experienced high-quality team member relationships. In contrast, Mostert and Rothmann (2006) found conscientiousness correlated at .38 ($p < .01$) and extraversion at .33 ($p < .05$) with engagement (Schaufeli, Salanova, et al., 2002). In a sample of 1794 South African police members (officers and staff) including Whites, Blacks, Coloreds, and Indians. They concluded from regression analyses that employees reporting higher conscientiousness, emotional stability (low neuroticism), and extraversion reported higher engagement, even in their stressful job environment.

Although some initial research examining engagement and various personality traits shows positive correlations exist, it is unclear why or whether these correlations matter in determining or predicting a predisposition to engagement. For example, why would someone scoring low in conscientiousness or extraversion not be able to become engaged at work? Is it just the being conscientious predisposes a person to take advantage of resources and a climate for engagement more so than someone who is not predisposed?

Conclusion

No research today offers a single-point confirmation or solid evidence providing the type of comprehensive and complex culture as described earlier that will ensure (a) an engaged workforce or (b) a competitive advantage. Such a study would be challenging, to say the least, to conduct given all the variables that would have to be simultaneously studied and the number of controls required to isolate which factor played what role in engagement and in competitive advantage. There are many case studies of organizational successes in improving engagement and competitive advantage offered by consulting firms such as Kenexa, Gallup, Towers-Watson, Deloitte, BlessingWhite, Inward Strategic, Hay Group, and Gagen MacDonald to name a small few.[1] However, none indicates how engagement was defined or measured (most hint or state that engagement is synonymous with job satisfaction), nor do they provide data regarding how they evaluated improvements. Thus, even though many report increases of 50% or more in engagement scores, organizational performance, or even financial gains, none provides the actual evidence.

However, results from many individual studies as reviewed earlier, when taken together, suggest that the noted factors independently support the right environment for engagement. Not all solutions are ripe for combining—it may be that some factors interact with others to set up conditions that are not as conducive to engagement as one might think. For example, research has shown cynical employees, those who believe their voice is unheard and suggestions discarded, tend to view organizational support negatively (Byrne & Hochwarter, 2008). Those exhibiting cynicism in their study were not the same as those suffering burnout; rather, they were assessed as those who have given up trying to offer their positive suggestions to improve the organization (most likely from lack of psychological safety or perceived value).

Walk-Away Points

- Engaged employees may be a one way to achieve competitive advantage.
- Organizations may be able to select for personality characteristics that predispose employees to become engaged.
- Organizations can create a culture for engagement.
- There is a big need for empirical evidence that demonstrates the actions recommended here and in other publications on culture for engagement are actually effective in building a culture that promotes engagement; engagement increases as a result, along with competitive advantage.

NOTE

1. There is no order to this list, and inclusion on the list is not representative of quality or size of offerings. It is simply an example list of consulting firms that offer engagement solutions and case studies of their reported successes.

8

HOW DO WE USE ENGAGEMENT TO CREATE A HEALTHY-THRIVING ORGANIZATION?

The study of psychology originally focused on understanding what prevents people from enjoying positive well-being, employing a medical model perspective on diagnosing and treating mental illness (Koch & Leary, 1985), and many still focus their attention today on resolving negative experiences that have lasting psychological effects. However, since about the late 1940s and early 1950s, attention has also been placed on understanding and helping normal people flourish. This positive approach to understanding the human existence, labeled positive psychology (M. P. Seligman & Csikszentmihalyi, 2000), has been active on both an individual and a group level. At the individual level of focus, researchers have studied individuals' traits that predispose them to happiness and hope, whereas at the group level, the focus is on how institutions promote citizenship, altruism, and a positive strong work ethic (Maddux, 2002).

Occupational health psychology has as a primary aim to identify and remove individual and organizational health risks (Quick & Tetrick, 2011; Tetrick, Quick, & Gilmore, 2012). Psychologists within this field focus on improvements to the workplace that eliminate or reduce stressors, prevent accidents and illness, and strive for healthy employees. Thus, one could describe occupational health psychology as an arm of psychology focused on the creation of healthy organizations (a term once reserved for describing the financial survivability of an organization; Graham, Howard, & Dougall, 2012), including creating healthy employees within.

Healthy-thriving organizations not only prevent health risks for employees, but they also grow their employees' health. Healthy organizations implement interventions specifically designed to create and protect the health and welfare of their employees (Cooper & Cartwright, 1994; Ganster, 1995), seeing employees as valuable renewable resources rather than expendable throwaways.

One approach to the study of employee engagement that has, to a degree, followed the history of psychology and trended towards the aim of occupational health psychology was launched by Maslach and colleagues (Maslach & Leiter, 1997; Maslach, Schaufeli, & Leiter, 2001). Maslach and colleagues proposed that employee engagement was a movement away from burnout to the state in which burnout is not experienced, in essence framing engagement as the opposite of burnout. We can describe their purpose as an attempt to find the construct space that captured what it meant to be not paying attention only to the lack of fulfillment and personal connection, but rather enjoying and fulfilling a positive existence marked by productivity and growth. This attempt to get away from or describe an opposite state of being, one that was positive as opposed to negative, was carried forward by Schaufeli, Salanova, González-Romá, and Bakker (2002) and other researchers studying health.

Thus far, the theoretical approach and research focused on the relationship between engagement and stress has studied the effects of the work environment on employee engagement—whether stress conditions negatively affect levels of engagement. But what if we flipped that causal direction the other way around—why not consider how engaged employees create a healthy organization?

Engagement Contagion

Theory and research on contagions, shared cognitions, social information processing, and the perception–behavior link suggest that engaged employees create engagement in those around them through a process I call *engagement contagion*. Others who are nearby those expressing their engagement at work "catch" the emotions, behaviors, and cognitions of engaged employees, thereby creating their own engagement. Thus, those who are fully expressing the characteristic state of employee engagement create engagement around them, increasing the number of employees who engaged at work and ultimately creating a healthy and thriving organization. As mentioned in previous chapters, engagement is positively related to performance and well-being. Thus, engagement contagion explains why organizations with more engaged than unengaged employees continue to report higher earnings, revenue, and overall financial health (Gallup Organization, 2002, 2013a, 2013b); it is because those who are engaged infect others with engagement and, given the right organizational culture (described in Chapters 4 and 7), are able to build an organizational army of engaged workers.

I explain in the following how this engagement contagion effect occurs by first explaining emotional and social cognitions contagions, social information processing theory, and the perception–behavior link. The synergistic and simultaneous activation of these contagions and transference theories create the foundation for engagement contagion.

Emotional Contagion

Emotional contagion refers to a tendency to mimic and adopt the emotions of others (Hatfield, Cacioppo, & Rapson, 1993). It is the automatic (either conscious or unconscious) mimicry and synchronization of people's expressions, vocalizations, and behaviors with others that results in an emotional convergence (Hatfield et al., 1993; Hatfield, Cacioppo, & Rapson, 1994). As described by Hatfield et al. (1993), emotions are considered integrated packages of facial, vocal, and physical expressions of neurophysiological and nervous system activity that triggers various behaviors in response to the environment or one's thoughts. Thus, emotional contagion includes the mimicry of facial expressions, vocal tones, speech patterns, and body language of others. Mimicking others is not a new phenomenon in human history—in fact, research on how babies learn demonstrates that we begin mimicking the expressions of others shortly after birth (Hatfield et al., 1994; O'Toole & Dubin, 1968).

During conversation, people tend to automatically synchronize their movements and expressions with others, posturing and speaking similarly to one another without conscious awareness of doing so (Hatfield et al., 1993; Kendon, 1970; LaFrance & Broadbent, 1976). The physical act of mimicking creates changes in one's own body, resulting in the physical and affective experience of the emotion and not just mirroring the emotion. The physiological feedback from muscles, visceral, and glandular mechanisms creates the full experience of the emotion, making the emotion one's own (Adelmann & Zajonc, 1989; Hatfield et al., 1994). Similarly, vocal feedback in the form of rhythm, pauses, and intonation from mimicry influences one's experience of the emotion (Hatfield, Hsee, Costello, & Weisman, 1995). As a result of mimicry, people "catch" the emotions of others and experience them as fully as if they were originally their own (Hatfield et al., 1993). We cannot help ourselves—yawning elicits yawning, seeing someone in pain causes us to wince in as if in pain, and we mimic the facial expressions and behaviors we see on television (Bavelas, Black, Lemery, & Mullet, 1986; Hsee, Hatfield, Carlson, & Chemtob, 1990; Provine, 1986).

Cognitive Contagion

Shared cognitions. Whereas emotional contagion is primarily unconscious, it has been suggested that shared cognitions, the learned understanding of group members' knowledge and approaches (Barsade, 2002; Cannon-Bowers & Salas, 2001; Hatfield et al., 1993), is accomplished through language. Therefore, sharing cognitions does not require face-to-face interactions and tends more toward a conscious process (Cannon-Bowers & Salas, 2001; Ilgen & Klein, 1989; Salancik & Pfeffer, 1978). Typically referred to with regard to teams or groups, shared cognitions include task-specific knowledge, task-related knowledge, team attitudes/beliefs and judgments, and knowledge of each other (Cannon & Edmondson, 2001; Cannon-Bowers & Salas, 2001; Klimoski & Mohammed, 1994). By understanding each other's expertise and by learning over time how members solve problems, group members can compensate for and support each other without first having to discuss the situation (Cannon-Bowers & Salas, 2001). Similarly, group members adjust their behavior to allow for the strengths of others to compliment their own, maximizing group performance. What is shared is the understanding of the knowledge base or compatible knowledge, such that individuals can draw the same or a common interpretation from the situation, even if they do not each possess the exact same structure of information. One's understanding of how others' think or what approach they use to think through problems or situations essentially creating shared meaning, forms the shared cognition. Collective meaning is another descriptor for the product of social interactions that include shared perceptions, behaviors, norms, belief systems, and interpretations (Gruenfeld & Hollingshead, 1993; Zajonc & Adelmann, 1987).

Social information processing theory. Social information processing theory (Salancik & Pfeffer, 1978), a special case of social cognition theories (Ilgen & Klein, 1988), suggests that people construct and share thoughts, judgments, attitudes, and cognitions through their interactions with each other in their work environment. People spend considerable time together at work or in work interactions (and not necessarily face-to-face, although cues have a stronger impact when transmitted in face-to-face interactions; Ilgen & Klein, 1989), and this social context provides information and insight into people's attitudes and thoughts. Through a need to fit into and make sense of the social environment (Baumeister & Leary, 1995), people adapt their attitudes, behaviors, and beliefs accordingly, using the cues from others around them to determine how and in what way that adaptation should occur (Salancik & Pfeffer, 1978). As a result, they take on each other's attitudes and judgments, forming a shared social cognition (Bateman, Griffin, & Rubinstein, 1987). Thus, shared social cognitions involve a process by which people share and construct memories, judgments, ideas, and thoughts, in general (Klimoski & Mohammed, 1994; Moreland, Argote, & Krishnan, 1996).

Many have used a variety of terms for describing collective or shared cognitions (e.g., Cannon-Bowers, Salas, & Converse, 1993; Hardin & Higgins, 1995; Hutchins, 1991; Ickes & Gonzalez, 1994; Klimoski & Mohammed, 1994; Levine, Resnick, & Higgins, 1993; Resnick, Levine, & Teasley, 1991). To date, even though the term has been used in conjunction with emotional contagion, no definition of cognitive contagion appears to have been offered (Barsade, 2002; Hatfield et al., 1993). Therefore, drawing on the frameworks of shared cognitions, social information processing theory, and the concept of a contagion, I propose *cognitive contagion* is the shared creation of meaning, an understanding of how to make sense of the work tasks and work environment, while drawing on compatible or shared knowledge structures. I further propose that cognitive contagion is similar to emotional contagion in that one can adopt, synchronize, or absorb the cognitive approach, beliefs, and judgment patterns of others, in essence "catching" their perspective and way of thinking to create meaning of the work environment.

Cognitive contagion is different from emotional contagion in that shared cognitions are not transferred via mimicry. Instead, cognitive contagion is caught through the process of sharing judgments, ideas, and thoughts about problems and tasks at work and conveying emotionally infused thought patterns. Cognitive contagion is passed or transmitted through the behavioral and communication cues of others.

Like cognitive contagion, emotional contagion can occur in groups where members of a group or individuals who work together influence the moods and judgments of those around them (Barsade, 2002). Collective emotion has been shown to positively affect work outcomes (George, 1990, 2002). That is, greater cognitive effort at work is displayed during complex reasoning and problem-solving tasks, and individuals tend to increase performance regardless of occupation (M. E. Seligman & Schulman, 1986; Staw, Sutton, & Pelled, 1994; Sullivan & Conway, 1989; T. Wright & Staw, 1999). Thus, the consequences of both emotional and cognitive contagion are positive for both individual and organization.

Behavioral Contagion

A viable explanation for the transmission (i.e., infection) and adoption of others' behaviors is the perception-behavior link. Chartrand and Bargh (1999) noted that people take on the behaviors of others, called the chameleon effect, and explained this effect using the perception–behavior link (Bargh, Chen, & Burrows, 1996). Similar to mimicry, a key aspect of emotional contagion, the perception–behavior link states people unintentionally mimic the postures, expressions, and behaviors of others, unconsciously matching their behavior to others and changing how they interact in the social environment. Just perceiving how another behaves, not even interpreting or processing the social context as proposed by symbolic interactionism, is enough to trigger changing one's own behavior to match (Chartrand & Bargh, 1999). The process of thinking about acting in a particular way actually triggers the same regions of the brain that doing the behavior activates, an explanation for why visualization is so powerful (Suinn, 1984). The act of thinking about the behavior leads to a tendency to engage in the behavior because of the muscular response thinking triggers (Chartand, Maddux, & Lakin, 2005).

Chartrand, Maddux, and Lakin (2005) suggested that perceiving the actions of others triggers associated representations in memory that in turn make one likely to enact the same behaviors. They argue that the main difference between perception–behavior link and mimicry is that mimicry requires no interpretation or translation of traits into behaviors, whereas perceiving the actions of others leads to spontaneous attributions and activation of stereotypes. Thus, the invocation of trait constructs and stereotypes or schemas trigger such as behaviors, a process that does not exist with simple mimicry. We can see evidence of this in the mimicking demonstrated by babies, who lack trait constructs and stereotypes on which to draw when mimicking their mother's or father's expressions or behavior. The difference is subtle, yet Chartrand et al. suggest it is important.

Substantial research evidence supports the perception–behavior link (Chartrand et al., 2005). The research evidence not only supports behavioral matching between not only people who care about one another, such as a mother and a child, but also strangers. For example, Chartrand and Bargh (1999) conducted a lab study wherein strangers were placed with confederates. Half of the participants were first with a confederate who rubbed her face and then later with a confederate who shook her foot during the sessions. The other half of participants were exposed to the foot-shaking confederate first followed by the face-rubbing confederate. Chartrand and Bargh found participants demonstrated the same behaviors as their confederates, shaking their foot with the foot-shaking confederate *and* rubbing their face with the face-rubbing confederate. At the end of the study, participants were asked about their behaviors and none noticed either the confederates' behaviors or their own mimicry of the behaviors. The authors also found participants mimicked confederates they reportedly did not like, demonstrating the perception–behavior link is not simply about adopting behaviors from those you like.

Combining Contagions to Make Engagement Contagion

Employee engagement has been defined by Kahn (1990) as a three-part multidimensional construct: affective, cognitive, and physical or physiological. Using this definition, it has integrated, interdependent components, and as such, engagement contagion relies on the synergistic integration of key theories and research to explain how these three components are transmitted and caught by others. The transmission of affective, cognition, and physiology does not occur in isolation; however, it helps to break the three apart to explain how the transmission or "infection" occurs. Additionally, if using Schaufeli, Salanova, et al.'s (2002) definition of engagement, the three components of engagement—vigor, dedication, and absorption—have been considered and assessed as independent representations of the full engagement construct (in particular vigor). Thus, considering the independent infection of emotional, cognitive, and physiological or physical components of engagement contagion provides an understanding of how engagement contagion works when using Schaufeli, Salanova, et al.'s definition.

To date, no one has described engaged employees as apathetic, zombielike, or foggy-brained. Rather, engaged employees are described as expressing enthusiasm, energy, playfulness, and generally displaying positive attitudes (Kahn, 1990; Schaufeli, Salanova, et al., 2002). Engaged employees are characterized as expressive, vigorous, energetic, cognitively focused, empathetic, and active (Kahn, 1990; Macey et al., 2009; Saks, 2006; Schaufeli, Salanova, et al., 2002). Because of how visible emotions are in comparison to what one may be thinking (which can be expressed to some degree) or whether one is internally physiologically aroused (if strong enough, we may be very active behaviorally), engagement may be more strongly transmitted through its emotional component than its cognitive or physiological, although all three operate in synergy and are transmitted simultaneously.

Transmitting affect. Through their interactions with others at work, engaged employees transmit their positive emotions, their physiological arousal associated with their emotions, and their sense of meaning and interpretation of what is meaningful at work. In doing so, employees who are around those who are engaged, "catch" engagement through the mechanism of engagement contagion. Unless one deliberately runs away from, avoids, argues with, fights, or purposefully ignores and resists engaged employees, the engaged employee's emotions are visible and can infect others. Even skeptical coworkers or colleagues who question the validity of the engaged employee's thoughts may become engaged themselves by diving into a heated debate or disagreement about the ideas, demonstrating their own fully focused and embraced attention on their view point. Engaged employees express enthusiasm and excitement that can be caught by others as explained by emotional contagion. Emotional contagion infuses in others an emotional response, influencing cognitions, attitudes, and behaviors (Hatfield et al., 1993).

Transmitting cognition. Employee engagement also comprises a cognitive component to which cognitive contagion applies. Engaged employees share their focus, their cognitive absorption and persistence in problem solving, such that others working with them and around them are infected and pulled into that problem-solving space. Through conversation, brainstorming, hearing how one makes meaning from the work environment and job tasks, and exploring thought processes together, the engaged employee infects others with a shared cognition and shared meaning of the work.

Not adopting the mental models, the schemas or thinking that engaged employees bring to the table while focused and in a state of flow would require ignoring the engaged employee, not joining in the problem-solving space, and removing oneself from the active discussion or brainstorming.

Transmitting physiology. Finally, engaged employees are physiologically aroused, excited, and energetic; they express an arousal level even if they are not physically darting around a room. Engaged employees might convey their internal arousal by punctuating their words, increasing or actively decreasing their volume to make a point, demonstrating fast reaction or response times with comments or actions, using expressive body language, and varying their intonations. Moreover, energy intensifies emotions, such that high arousal levels are associated with high energy emotions; heart rate is accelerated, skin conductance is high, and facial activity increases indicating affective involvement (Jacob et al., 1999). Through the perception–behavior link, engaged employees infect others with an aroused physiology, matching pace, body language, and expressions.

Working in groups. Employees who are engaged most likely connect with others at work. Research suggests connection and relations with others promotes engagement within individuals, as do friends and close coworker relations (Kahn, 1990). Relationships at work provide support that facilitates becoming engaged (Bakker & Demerouti, 2008). People are attracted to emotionally expressive people (H. Friedman, Riggio, & Casella, 1988). This means engaged employees are not work hermits— they attract and interact positively and frequently with others at work. Moreover, expectations for working together increases mimicking (Lakin & Chartrand, 2003), which suggests engaged colleagues activate engagement contagion on a consistent and ongoing basis; it is not a onetime infection.

In summary, engagement contagion occurs through the mechanisms of emotional, cognitive, and physiological contagions and is unique in that it synergistically combines these other forms of contagion to infect others.

Why Some May Not Catch Engagement From Others

Dynamic social impact theory (Latané, 1997) suggests when people work together, even minimally, there is a natural tendency toward (a) consolidation: as the proportion of the people who hold a minority perspective shrinks, the diversity in the group shrinks; (b) clustering: people become more similar to those near them than to those farther away; and (c) continuing diversity: a few holding minority views persist within the group. Evidence supports these natural tendencies (e.g.,

Latané & L'Herrou, 1996) indicating that shared cognitions and behaviors are natural and common phenomena when people participate in groups or work with others. Those who do not catch engagement may make up the minority group or the minority perspective.

There may be several reasons why engagement contagion is not fully passed onto others. Some reasons may be motivational, situational, or dispositional. Like those in Latané's (1997) continuing diversity group, some may purposefully choose to remain uninfected.

Motivational. Those who do not catch engagement to its fullest extent may be motivated to deflect the emotional or behavioral influences because they have instrumental reasons, such as political battles or retaliatory behavior, not being excited or involved in the tasks or project, or for purposefully shutting down and withdrawing from work. If people have a reason for not wanting to be a part of a team or group, part of a solution, or open to the excitement of others, they may be less inclined to pay attention to the emotions of others and to the thoughts or comments from others and may not notice others' behaviors. In this case, the mechanisms of emotional and cognitive contagion, as well as perception–behavior links are deflected and unable to have their effect.

Reasons for deflecting engagement from others may also include depression or emotional exhaustion, which affects one's motivation to participate at work (Maslach & Leiter, 1997). As long as people interpret their work environment as supporting their feelings of competence and a sense of relatedness, they should feel self-determined and intrinsically motivated (Ryan & Deci, 2000). However, when external motivators, in particular introjected regulation (attempts to push guilt) or external regulation (attempts to get compliance), are used, feelings of being controlled reduce motivation and lead to less intrinsic motivation to perform (Ryan & Deci, 2000). Therefore, if engagement contagion feels staged or pushed by the organization, as could occur in a training session or a team-building intervention, results may lead to less engagement than otherwise would be achieved through natural interactions.

Situational. Researchers studying emotional contagion have shown people who we considered our opponents are unlikely to infect us (McHugo, Lanzetta, Sullivan, Masters, & Englis, 1985), suggesting it is possible to deflect absorbing others' emotions, cognitions, and behaviors. Thus, a possible situational boundary condition to engagement contagion may be situations wherein interactions involve individuals with whom one has a conflicting or negative relationship, like opponents, enemies, or nemeses.

Sensitivity to rejection (Mehrabian & Ksionzky, 1970), a determinant of affiliative behavior, refers to a tendency to struggle with interactions with others over a fear of rejection and strong desire for belongingness. High sensitivity to rejection, hypothesized to stem from attachment issues with parental figures (hence, situational; Butler, Doherty, & Potter, 2007), would lead one to avoid extensive contact with others (this does not require that contact be face-to-face), making engagement contagion challenging and less likely.

Dispositional.   There may be personality traits, such as neuroticism or emotional instability that when expressed result in withdrawing from others at work or avoiding strong connection with others. For example, individuals strongly endorsing facets of neuroticism such as self-consciousness or depression may struggle with work relationships (Costa & McCrae, 1992, 2009).

Another personality trait, social anxiety (called social phobia in the *Diagnostic and Statistical Manual of Mental Disorders*, 1994), can manifest itself in different ways and refers to a persistent fear of social or performance situations. Shyness may be considered related to social phobia (Van Ameringen, Mancini, & Oakman, 1998); thus, not all anxiety issues have to manifest themselves at a clinically diagnostic level such as social phobia. For those who are either very shy or experience a manageable yet challenging level of social anxiety, interactions with others become very uncomfortable and difficult and, thus, are kept to a minimum, reducing opportunity for engagement contagion.

Weakened Effect of Engagement Contagion?

The engagement contagion effect is strongest for employees working in similar occupations and units as compared to those working in different fields of study. Namely, for the cognitive contagion effect of engagement contagion to work, employees must understand each other's work environment and fundamental knowledge base. Thus, lawyers working with nurses are unlikely to cognitively infect each other because they do not understand each other's workload, tasks, and content language. It may be possible to transmit one's enthusiasm and physical energy for work in general, but shared meaning and thinking are less likely and weaker across occupational boundaries.

One could hypothesize engagement contagion may be weakened for workers from different countries who do not share a common language. However, my own experience suggests that this hypothesis needs extensive testing. When I visited Russia in both 2012 and 2013, although the university leaders told me that they felt their students and faculty members were more excited and bubbling with energy for research because of my visit and because of being around me, we could not share our thinking about research because we could not speak each other's language.

Our communication was through interpreters and that boundary through which we spoke prevented our ability to share direct meaning, understanding, problem-solving strategies, or ways of thinking about our fields of interest. Language is critical to cognitive contagion and language barriers constrain or prohibit shared meaning through cognitive contagion. What I found particularly fascinating, however, was that even though I could not speak Russian and my contemporary could not speak English, we seemed to understand each other's intention through our emotional expressions, excitement, and touch. By connecting on all other levels, our shared feelings and energy seemed to provide us some feeling of shared meaning, even if not as fully as if we could understand each other's words. It felt almost as if we could actually understand each other's words at times; however, once the interpreter translated our words, we realized what we thought was said was not. Instead, what we seemed to accurately understand was the emotion (e.g., positive, affiliative, excited), the intent of the thoughts and content (e.g., making progress, collaboration, resolving differences), and the behavioral messages (e.g., energy, impatience to get started, impatience to understand each other).

In addition to language barriers, one could hypothesize physical boundaries to accurately perceiving behavior, such as virtual work environments (even those that incorporate audio-visual communication mechanisms) that may weaken the engagement contagion effect. Although employees can perceive each other's behaviors, expressions, and vocal tones across virtual work boundaries when audio-visual communication media are available, the strength of contagion effect is dependent on the quality of transmission. One must be able to adequately see behaviors, body language, and expressions to mimic or match them. However, recent research on the use of digital avatars (computerized representation of people) has shown that animated avatars mimicking their communication partner's nonverbal cues (i.e., head movements) were more persuasive and likeable than were nonmimicking avatars (Bailenson & Yee, 2005).

Can You Train Others to Catch Engagement?

Organizational consultants, no doubt, want an answer to the next logical question, "Can it be trained?" That is, can you train engaged employees to "infect" others around them, or train employees to catch engagement? Hatfield et al. (1993) argued that people cannot consciously mirror others without coming across as phony because of the amount of time it takes to synchronize one's movements. When done unconsciously, mimicry and synchronization of facial expressions, movements, postures, and vocal intonations can occur very quickly (Hatfield et al., 1994). The research on mimicking avatars suggests, however, that some learned mimicry may be sufficient for at least low amounts of engagement contagion.

In support, recent research in digital mimicry suggests people cannot decipher faked mimicry from general behaviors (Bailenson & Yee, 2005). The implications of the digital chameleon effect studies are that people can be taught to mimic others, which has promise for the idea of training employees to catch engagement. By mimicking the behaviors and emotions of engaged employees, and collaborating on projects where the engaged employees share their thought processes and problem-solving approaches, non-engaged employees may be exposed to the engagement contagion. A challenge with any training that may not necessarily be voluntary on the part of the employee is motivation—in this case, training to mimic others need not be positioned as a training program in how to become engaged.

Chartrand et al. (2005) suggest that rapport, goals to affiliate, interdependent self-construals, and perspective taking act as facilitators of nonconscious mimicry, which I argue are therefore facilitators of engagement contagion. People use body language to convey liking and to build rapport (Scheflen, 1964). Thus, posture sharing, an indicator of rapport, leads to behavioral mimicry (Chartrand et al., 2005), which leads to engagement contagion. Likewise, rapport increases posture sharing (LaFrance & Broadbent, 1976), again leading to engagement contagion.

In a series of experiments, Lakin and Chartrand (2003) exposed a group of participants to words related to goal affiliation (e.g., friends, together) and a control group to neutral words and exposed another group to an explicit goal of affiliating with another person and a control group to neutral words. Participants in the two experimental groups were asked to complete a fairly mundane distractor task before being asked to watch a live feed of a person in the next room (a confederate) with whom they would soon be working. The confederate touched her face throughout the live feed, which resulted in participants (who were being videotaped) mimicking her behavior. Independent coders watched these video recordings of participants and measured the extent to which they mimicked the face-rubbing behavior of the confederate. Results showed that those who were exposed to the goal affiliation words and the explicit goal of affiliation rubbed their faces more than those in the control groups who were exposed to neutral words prior to the mundane task. Lakin and Chartrand's results confirmed that individuals mimic more when given an implicit or explicit goal to affiliate, suggesting that goals to affiliate (whether implicit or explicit) lead to increased mimicry. Thus, I propose an implicit or explicit goal to affiliate with an engaged employee will result in higher levels of or a stronger likelihood of engagement contagion. Lakin and Chartrand's results have implications for training programs in producing engagement contagion.

Training programs can be conducted globally within non-U.S. countries. Construals of the self are how people view themselves relative to others, whether as independent, self-contained, and autonomous as in the Western view, or as interdependent, related, or part of a larger social world as in the Eastern or African view (Markus & Kitayama, 1991; see more on International in Chapter 9). Those with an interdependent self-construal tend to seek harmonious relationships, connection, and meaning in being identified with others (Markus & Kitayama, 1991). In a series of studies, Chartrand and colleagues (van Baaren, Maddux, Chartrand, de Bouter, & van Knippenberg, 2003) demonstrated those with an interdependent self-construal were more likely to match the behavior of confederates than were those with an independent self-construal. Consistent with rapport and goals to affiliate, interdependent self-construals facilitate engagement contagion.

Furthermore, training across cultures can also be effective. Chartrand et al. (2005) suggest that perspective taking facilitates mimicry. The ability to see things from another's point of view makes one susceptible to the influence of mimicry; by focusing attention on perceiving what others perceive, one adopts their viewpoint and experiences their emotions, thoughts, and intentions toward specific behaviors. Indeed, Chartrand and Bargh (1999) found that those who scored high on an empathy scale (perspective taking is a component of empathy) were more likely to mimic compared to those scoring lower on the measure of empathy.

Last, training others to catch engagement may involve training them on how to build rapport with others (Utay & Utay, 1999), helping them to set goals for affiliation, taking others' perspective (Ray & Ray, 1986), and developing an appreciation for a self-construal other than one's own (Constantine, 2001).

Benefits to the Organization of Engagement Contagion

Positive affect leads to collaborative and supportive prosocial behavior (George & Brief, 1992), which increases prosocial behavior in others as a result of social exchange relationships at work (Blau, 1964). Likewise, engagement contagion will increase prosocial behavior between individuals because of the exchange of the emotional and physical aspects of engagement via emotional and physiological contagion (e.g., Chartrand & Bargh, 1999; Chartrand et al., 2005; van Baaren, Holland, Kawakami, & van Knippenberg, 2004). The promotion of prosocial behavior results in higher employee performance, reduced turnover intentions and withdrawal behaviors, and higher organizational-level performance and customer satisfaction (N. Podsakoff, Whiting, Podsakoff, & Blume, 2009).

Engaged employees experience positive emotions, which serve to broaden their ability to cope with higher levels of stress, enabling them to maintain high levels of engagement even when working in otherwise stressful conditions (Fredrickson, Tugade, Waugh, & Larkin, 2003). Thus, engagement may promote a healthy organization by helping employees to cope with stress and through engagement contagion, passing engagement along to others, making them more capable of coping with stress. Leaders supervising engaged employees are more capable of leading and moving their workforce to achieve innovation and higher levels of performance because the engaged employee infect their colleagues with such desires and capabilities.

What Does Engagement Contagion Look Like?

Elsabee Krüger is a new doctoral student at Ludwig-Maximillians Universität München, also known as the University of Munich, Germany. She has chosen to work with one of the professors in the graduate school of systemic neurosciences, mainly because of his enthusiasm about his research topic. There are other more-well-known professors in the same department, but she was drawn to this professor because of his high energy. Although she has never been that interested in research per se, she finds that when she and her advisor meet to discuss how they will design their studies, what recent publications have come out in print, and to which conferences they will submit their current research findings, she is drawn into his high-energy, nearly nervous behavior and excited speech.

Normally a soft-spoken, somewhat slow to speak person, Elsabee becomes a new person when working with her advisor—she is animated, loud at times, anxious to speak, and just as excited as he is. The enthusiasm and passion of her advisor is contagious, and it is not just Elsabee who "catches" it; the other students on the research team are the same. In fact, a key differentiator between her advisor's research team and all others in their department is their team is excited, energetic, and very research active. One could argue the excitement over the research area has nothing to do with engagement contagion—students entering doctoral programs are, in general, excited about advancing into their new careers. But how then do we explain the excitement and energy displayed by those students who dislike research, struggle with it, and have no aspirations for a research oriented careers, but who become completely engaged in the academic track when working with this advisor. The most notable characteristic about this advisor is his engagement—he is completely engaged in his work and he infects the students with whom he works, with engagement. As we look further into the graduate school, we see that other students who are office mates of those who work with Elsabee's advisor are also engaged at work.

Walk-Away Points

- Engagement is contagious. Engagement contagion incorporates emotional, behavioral, and cognitive contagions.
- Engaged employees *can make* a more engaged and healthy organization by infecting others with the ability to do more, be excited, and cope with work challenges beyond what they could do without catching engagement.
- Employees can be taught to infect each other and how to catch engagement from others around them, and leaders of engaged employees can capitalize on engagement contagion, creating a more productive and innovative workforce.

Part IV

THE NEW FRONTIERS OF EMPLOYEE ENGAGEMENT

9

SHINING AN INTERNATIONAL LIGHT

Is Engagement the Same Everywhere?

The practical reality of the worldwide marketplace is engagement crosses cultural boundaries in very complex ways. Take, for example, the following real organizational situations (names and exact countries changed):

> Jian-Xi Guo is the Vice-President of South-Eastern Asia Sales with an International company. He is based in China and manages several regional sales managers including Hitesh Dhingra in India, Hae Sim Kwon in Korea, Seo-yeon Daeng in Malaysia, and Loi Pham in Vietnam, not to mention sales managers in Thailand, Indonesia, and Japan. Some of his managers are from countries that dislike one another and have multiple cultures within their country. They all work for a U.S.-based organization and as such are expected to conform to the norms prescribed by U.S. culture during their interactions with each other and their U.S. colleagues. In a similar situation, Matías González is the Vice-President for Sales in South America for a company based in Brazil. He lives in Argentina. He manages sales managers in Chile, Bolivia, Brazil, Peru, and Colombia. Like Jian-Xi, he is challenged with supervising people from a number of different cultures all working for the same organization.

What can we tell Jian-Xi and Matías about how to foster engagement within their sales groups and across their diverse management teams? Not only do they and their staff have country cultures to deal with, but they also have an organizational culture that transcends the country cultures, and as managers, they are expected to abide by the organizational norms. At this time, there seems to be little we can tell these managers about how to foster engagement in their situations; there simply is not much research on engagement, not to mention how to deal with the interaction of country culture and organizational culture, across the globe.

I have structured this chapter to share what is currently known about engagement across the globe, and what can be hypothesized given the theories that exist today for our understanding of culture. None, however, adequately addresses the challenges outlined in the preceding scenarios. What is known today is a good place to start and I challenge the research community to develop and grow our knowledge so we have answers for people such as Jian-Xi, Matías, and others in similar situations.

What Do We Know so Far About Engagement Internationally?

A number of studies looking at employee engagement have incorporated international samples (at least 48 different studies published between 2002 and 2013 and indexed in electronic databases such as PsychInfo and Academic Search Premier). However, only two have reported comparative results between the different samples on perceptions of employee engagement. Namely, Garczynski, Waldrop, Rupprecht, and Grawitch (2013) noted Indians (mean engagement score = 4.41) reported higher levels of employee engagement than did Americans (mean engagement score = 3.54; after converting their 1–7 response scale to a 0–6 scale as is typically used for the Utrecht Work Engagement Scale [UWES]; Schaufeli & Bakker, 2003). Kożusznik, Rodríguez, and Peiró (2012) reported that Polish workers have lower employee engagement (mean engagement score = 3.37) than do Spanish workers (mean engagement score = 3.94).

Although the means cannot be compared because they are from a number of different studies, Figure 9.1 shows the average engagement scores reported in 31 of the 48 studies (not all studies reported means)[1] on a scale from 0 to 6. A number of studies provided several means, and all studies illustrated in the graph used the UWES to assess employee engagement.[2] Countries that are numbered represent different studies of the same country, countries with T# are a single study with multiple times in which engagement scores were assessed, and countries with S# are the same study with multiple samples.

Although more studies exist than covered here, evident from Figure 9.1 is most studies conducted in these various studies report engagement scores above the mid-point (3 = *sometimes/a few times a month*, 4 = *often/once a week*), on a scale of 0 (*never*) to 6 (*always/every day*). At a glance, studies suggest engagement varies somewhat across countries with some countries reporting higher engagement scores than others. For example, engagement scores in Japan seem quite a bit lower than those in Switzerland or in Finland. The challenge with using and interpreting these types of data is comparisons across countries are actually cross-national and not necessarily across *cultures*, although cross-national and cross-cultural comparisons are often correlated (Javidan, House, & Dorfman, 2004). Several cultures can exist within one country, and cultures can cross country boundaries, which are not reflected in any of these studies.

160

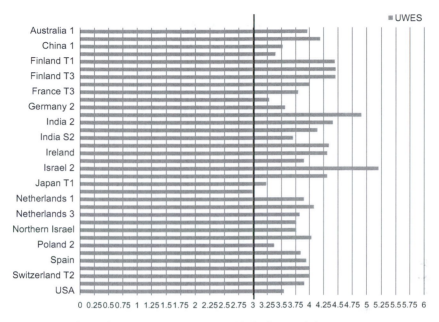

Figure 9.1 Chart of International Studies Published in English Between 2002–2013 (N = 48)

What Does This Mean for Engagement on an International Level?

First, we know little about whether or how engagement truly varies (or does not) from country to country or whether it is a concept that retains its conceptualization across countries; cross-cultural studies are sorely needed. Although the preceding data suggest engagement scores are similar, cross-culture comparisons were not made in those data, and there are some questions about how engagement was assessed. Additionally, the majority of the countries noted in Figure 9.1 are considered similar to one another along dimensions of culture as discussed in the next section, with only a few exceptions. Actual cross-cultural studies, not just studies in different countries, are needed to clarify what cultural effects exist or do not exist for employee engagement.

Second, we can hypothesize that country differences in engagement based on theory and findings on constructs related to engagement. The literature on cross-cultural psychology and cross-cultural research is extensive, and even a brief review here cannot adequately capture its depth or breadth. Therefore, only a brief and selective review is offered here, with the focus on theoretical models and studies that shed light on how we might hypothesize cultural differences with employee engagement.

Hofstede Dimensions of Culture

In general, when researchers seek to hypothesize cultural differences between constructs, many rely on Hofstede's collective works. Hofstede (1980) defined country culture as "the collective programming of the mind which distinguishes the members of one human group from another" (p. 260), and proposed cultures can be described along four primary dimensions: individualism versus collectivism, power distance, masculinity versus femininity, and uncertainty avoidance. Hofstede and Bond (1988) later proposed a fifth dimension: long-term versus short-term orientation. Culture can also be defined as a set of norms, beliefs, and behaviors that guide and maintain society and its products and people (Triandis, 1994). In this chapter, I refer to *country* culture (see the aforementioned definition), as opposed to *organizational* culture, which refers to the experience of employees within an organization, and the norms, beliefs, and behaviors that guide organizational behavior (Schein, 1990; Schneider, 2000).

Hofstede (1980) developed his dimensions based on data collected in one large U.S.-based multinational corporation (later revealed to be IBM), across its 40 country locations. Data were collected at two time points (Time 1: 1967–1969, Time 2: 1971–1973), and participants in each country received the survey in their native language (versions in 20 languages were made available; Hofstede, 1980). Each of the 40 countries was given a score on each of Hofstede's dimensions (excluding long-term vs. short-term). After several other validation studies incorporating 10 more countries (e.g., Hofstede, 1983), Hofstede settled on the four dimensions, which were later extended to five (adding short-term orientation) by Hofstede and Bond (1984).

Individualism/collectivism. Individualism versus collectivism, probably the most popular and recognized component of culture, has been considered a unidimensional, bipolar construct, with individualism occupying the one pole and representing individuals who prefer to operate on their own and be considered distinct and unique. Individualism embraces the idea of freedom of speech, autonomy, little attachment to the in-group, and little attention to contextual factors (M. Erez, 1994; Triandis, 1994). In contrast, collectivism is represented by value for in-group solidarity, preference to do things in a group or with others, subordinate personal goals for those of the group, and preference to be considered like others and nondistinct (M. Erez, 1994; Triandis, 1994). Collectivism embraces attention to social relations and contextual factors that influence behavior. Although generally considered opposites, research shows that the two poles can coexist; thus, they are not exclusive of one another, and may be best viewed as a probability for behavior in one direction or the other, depending on the situation (see Kâğitçibaşi, 1994).

Originally proposed as a country or societal level construct, research has shown cultural differences along this dimension also exist at the individual level. However, as Kâğitçibaşi (1994) pointed out, a lack of clarity between macro- and micro-level views of individualism and collectivism resulted in conceptual confusion that sparked the creation of other terms for this dimension at the individual (micro) level of analyses. Specifically, Triandis, Leung, Villareal, and Clack (1985) delineated individualism versus collectivism as idiocentric versus allocentric (respectively) at the individual level (as opposed to a group- or country-level construct in Hofstede's work). Triandis and colleagues assumed individuals vary *within* countries on their level of idiocentrism and allocentrism. Results across three studies showed that allocentric values include cooperation, equality, and honesty, whereas idiocentric values include competition and social recognition (Triandis et al., 1985).

Another way to view the individualism/collectivism dimension of culture is using Kâğitçibaşi's (1987) terms, culture of separateness/culture of relatedness. Culture of separateness captures the independent, individualistic view that one is distinct from others and the environment. Culture of relatedness reflects the interdependent, collectivistic, or group-oriented perspective; one is intertwined with others and the environment and prefers to be related to others rather than distinct from others.

Power distance. Power distance refers to the preference for, or acceptance of, an unequal distribution of authority, resources, and power. In societies with a large power distance, the norm is to accept formal orders and mandatory in-role job performance expectations and to respect hierarchy. In contrast, societies with a small power distance believe everyone should have equal rights, everyone relies on each other as opposed to dependent on those in positions of authority, and superiors are accessible to those beneath them in the hierarchical chain (Hofstede, 1980). Within organizations, Hofstede (2001) described power distance as "a measure of the interpersonal power or influence between B and S as perceived by the less powerful of the two, S" (p. 83), where B stands for boss and S stands for subordinate. Hofstede's (1980) power distance construct is considered a property or description of a society, whereas Schwartz and colleagues (S. Schwartz, 1992; S. Schwartz & Bilsky, 1987, 1990) have defined power as a personal value associated with wealth and authority over guiding others lives (e.g., "it is important to me to be rich"; Davidov, Schmidt, & Schwartz, 2008).

Masculinity/femininity. Masculinity/femininity may be Hofstede's most controversial dimension, mainly because of the label. Hofstede (2001) argued that societies hold assumptions and normative beliefs over what behaviors, values, and choices are most indicative of women and men.

According to Hofstede, masculinity reflects the extent to which the society values dominance, assertiveness, and money. Hofstede (1980) suggested the label came from the difference between how men and women tended to score in terms of their value of these items—within nearly all groups he studied, men reported more positive values for dominance and assertiveness than did the women. As others summarize this dimension (e.g., M. Erez, 1994), men within masculine cultures are expected to be aggressive, tough, and focus on success, and women are expected to be modest and soft-spoken. Relying on sex roles (roles tied to biological functions as opposed to gender, which is tied to societal functions), Hofstede (2001) proposed that because women bear children and tend to be responsible for the first months of feedback and direct care, they are naturally more oriented toward taking care of people and connecting with others. Men, lacking the ability to bear children, are concerned with economic support for the family and for achievement. In support, Tannen (1990), a sociolinguist, proposed communication styles of men and women differ significantly and essentially that women talk to connect and to build community, whereas men talk to convey information and achieve separateness. Although described in ways that suggest this dimension is non-distinguishable from individualism/collectivism, Hofstede (2001) provided empirical evidence of the distinctiveness of the dimensions. He argued masculinity/femininity "is about ego enhancement versus relationship enhancement, regardless of group ties" (p. 293). Finally, to further clarify, Hofstede (2001) suggested masculinity refers to a society wherein the gender roles are distinct, with men expected to be assertive and women expected to be nurturing. Femininity refers to a society in which gender roles are overlapping, where expectations for both men and women are that they be modest and caring.

Uncertainty avoidance. Uncertainty avoidance describes how much ambiguity about the future a culture can tolerate before it feels threatened. When uncertainty avoidance is strong, people tend to gravitate to more formal rules, structure, career stability versus changeability, and are not tolerant of new ideas or deviant behaviors. By using rules, standard operating procedures, and contracts, organizations can (to a degree) avoid the uncertainty of the future. Hofstede (1980) suggested societies with strong uncertainty avoidance tend to experience high levels of anxiety and aggression, resulting in a strong internal drive to work hard. Additionally, he offered that religious prescriptions, bureaucracy, traditions, and rituals (e.g., business meetings, training programs, memos, and reports) are all mechanisms for coping with the uncertainty of the future (Hofstede, 2001). Hofstede (2001) emphasized uncertainty avoidance is not the same as risk avoidance. He argued risk is a probability function specific to an event, whereas uncertainty is a diffuse feeling with no associated probability.

Uncertainty avoidance is about ambiguity; hence, cultures with high or strong uncertainty avoidance adopt traditions, ceremonies, plans, structure, and rules to remove ambiguity and thereby reduce uncertainty.

Long-term versus short-term orientation. Influenced by his collaborations with Bond in Hong Kong, Hofstede added a fifth dimension called long-term versus short-term orientation. Long-term versus short-term orientation is about perspective taking in reference to time. Long-term orientation refers to focusing on the future and participating in practices such as persistence or thriftiness that support sustenance in the future. A short-term orientation is the opposite of long-term orientation, in which the focus is on the immediate or present moment. Ignoring the future ramification of today's decisions and sacrificing the future for today's gain are behaviors indicative of a short-term orientation. Hofstede (2001) defined long-term orientation as a "fostering of virtues oriented towards future rewards, in particular, perseverance and thrift. Its opposite pole, Short Term Orientation, stands for the fostering of virtues related to the past and present, in particular, respect for tradition, preservation of 'face' and fulfilling social obligations" (p. 359). Low long-term-oriented (i.e., short-term-oriented) cultures are characterized by expectations for fast response, value of leisure time, lack of value for persistence as a personality trait, spending, and reciprocity of greetings and gifts. High long-term-oriented cultures are characterized by persistence and perseverance, thriftiness, saving, and a value for personal adaptability.

Other Theoretical Perspectives

In efforts to advance Hofstede's work, power distance has been combined with the individualism/collectivism dimension and referred to as horizontal vs. vertical orientations, resulting in four cells of a 2 × 2 matrix (Singelis, Triandis, Bhawuk, & Gelfand, 1995; Triandis, 1995). According to Torelli and Shavitt (2010),[3] vertical individualistic cultures (e.g., United States) are characterized by people attempting to be unique and seeking power and status through competition with everyone (regardless of in-group or out-group). Having a vertical individualistic orientation is correlated with using power to benefit oneself at the expense of others (Torelli & Shavitt, 2010) thus may be consistent with politicized organizational climates (see organizational politics; Ferris, Russ, & Fandt, 1989). People in horizontal individualistic cultures (e.g., Sweden) value distinctiveness and separateness but do not seek status. Vertical collectivistic cultures (e.g., Japan) are characterized by people seeking to fulfill the in-group's goals, obeying authority, and competing with the out-group. Last, people in horizontal collectivistic cultures (e.g., Israel) tend to emphasize connection, goal congruency, and responsibility for others but fail to subordinate to authority. Having a horizontal collectivistic orientation is positively associated with using one's power to help others (Torelli & Shavitt, 2010).

Individualism versus collectivism has also been framed as the independent versus interdependent self-construal (Markus & Kitayama, 1991). Self-construal refers to one's self schema or the cognitive framework one holds about the self. A schema is a stable mental or cognitive structure or organization that explains and represents our knowledge about a concept (S. Fiske & Taylor, 1991); thus, a self-schema is the cognitive representation of what we know and understand about who we are and how we fit into the world. Self-schemata are derived from past experiences and are socially constructed using information others provide about the self (Markus, 1977). According to Markus and Kitayama (1991), an independent self-construal refers to thinking of the self as independent of the surrounding environment and from others. The self becomes the target and referent for all experiences (cognitive, emotional, physical), such that actions and feelings are generated from within and are not situationally bound nor connected with others. In this context, actions are seen as self-serving. To the contrary, the interdependent self-construal describes one's experience in relation to others, situationally bound, and interdependent or intertwined with the surrounding context. One's actions are seen as other-serving and in connection with others. Western Europe and the United States exemplify the independent view of the self; in contrast, Asian cultures as well as African and Latin American cultures exemplify the interdependent view (Markus & Kitayama, 1991). Akin to people with a collectivistic orientation, those with an interdependent orientation do not seek to connect with *everyone*—rather their desire for group connection is within their own group, the in-group, as opposed to members of the out-group.

Markus and Kitayama (1991) suggest one's self-construal has significant implications for motivation. With the independent self, motivation is self-directed, expressing one's internal needs and competency, and is self-enhancing, self-consistent, self-affirming, self-verifying, and self-determined. In contrast, with the interdependent self, motivation is other-directed, expresses social motives, and is other-referent; one is driven to achieve connection, consistency with others, and to affirm others. These differences also have implications for engagement. Specifically, affiliation, connection, and fulfilling the desires of the group may be more influential in promoting engagement among those with an interdependent self-construal than among those with an independent self-construal who may be more likely to seek autonomy, self-fulfillment, and self-significance. Thus, research showing core job dimensions such as autonomy positively relate to engagement (e.g., Christian, Garza, & Slaughter, 2011; Menguc, Auh, Fisher, & Haddad, 2013) may not hold up in interdependent cultures, in which the search for autonomy is of less value. Although engagement is not the same as motivation, engagement has motivational principles and is often defined as a motivational state (e.g., Macey & Schneider, 2008; Rich, LePine, & Crawford, 2010). Thus, studies about motivation and cultural effects on motivation may translate to effects on engagement.

Conclusion Regarding Typologies

Although I have briefly described only two popular typologies of culture, most definitions of culture focus on the shared meaning of norms that are adaptive and transmitted over time (Triandis, 1994). The two primary typologies offered here were chosen because of their potential for deriving hypotheses for how we might consider the effects of culture on employee engagement. Readers interested in more in-depth and broader reviews of culture may look at Cross and Gore (2012); Triandis et al. (1985, 1993); A. Fiske, Kitayama, Markus, and Nisbett (1998); Markus, Kitayama, and Heiman (1996); Ronen and Shenkar (1985, 2013); and Oyserman, Coon, and Kemmelmeier (2002).

Cross-Cultural Findings for Constructs Similar to Engagement

Before using the theoretical frameworks reviewed earlier to develop hypotheses about how engagement may vary across cultures, a quick look at several empirical cross-culture findings on constructs similar to engagement such as motivation, job involvement, commitment, and organizational citizenship behaviors (OCBs) may prove useful. Although few studies have been conducted, those that have been done provide some valuable insight.

Motivation

Employee engagement is considered a motivational state; therefore, cultural studies examining various motivational states may provide insight into how engagement may (or may not) vary across cultures. In the following three studies, research has shown that cultural perspective affects the interpretation of the situation, goals, and expected outcomes of motivation, which provides information about designing interventions and implications for the study of engagement.

First, research has shown both Chinese and U.S. individuals are intrinsically motivated by challenging situations, but for Chinese individuals the challenge must be well within their level of mastery to positively affect their intrinsic motivation otherwise it become a negative factor.

In contrast, U.S. individuals are motivated by challenge even when the challenge is extreme (Moneta, 2004). Similarly, people from collectivistic/high power-distance cultures (i.e., Singapore) are more motivated by moderately challenging, achievable goals than are people from individualistic/low power-distance cultures (i.e., Israel; Kurman, 2001). They do not seek the desire to stand out either in achieving a hard goal or failing to achieve one.

Second, B. Kim, Williams, and Gill (2003) examined goal orientation between young athletes (ages 11–16 years old) in the United States and South Korea. The authors explored whether student athletes would differ on their goal-orientation and intrinsic motivation because of their independent and interdependent culture perspectives. The authors assessed task and ego goal orientations, in which task goal orientation refers to choosing goals that are challenging, exerting maximum effort to achieve those goals, and persisting in the face of difficulty. Ego goal orientation refers to choosing goals that preserve the ego by being easily achieved and requiring little effort; high ego goal orientation results in quickly giving up when it appears that failure is imminent (B. Kim et al., 2003). Results from the study showed American athletes reported high task goal orientation and low ego goal orientation, and the two orientations were negatively correlated. The American athletes reported higher intrinsic motivation than did the Korean athletes. In comparison, Korean athletes reported moderately high task goal orientation and average ego goal orientation (higher than American athletes), but the two orientations were positively (although not strongly) correlated. For both athlete groups, task orientation was positively related to intrinsic motivation. The authors suggested in their findings that the Korean athletes have both task and ego goal-orientations because of the school sport system. Specifically, the Korean students compete in athletics to gain entry into high school, and such competition naturally promotes a strong social comparison, which ultimately boosts an ego orientation (i.e., competition to preserve one's ego relative to how one sees oneself compared to others). Hence, their goal orientation did not necessarily determine or strongly relate to their intrinsic motivation, but rather it changed their interpretation of the goal. Choosing the challenging goal and needing to persist were necessary for entry into high school, thus not a task goal per se but rather an ego goal—they wanted to get into school to fit in with their peers. Kim et al.'s findings suggest the actual construct of intrinsic motivation itself may not differ along cultural lines but how one interprets or frames the antecedents of intrinsic motivation may differ. Thus, just assessing intrinsic motivation between the American and Korean athletes would have resulted in similar scores and no cultural difference effects; measures of the antecedent to motivation, however, would not produce the same scores.

Third, choice is often studied in the context of motivation, especially in studies of intrinsic motivation, and when placed under the cross-cultural lens provides additional perspective to the findings reviewed above. In a study of Asian children (Chinese and Japanese, 7–9 years old) compared to American children (7–9 years old), Lepper, Sethi, and Dialdin, and Drake (1997) examined whether being assigned to a choice by one's mother, selecting one's own choice, or having no choice on a task was more motivating. The task was solving various anagrams and motivation was assessed by the time spent and number of anagrams solved. Asian children scored highest on the mother-assigned choice condition and lowest on the no-choice condition. In contrast, American children scored highest on the free-choice option and lowest on the mother-assigned choice. Similarly, Iyengar and Lepper (1999) found personal choice (autonomy) positively affected intrinsic motivation for Anglo-Americans, whereas it was less important for Asian Americans who were more intrinsically motivated by choices made for them by authority figures or peers. J. Miller and Bersoff (1994) suggest from an interdependent perspective, the choice of others is not inconsistent with one's own desires; thus, in the Lepper et al. study, one might conclude that the Asian children did not view their own choice as being in conflict with the choice assigned by their mother.

The implications for engagement of the combined studies reviewed earlier are engagement scores may be similar across cultures, but the antecedents or how the antecedents are framed and interpreted may differ. Such differences are important to understand because even if the engagement scores are the same, how we get them differs—interventions designed for one culture will not work in another. Furthermore, many interventions are implemented in organizations as a no-choice event; that is, employees are required to attend the workshops or training sessions put in place to increase engagement scores. Thus, applying equivalent reasoning to the choice studies reviewed earlier suggests that employees holding an interdependent perspective may be less put off by an organization's choice to send them to training to increase employee engagement as compared to employees who are independent and may view such efforts as being assigned the choice of whether to be engaged or not. Being given a choice reflects the opportunity for self-expression—a decision that mirrors the independent self (Iyengar & DeVoe, 2003; Iyengar & Lepper, 1999); hence, for the employees from an independent/individualistic culture, being assigned the intervention may not result in the desired effect on engagement levels.

Other influences on motivation and other forms of motivation have been studied cross-culturally, and the results of those studies may also provide insight into studying engagement cross-culturally. For example, S. Schwartz and Bilsky (1990) determined people from Hong Kong can experience both a strong need for achievement and a strong need for interdependence. Historically, the need for achievement has been considered indicative of an independent or individualistic value system, marked by a drive for mastery and power (Hilgard, 1987). Schwartz and Bilsky speculated that in Hong Kong the need for achievement may be experienced as a drive to do what is expected. Thus, their Hong Kong sample seemed to dissolve any potential inconsistency between the need for achievement (independent/individualism) and need for fulfilling others' expectations (interdependence/collectivism) by considering the results of the need for achievement relative to their culture (expectation vs. demonstration of independence). The study showed that the need for achievement should not be automatically associated with independent/individualistic cultures.

Individuals with an independent versus interdependent self-construal tend towards a promotion as opposed to a prevention motive, respectively (Heine et al., 2001; A. Lee, Aaker, & Gardner, 2000). A promotion motive refers to a motivational pattern marked by the pursuit of ideals and towards gains, whereas a prevention motive refers to a pattern marked by avoiding losses and meeting obligations. These motivational patterns are activated by one's self-construal, which has an impact on individuals' social perceptions and behaviors (A. Lee et al., 2000). Thus, according to Heine et al. (2001) and A. Lee et al. (2000), the tendency is for people with an independent self-construal to pursue ideals and advancement, whereas those with an interdependent self-construal take the conservative route avoiding risk. This seems a somewhat broad overstatement and deserves additional research; however, the implication for engagement research is that different cultural perspectives may trigger different motives, influencing the degree to which engagement is manifested in advancing behaviors (e.g., job performance to get ahead) versus maintenance behaviors (e.g., OCBs in the form of voice extra-role behaviors; Van Dyne & LePine, 1998).

Organizational antecedents of motivation include leadership and core job dimensions; thus, cross-cultural research examining these constructs is particularly relevant for considering how engagement may vary cross-culturally.

Leadership is considered a predictor of engagement, and when looked at through the cross-cultural lens within motivation studies could provide insights into engagement across cultures. For example, Misumi (1989, 1995) and colleagues (Misumi & Peterson, 1985a, 1985b) collectively demonstrated Japanese leaders who are both transactional or performance oriented and personally caring of their employees in and outside of work were considered the most effective, as compared to those leaders who were task oriented only and who separated personal matters from work-related matters. In their review of Misumi and colleague's findings, Markus and Kitayama (1991) suggested in interdependent cultures such as

Japan, employees' personal attachment to their leader is more important in fostering motivation than are the strong independent leadership skills and characteristics considered essential of good leaders in independent cultures such as the United States. However, Misumi and colleagues' findings suggest leaders who are balanced in both transactional and relational tasks will fare better than those focused on personal attachments only. Misumi and his colleagues did not study American leaders, and therefore, the converse of this hypothesis may not necessarily be appropriate.

Job characteristics theory (Hackman & Oldham, 1976) has been used to explain predictors of engagement (e.g., Kahn, 1990), and cross-cultural research on the effects of job characteristics on motivation may shed light on what can be expected with regards to engagement. Specifically, core job dimensions—job autonomy and task complexity—have been shown to increase initiative taking behaviors in both East and West Germany (Frese, Kring, Soose, & Zempel, 1996). Research has shown core job dimensions, in general, were positively related to motivation in Dutch, Bulgarian, and Hungarian samples, although comparatively, autonomy had a more pronounced effect on responsibility in the Netherlands than in the other two countries (Roe, Zinovieva, Dienes, & Ten Horn, 2000). Notably in Roe et al.'s (2000) study, core job dimensions did not influence psychological meaningfulness or job involvement in the same way across the Netherlands, Bulgaria, and Hungry, suggesting that engagement may not be fostered in the same way between independent or individualistic cultures such as the Netherlands as it is in interdependent or collectivistic cultures such as Bulgaria or Hungary (although Hofstede, 1980, 2001, did not examine former communist countries, he does suggest most communist countries would rate collectivism higher over individualism). Roe et al. considered Bulgaria and Hungary different from the Netherlands because of the countries' differing "political, cultural, and economic" (2000, p. 660) views. A conclusion from these studies on core job dimensions is that autonomy, task identity, and skill variety may influence engagement levels more in individualistic/independent cultures than in collectivistic/interdependent cultures, where the desire to be known, distinct, and decide for oneself (essentially what core job dimensions provide) are not as highly valued as in individualistic cultures.

Implications of Cross-Cultural Motivation Research for Engagement

The cross-culture literature reviewed here suggests that how one interprets predictors or antecedents of motivation determines whether motivation is fostered, and those interpretations rely heavily on one's cultural framework. Extrapolating from this literature suggests it may be engagement itself is viewed similarly from culture to culture, but what fosters it is culturally influenced. For example, achievement motivation as assessed using the Achievement Motivation Inventory appears invariant across country samples, implying achievement motivation is interpreted to have the same meaning from country to country (see Byrne et al., 2004). However, as noted by Schwartz and Bilsky (1990), what achievement motivation results in (fulfillment of expectations of group vs. demonstration of independence) may vary by culture. Similarly, what fosters motivation, such as the type of leader behavior displayed, the job characteristics (high autonomy or not; free choice or assigned), and type of goal (easy vs. challenging) may vary by culture, or at least how these antecedents are interpreted may differ, thereby ultimately affecting the level of motivation displayed.

Another broad conclusion from the motivation research and current engagement literature is much of what we currently know about antecedents to engagement are grounded in the individualistic/independent, low power distance, masculine, and high tolerance for ambiguity culture perspectives. Concepts such as autonomy, freedom of speech (as with psychological safety), and being in control of creating one's own meaning, as well as feeling significant are all values representative of these culture dimensions.

Commitment, Job Involvement, and Citizenship Behaviors

As noted in Chapter 3, employee engagement has, at times, been confused with organizational commitment, job involvement, and OCBs. Although enough accumulated research has demonstrated these constructs are distinct (see Chapters 2 and 3), they still overlap and share some of the same antecedents. Thus, examining cross-cultural research on organizational commitment, job involvement, and citizenship behaviors may provide insight into the development of hypotheses about engagement across cultures.

In a study of South Koreans in comparison to German participants, Steinmetz, Park, and Kabst (2011) set out to evaluate the predictive validity of need for achievement, the need for affiliation, and the need for power regarding job involvement and organizational commitment. After first determining the two countries' cultures differed (South Korea scored higher on power distance and collectivism than Germany), the authors reported scores on job involvement ($M = 2.06, 2.46$) and organizational commitment ($M = 2.53, 2.11$) for the South Korean and German samples, respectively. Using structural equation modeling, the authors demonstrated the three needs were similarly related (nearly identical path coefficients and standard errors) to both job involvement and commitment in each country. Specifically, need for achievement was positively related to both involvement and commitment $\beta = .27$ and $\beta = .33$, respectively, in both the South Korean and German samples. The need for affiliation was unrelated to both outcomes in both samples, and the need for power was only positively related to job involvement ($\beta = .36$) in both samples. The study findings suggest that for this sample of 209 South Korean and 198 German executive MBA students and alumni, there are no significant cross-cultural differences in how the three needs predict job involvement and commitment. The authors concluded interventions designed to motivate employees to be more involved and committed at work, via their need for achievement and power, should be universal across cultures that differ on collectivism and power distance. The authors did not examine the other Hofstede dimensions of culture.

Similarly, an examination of job involvement across an Indian and United States sample also showed predictors of job involvement do not vary between the two cultures (Sekaran, 1981). Sekaran examined 20 predictors including demographic variables, personality characteristics such as need for achievement and affiliation, and core job dimensions such as autonomy.

However, though the results above suggest there are no differences across culture for predictors of job involvement and commitment, country differences are not necessarily reflective of cultural differences, although they are related (Javidan et al., 2004). Looking at multiple cultures within one country, Cohen (2007) examined job involvement, organizational commitment, and OCBs in Northern Israel, a region he divided into at least five different cultural groups: secular Jews, Orthodox Jews, kibbutz members, Druze, and Arabs. His results are detailed and one must read his study to see the specific results; but I summarize a few findings relevant to my review. The cultural groups differed significantly in their ratings of Hofstede's (1980) four original dimensions (excluding time orientation), indicating they should be considered different cultures from each other. Druze and Arabs rated highest on collectivism, whereas kibbutz members and secular Jews could be considered more individualistic given their significantly lower ratings on collectivism than the other groups. Arabs were highest in power distance, and kibbutz members were lowest. Arabs and Druze were highest in masculinity, whereas kibbutz members were lowest (indicating high femininity scores). Last, secular Jews were highest in uncertainty avoidance, and kibbutz members were lowest. Results for analysis of variance comparisons of mean scores on job involvement, organizational commitment, and OCBs indicated some of the cultures differed from one another on their job attitude scores, though not all. For example, on organizational commitment, the secular Jews differed from the kibbutz members, but not from the Orthodox Jews. For job involvement, the secular Jews differed from all other groups, but the other groups did not significantly differ from each other (e.g., Arabs did not score job involvement significantly different from Druze). Ratings of citizenship behavior, specifically altruism and conscientiousness, differed across cultures. Finally, Cohen (2007) concluded from his findings that collectivism is strongly related to citizenship behaviors, namely, altruism and civic virtue.

Overall, Cohen's (2007) results indicate that scores on job involvement, commitment, and OCBs *do* differ by culture. Using regression analysis, Cohen additionally determined collectivism was positively related to altruism and civic virtue, and low power distance was related to higher levels of conscientiousness. Because the focus of his study was primarily on OCBs and in-role job performance, Cohen did not run regression analyses on job involvement or commitment with culture because his primary goal was to examine predictors of OCB and in-role performance.

OCBs have been compared across cultures, even though what constitutes extra-role behaviors may vary across cultures (e.g., Lam, Hui, & Law, 1999). Research has shown Canadians, in general, demonstrate fewer OCBs than do those in Iran or Turkey (Kabasakal, Dastmalchian, & Imer, 2011). OCB was assessed by three dimensions: helping, civic virtue, and sportsmanship. In the same study, Iranians' scores were higher on helping behaviors, whereas the Turkish participants scored highest on civic virtue OCBs. In Cohen's (2007) study, OCB was assessed by three dimensions—altruism, civic virtue, and conscientiousness—and levels of each dimension varied by cultural group (although not all groups were significantly different from each other). Whether OCB is defined using Organ's (1988) or Williams and Anderson's (1991) definition matters, and which dimensions of OCB are measured makes a difference in how results are interpreted.

In summary, the findings reviewed from a number of cross-cultural studies examining organizational commitment, job involvement, and OCBs are mixed. The constructs were not all assessed using the same instruments or in the same manner (e.g., one overall score combining dimensions versus dimensions separated into individual scores). Perhaps the clearest pattern of results is antecedents to job attitudes did not seem to vary across countries, but levels of the job attitudes themselves did vary by culture. This pattern suggests a number of conclusions: (a) What predicts job attitudes may not vary by country, (b) we have not yet examined predictors expected to vary by country, (c) we have not yet examined contrasting cultures or we are looking at irrelevant dimensions of culture (these studies were across country and did not comment on culture per se), or (d) the meaning of the actual job attitude itself varies by culture. It may be organizational commitment does not quite mean the same thing across countries or cultures and our failure to examine scale invariance in every cross-cultural study hides this issue. In my trips to Russia in 2012 and 2013, after many hours of conversation and presentations, while trying to understand what employee engagement is in Russia, I finally determined engagement may not the same between the United States and Russia, and this has implications for understanding what is engagement, if anything, in Russia.

Implications for Employee Engagement

In the preceding review, I offered several implications of the cross-cultural research findings in other areas of organizational behavior related to engagement. In this next section, I develop several propositions about what employee engagement may look like across cultures. I relied on the two theoretical frameworks of culture described earlier in this chapter, in addition to the overall patterns of findings from empirical literature applicable to engagement. For this discussion, I assume the current dominant definitions of employee engagement (both Kahn's, 1990, and Schaufeli, Salanova, et al.'s, 2002) and leverage the extant literature in engagement on what predicts or fosters engagement levels.

Employees in individualistic cultures value work and their role at work, viewing outside demands such as family as distractions to personal achievement. Work is given more emphasis than is leisure, and meaningfulness is achieved through one's role and accomplishment at work, as opposed to one's contribution to society (Spector et al., 2007). In contrast, employees in collectivistic cultures view their connection with others as central to their personal fulfillment, and work is a means to serving one's value in the group. Becoming completely absorbed at work to the detriment of outside distraction (such as requests for help from others in the group) may be considered more of an individualistic value than a collectivistic one. Because of the difference in focus of the individualistic versus collectivistic perspective, one could hypothesize those in individualistic cultures are more engaged at work than those in collectivistic cultures.

In support of work playing a central role at the expense of family, Spector and colleagues (2007) showed the association between work demands and work interference with family was stronger in individualistic cultures than collectivistic cultures. However, one could also argue because of the social support those in collectivistic cultures receive from their social network and the sense of communal meaningfulness one can derive from working with others to achieve a common goal (goal of the unit or organization), employees from collectivistic cultures are more engaged at work than are those from individualistic cultures who shun support as a sign of lack of independence. Consequently, I propose two competing propositions:

Proposition 1a: Individualistic cultures where autonomy, one's significance, achieving meaningfulness for the self, and one's personal achievement is valued, report higher employee engagement than collectivistic cultures where fitting into the group, serving the meaningfulness of others, and social relations are valued above self-promotion.

Proposition 1b: Collectivistic cultures valuing social support, connection at work, and the meaningfulness of community are more engaged than their individualistic counterparts because they receive support to offset job demands.

High power-distance cultures most likely have organizations support-ing a steep hierarchy (i.e., many levels of management) because of their acceptance and expectation for authority and inequality. In such orga-nizations, subordinates are unlikely to speak out or feel safe expressing their ideas (M. Erez, 1994). Thus, they would report low psychologi-cal safety, which is one of Kahn's (1990) psychological states leading to engagement; hence, engagement is probably lower in organizations based in high power-distance cultures than in low power-distance cultures:

> **Proposition 2:** High or large power-distance cultures in which fol-lowing orders, doing what you are told versus what you think, and working without clear task identity or significance report lower employee engagement than do low or small power-distance cul-tures where equal rights for everyone, voice opportunity, and the ability to step outside of the line of authority to do something that would create greater meaning are valued.

Organizations in masculine cultures endorse strong masculine gen-der roles in which promotional opportunities are favored for men over women, support higher salaries for men under the assumption they are the main source of household income, and stress work over family life, judgment over intuition, assertiveness over consideration, and results over process (M. Erez, 1994). As such, we might hypothesize social support in masculine cultures is minimal, and transactional leadership may be preferred over transformational or servant leadership, in which one focuses on the relationship and development of employees more so than on just getting the job done. Consequently, one would expect employee engagement to be higher in feminine cultures than in mascu-line cultures because of the support, community, and relational com-ponents of feminine cultures, components shown as positively related to engagement:

> **Proposition 3:** Cultures rated as masculine, in which the culture is aggressive, work is stressed over family life and balance, and the focus of work is on ego enhancement may inhibit employee engagement, result in lower scores than do feminine cultures, in which opportunities are equal, balance between work and family is encouraged (promoting psychological availability), and a focus on meaningfulness may be more valued.

M. Erez (1994) suggests that in cultures with high uncertainty avoid-ance, organizations put efforts in place to formalize rules, regulations, and control employee actions. In organizations with many constraints on employees, autonomy is most likely limited. Furthermore, regulated work environments may stifle employees' ability to derive meaningfulness from the work because efforts to feel valued may be seen as working outside regulations. One could hypothesize, as a result of such control, engagement would be lower than in cultures where uncertainty avoidance is low. Furthermore, current research on engagement suggests autonomy is important to promoting high levels of engagement. Having the freedom to choose to invest oneself into the work role is constrained in a culture of high uncertainty avoidance. Freedom of choice, however, is a value of the independent self-construal. Thus, those with an interdependent self-construal may not feel as constrained in a high uncertainty avoidance culture as may those with an independent self-construal. Thus, self-construal and uncertainty avoidance interact to determine employee engagement levels:

> **Proposition 4:** In cultures with high uncertainty avoidance, in which formal rules, structure, and tight policies are in place to minimize ambiguity, employee engagement may be stifled because of the inability to create a meaningful workplace. However, the effects of uncertainty avoidance on engagement are moderated by one's self-construal.

Hofstede and Bond's (1984) fifth dimension of culture, short-term versus long-term orientation, is a challenging dimension to tie to engagement. A culture of long-term orientation focuses on the future, on the sustainability of effort, gains over the long run, high persistence, and perseverance. Although both Kahn's (1990) and Schaufeli, Salanova, et al.'s (2002) definitions of engagement incorporate persistence and perseverance, neither is time based. Kahn's engagement is a moment-to-moment state, whereas Schaufeli, Salanova, et al.'s engagement is a stable state. Neither suggests a trade-off of the present for the future, which is indicative of a long-term versus short-term orientation. One could argue the thriftiness of the long-term orientation, the holding back of resources for a future need, may be counterproductive to engagement, which requires giving all of oneself in the present moment. Kahn (1992) proposed psychological presence is an essential antecedent to engagement. Thus, holding back and conserving would appear to be the opposite of employee engagement. Therefore, we could hypothesize engagement should be higher in short-term-oriented cultures:

> **Proposition 5:** Short-term-oriented cultures, in which giving all your effort for the immediate need, encourage higher levels of employee engagement than do long-term-oriented cultures, in which conserving resources for the future encourages not giving all your effort to the immediate role performance.

The preceding propositions assume that employee engagement is defined using either Kahn's (1990) or Schaufeli, Salanova, et al.'s (2002) conceptualization. If, instead I use my definition offered in Chapter 2,[4] cultural effects on employee engagement may diminish. Specifically, by providing a target for motivation, in particular *the goals of the organization*, both individualistic and collectivistic cultures have equal influence because how the goal is defined seems to matter in motivation (as concluded from the review of the literature in this chapter). Another component of my definition, *focus*, refers to alignment with organizational goals, goals established within a particular culture. Thus, the meaning of the goal itself may differ across cultures, but focusing on the goal does not, as just as identified in the literature reviewed previously; hence, engagement would remain the same. This focus is different from how it is conceptualized in current definitions of engagement, where focus is a part of absorption or flow requires detachment from others or time. Other elements of my definition, *psychophysiological arousal* and *physiological arousal*, as opposed to physical vigor or activity, allow for conservative expression of engagement such as might be expected in collectivistic/interdependent cultures in which one wishes to blend in with the group. For the expression of one's *affective and cognitive self* in transforming work into meaningful accomplishment, it is similar. By specifically incorporating the idea of *transforming* work activity into what the individual finds meaningful, my definition allows for meaningfulness to be culturally based. Specifically, in collectivistic cultures, *meaningfulness* is in service to the goals of the group versus one's own significance. Likewise, *purposeful accomplishment* may be completing the assigned goal. Last, in contrast to the other more culture-free aspects of the definition, the incorporation of *psychological presence* may suggest engagement would be higher in short-term- versus long-term-oriented cultures because one must direct all attention and energy to the moment rather than to the future.

In defense of existing definitions of engagement, given my definition of engagement incorporates components of the two most dominant definitions, Kahn's (1990) and Schaufeli, Salanova, et al.'s (2002), one could argue their definitions should be as culturally free as mine, and mine is not completely culture-free (i.e., not biased toward one culture versus another). I agree with this criticism, although other aspects of Kahn's and Schaufeli, Salanova, et al.'s definitions render them potentially less portable. Specifically, the perspective and framing of their definitions ties them to a number of the cultural dimensions identified by Hofstede (1980). For example, Kahn's foundation of the job characteristics theory, which suggests that core job dimensions lead to psychological states that then lead to motivation, is somewhat problematic from a cross-cultural perspective. The core job dimensions of autonomy, task significance, and task identity suggest that an independent/individualistic orientation. Psychological states such as psychological safety, which refers to the freedom to express oneself honestly and without career threat, is inherently a low power distance, individualistic, and possibly masculine value. Likewise, Schaufeli, Salanova, et al.'s definition is based on original conceptualizations of engagement as the opposite of burnout (Maslach & Leiter, 1997), an experience grounded in how an individual withdraws from the environment, others, and the self. Consequently, Schaufeli, Salanova et al.'s conceptualization of engagement relies on expressions of energy and connection as a way of demonstrating the opposite of withdrawal and depression. Schaufeli, Salanova et al.'s definition also relies heavily on concepts of value in individualistic cultures such as self-absorption and intense focus on the job at the expense of all others around. Both definitions, Kahn's (1990) and Schaufeli, Salanova et al.'s (2002), in addition to my own, could be modified to accommodate a cross-cultural perspective, if research evidence suggests engagement has the same meaning around the globe.

Perhaps a cultural weakness of all the definitions, including my own and several others I reviewed in Chapter 2, is they are all derived from or based on studies of the individual, separate from the social environment, situational influences, and his or her values, thus placing the individual as the central referent point. On one hand, because engagement is an individual-level construct, it makes sense the construct would be studied from an individual's point of view. On the other hand, this self-referent approach to identifying the concept removes interpretations of engagement as placed in something other than an individualistic, low power distance, low uncertainty avoidance, masculine concept. Engagement may be more socially and situationally dependent than current conceptualizations allow.

What I Learned About Engagement From Non-U.S. Countries

I recently visited a number of countries, presenting on employee engagement and exploring whether the concept exists or is understood in other countries. Those countries included the United Kingdom, France, Russia, and South Africa. My observations that follow are all bounded by my limited exposure in each country.

In France and South Africa, the academicians I spoke with had heard of employee engagement, but very few were studying the construct. Their understanding of engagement was limited to the opposite of burnout, the definition grounding the UWES, the only measure they know of for assessing engagement. Others I spoke with in France thought that engagement was the same as commitment.

In the United Kingdom, my audience had heard of engagement but not in much detail. Most of the individuals who spoke with me after the talk were primarily interested in whether engagement was a fad or a long-lasting area of study.

I was left with the impression in both France and the United Kingdom, engagement is not as big of a phenomenon as it appears in the United States, but also it was not being ignored. In the United States, talks about engagement and, perhaps more important, *how* you engage employees seem in vogue. I did not get that impression in the United Kingdom or France.

In Russia, both academicians and practitioners with whom I spoke had either never heard of engagement or, if they had (which was rare), they had heard of the "opposite of burnout" definition from a few papers on the UWES translated into Russian. I found the Russians with whom I interacted to be fascinated with the concept. The students who I visited at Saratov State University began studying the concept as soon as my talks were over in 2012 and presented their findings during my visit in 2013.

Finally, in South Africa, a few academicians with whom I spoke knew of the concept, and I found a few papers published in the South African Journals; if engagement was defined at all, it was the opposite of burnout using the UWES. The practitioners with whom I spoke were not interested in the concept—they struggled with broader concepts relating to fairness in selection, diversity of cultures within organizations, and the very large disparity of income levels within a single business unit.

As best as I could determine from my conversations and exposure to the literature of the country, no one made efforts to determine whether engagement means the same in their country as that used to create the UWES.

Conclusion

A chapter about employee engagement across cultures may be premature, given the literature on engagement in any one single culture is not yet well established. As I pointed out in Chapters 2 and 3, there is still debate on what exactly engagement is and how it is fostered; however, some may disagree with this statement. Although there exist a number of studies looking at employee engagement in different countries, such examinations do not necessarily capture differences in culture and many boast a number of methodological weaknesses rendering their findings challenging to use. Perhaps what this chapter does best is highlight the need for cross-cultural studies of employee engagement.

Engagement needs to be defined and understood from within each country (and culture's) perspective. For example, there are 11 official languages in South Africa, with each reflecting a unique culture. China is geographically divided along east–west and north–south lines, essentially creating at least four different regions and four different cultures, and this does not capture the 55 minority groups or more than 200 dialects (see Gundling & Zanchettin, 2007, for more details on China and six other countries). To study engagement across these countries and cultures, accurate and careful translation cannot be overlooked. Additionally, to provide answers for Jian-Xi and Matías, studies of the interaction between cultures across countries, and country cultures with organizational culture are necessary.

Walk-Away Points

- Little cross-cultural research on engagement exists.
- Most studies of engagement in non-U.S. countries do not define engagement.
- Cross-cultural studies of related concepts provide some insight into whether engagement will vary by culture; what fosters engagement may vary because of how work environment, goals, leadership, and meaningfulness are interpreted across cultures.
- Studies assessing whether engagement is actually a U.S. phenomenon only, and cross-cultural comparisons are sorely needed, as well as studies of interactions between cultures and organizational culture.
- Language is culturally defined and grounded; translations are critical to how we understand and study engagement cross-culturally and cross-nationally.

NOTES

1. Special thanks to James Weston, Xuan Zheng, and Jackie Benson for their help coding International studies of employee engagement that provided the data for Figure 9.1.
2. Given recent challenges to the construct validity of the UWES (see Chapter 6; Cole, Walter, Bedeian, & O'Boyle, 2012; Wefald, Mills, Smith, & Downey, 2012), we cannot be certain whether the means reported are actually employee engagement. What we do know about the UWES with regards to these international data and studies by Schaufeli and colleagues (e.g., Schaufeli &

Bakker, 2004; Schaufeli, Bakker, & Salanova, 2006) is several studies have reported the invariance of the UWES across cultures—thus, whether engagement or perhaps some other very positive stable state of vigor, dedication, and absorption, the UWES is doing so similarly from culture to culture, employees in various cultures interpret the items similarly, and report moderate levels.

3. Remember from Chapter 2 that employee engagement is a state of motivation, wherein one is psychologically present (i.e., in the moment) and psychophysiologically aroused, is focused on the job and organizational goals, and is in a state wherein one brings all of oneself (emotionally, physiologically, cognitively) together to transform work into meaningful and purposeful accomplishment.

4. The example countries in this paragraph to represent the different combinations of individualism/collectivism by vertical/horizontal were taken directly from Torelli and Shavitt (2010).

10

THE PARADOX OF EMPLOYEE ENGAGEMENT

Is There a Dark Side?

Employee engagement is considered a positive state and one organizations desire of every employee. As noted in the beginning of Chapter 2, financial gains and losses attributed to engagement and disengaged employees, respectively, are too much for human resource managers and organizational leaders to ignore. As such, their focus on engagement thus far has been toward maximizing it and finding ways to ensure employees are consistently and constantly engaged. Research to date has followed suit by examining positive outcomes of engagement, focusing on the benefits of engaged employees such as customer satisfaction and organizational productivity (e.g., Harter, Schmidt, & Hayes, 2002), commitment and turnover intentions (e.g., Karatepe, 2013), and job, task, and extra-role performance (e.g., Rich, LePine, & Crawford, 2010; Saks, 2006). For those employees who do not "appear" engaged, leadership and organizational interventions have been, and are being designed, to "fix" their perceived lack of engagement (e.g., see various websites for consulting perspectives; Macey, Schneider, Barbera, & Young, 2009). All of the above assumes low, inconsistent, not continuous, or less than obvious engagement are all bad (e.g., Gallup Organization, 2002, 2013; Gebauer, Lowman, & Gordon, 2008). But is it really beneficial to have everyone engaged, all the time, at the highest intensity level? George (2010) suggests that it is not. Instead, she and others (e.g., Macey & Schneider, 2008) argue continuous engagement comes at a cost to the employee, a cost in the form of burnout and work–life conflict (Sonnentag, 2003).

In this chapter, I additionally argue that too much engagement is not in the organization's best interest and that there is a dark side to engagement. When does engagement come at the expense of other highly desirable organizational constructs? This chapter explores this fundamental question.

Too Much Engagement

Researchers have begun to question whether employees can become too engaged (Halbesleben, Harvey, & Bolino, 2009; Schaufeli, Taris, &

Bakker, 2006; van Beek, Taris, & Schaufeli, 2011; Van Wijhe, Peeters, & Schaufeli, 2011). Speculation is employees who are engaged frequently, over long periods of time, or at very high levels of intensity, may eventually become burned out (e.g., Halbesleben, Harvey, & Bolino, 2009). Thus, people who work at intense levels of concentration for consecutive periods, with little rest in-between, demonstrate emotional exhaustion and mental fatigue (Schaufeli, Taris, et al., 2006). However, other researchers have argued that rather than employee engagement leading to such negative outcomes, when employees work obsessively and to their own detriment, they are no longer demonstrating engagement, but rather they are demonstrating workaholism (Schaufeli, Taris, et al., 2006).

Workaholism

Various definitions of a workaholic or workaholism exist (see Burke, 2009), although most tend to include the notions of self-imposed demands that are compulsive, excessive, neglectful of other areas of life, unhealthy, and crippling (Burke, 2009). Workaholism was originally patterned after the term *alcoholism* (Oates, 1968), to capture the addictive and negative consequences of excessive work. However, few tend to consider workaholism in the same light as alcoholism, which falls under substance-related disorders, a category of mental disorders listed in the *Diagnostic Statistical Manual of Mental Disorders* (1994). Alcoholism is a substance-related mental disorder, whereas workaholism is not considered a mental disorder. Workaholics tend to feel driven to work because of an internal sense of guilt when not working, or an inner pressure to keep on working. Thus, working because it is enjoyable or fulfilling is not what characterizes workaholism (Spence & Robbins, 1992); however, others disagree and characterize workaholics as enjoying work but unable to disengage (McMillan & O'Driscoll, 2006; Ng, Sorensen, & Feldman, 2007). In studies comparing workaholics with individuals who are considered enthusiastic about their jobs (thus exhibiting some of the same work involvement tendencies), workaholics scored higher on scales of perfectionism, job stress, and inability to delegate (Spence & Robbins, 1992). Contrary to popular belief, working a lot (hour per week) is not necessarily characteristic of workaholics (Burke, 2009).

Although workaholics may report losing track of time while working, flow, often described as part of engagement (Kahn, 1990; Schaufeli, Salanova, et al., 2002) because of the intensity of focus and absorption, is not considered a component of workaholism (Burke & Matthiesen, 2004). As described in Chapter 3, flow is experienced as enjoyable and being lost in the pleasure of just doing the activity for the sake of doing it; there is no guilt or pressure to do the task (Csikszentmihalyi & Rathunde, 1993).

Some researchers have suggested "good" workaholics demonstrate high levels of engagement (Schaufeli, Taris, & Bakker, 2006). Across several studies, Schaufeli and colleagues (2007; Schaufeli, Taris, & van Rhenen, 2008) determined that engagement and workaholism, when operationalized as working excessively and compulsively, were similar yet distinct. Specifically, Schaufeli and colleagues (2007, 2008) measured working compulsively with items that capture working without enjoyment, feeling obligated to work, and feeling compelled to work rather than wanting to work. Working excessively was measured with items focusing on working beyond what others do, being overcommitted to work, and unable to take breaks from work. The authors concluded from their findings good workaholism can be operationalized as work engagement, even though they found correlations of only .27 between work engagement (measured using the UWES) and working excessively (which was correlated at .57 with working compulsively). However, whether called good or not, overcommitment at work is positively related to burnout (Philp, Egan, & Kane, 2012).

Like Spence and Robbins (1992); K. Scott, Moore, and Miceli (1997); and others, Schaufeli et al. (2008) divided their sample into multiple types of workaholics, with some displaying positive characteristics (enjoyment) and others displaying negative characteristics (guilt, lack of enjoyment). Across the various types of workaholics, those displaying more positive characteristics may be considered more like engaged workers, suggesting potential construct overlap. However, although some have suggested that workaholism has positive characteristics, workaholics create tense work environments around them, pushing others to work more (Machlowitz, 1980; K. Scott et al., 1997; Seybold & Salomone, 1994). Thus, even "good" workaholics are not necessarily great to have around.

Passion

Descriptions of workaholism and compulsive work seem similar to obsessive passion (see Vallerand & Houlfort, 2003). Passion is not typically considered a construct of excess or compulsivity; however, Vallerand and colleagues (Vallerand, 2008; Vallerand & Houlfort, 2003) proposed that individuals can demonstrate either *harmonious* or *obsessive* passion toward a number of activities, including work. Harmonious passion is defined as willing involvement in a task without the compelling need to do the task at all times (Vallerand, 2008). Obsessive passion, in contrast, refers to "rigid persistence toward the activity" (Vallerand, 2008, p. 2), describing an individual who becomes dependent on the activity such that his or her normal functioning is impaired by the obsessive need for continuous involvement in the activity. Working at the task may provide a boost to the ego and satisfy a need for feeling important, yet it controls the individual. Thus, obsessive passion is compulsive, whereas harmonious passion is considered "in harmony with other aspects of the person's life" (Vallerand, 2008, p. 2). Others have defined passion as incorporating a synthesis of one's affective and cognitive self-perception towards the job (e.g., Ho, Wong, & Lee, 2011). Although compulsive behaviors describe workaholism and obsessive passion, the compulsive behaviors are not indicative of a mental disorder, such as obsessive-compulsive mental disorder, a type of anxiety disorder (see the *Diagnostic and Statistical Manual of Mental Disorders* [1994], published by the American Psychiatric Association).

Across a series of studies conducted in three different countries, Burke and colleagues (Burke, Burgess, & Oberklaid, 2002; Burke & Matthiesen, 2004; Burke, Richardsen, & Martinussen, 2004) examined the relationship between passion and addiction to work (e.g., compulsive work). Results from all three studies showed that passion and addiction demonstrated opposite relationships with outcomes; passion was positively related to satisfaction and health outcomes, whereas addiction was negatively related to both. The authors concluded that obsessive passion and addiction may be considered opposite constructs to one another.

In terms of the relationship between passion and engagement, a recent study has shown that harmonious and obsessive passion are distinct constructs from engagement and related to engagement (Trépanier, Fernet, Austin, Forest, & Vallerand, 2013). Specifically, harmonious passion was positively related to engagement, whereas obsessive passion demonstrated no significant relationship to engagement (engagement was assessed using only the vigor component of the UWES). Moreover, both forms of passion were shown to mediate the relationship between job resources and job demands with engagement and burnout (see Trépanier et al., 2013).

In sum, neither workaholism nor passion seems to reflect the idea of too much engagement. As found in the studies reviewed above, engagement appears to be a separate construct from workaholism and passion. Engaged employees may at times be workaholics or experience either obsessive or harmonious passion.

If "Too Engaged" Is Not Workaholism or Passion, Then What Is It?

In her chapter on too much engagement, George (2010) suggested high levels of engagement interfere with conscious decision-making and problem-solving processes. Specifically, she argued that when an employee is in a state of high engagement, problem solving is limited because conscious thinking cannot access as much information as the nonconscious mind. Relying on the works of Wilson and colleagues' (Wilson, 2002; Wilson,

Dunn, Bybee, Hyman, & Rotundo, 1984; Wilson & Kraft, 1993a, 1993b; Wilson & Schooler, 1991), she concluded that

> high levels of engagement are necessary to acquire the knowledge and information relevant to decisions and judgments that come up on a job. When actually making complex decisions and judgments, perhaps, too much engagement and weighing pros and cons may be dysfunctional.
>
> (George, 2010, p. 257)

The argument here is when one allows the nonconscious mind to problem solve and make decisions, essentially following one's "gut" (George, 2010, p. 256), the greater capacity of the nonconscious mind is accessed and responds in a divergent, less restricted processing manner (Dijksterhuis & Nordgren, 2006; Dijksterhuis & van Olden, 2006; Wilson, 2002). Because most behavior is primarily nonconscious, driven by nonconscious thoughts and feelings, and performed automatically based on activated schemas, scripts, and predispositions (e.g., George, 2009; Glaser & Kihlstrom, 2005; Uleman & Bargh, 1989), using conscious thought to behave inhibits and limits access to the adaptive and accumulated knowledge stored in the nonconscious. One's thoughts, feelings, and behaviors can become faster, richer, and less structured or constrained if conscious intent is set aside. However, herein lies the problem according to George (2010); engagement has been defined as *conscious* thoughts, feelings, and behaviors (e.g., Kahn, 1990; Schaufeli, Salanova, et al., 2002).

Assuming George's (2010) reasoning is correct, that conscious engagement can be dysfunctional in decision-making, creative work, and complex problem solving, too much engagement can be detrimental to an organization. Some research has shown that better decisions are indeed made when relying on one's gut as opposed to simply relying on conscious problem solving (Wilson, 2002; Wilson et al., 1984; Wilson & Kraft, 1993a, 1993b; Wilson & Schooler, 1991); therefore, organizations would benefit from fluctuating levels of employee engagement; precisely what George (2010) argues is most beneficial for employees themselves.

George (2010) further proposed that although engagement has been defined as a positive affective state, negative affect may be just as important to experience during moments of engagement. She suggested negative affect signals a problem exists that must be solved, mobilizing the mind and body to work on changing behavior or changing the situation (Damasio, 1999; Frijda, 1988; George 2009). Thus, if engagement is limited to a positive affective state only, as is suggested in its definition (Kahn, 1990; Schaufeli et al., 2002), being engaged all the time may not be particularly beneficial to an organization. George's (2010) arguments are compelling in suggesting that how engagement is currently defined renders it a concept organizations should not want to continually push for from every employee at all times.

The Paradox of Engagement

However, there are other concerns for the dark side of engagement, the idea that perhaps engagement is not always a good thing, even if we retain its current definition. As reviewed in earlier chapters in this book, researchers have shown engagement is associated with commitment, job involvement, and extra-role behaviors (e.g., Christian, Garza, & Slaughter, 2011; Karatepe, 2013). Although these outcomes are generally considered good for the organization, taken to an extreme they become negative. For example, employees who are engaged in their current jobs and projects may become so committed to the project their commitment becomes rigid, so much that changes become unacceptable. Siegrist et al. (2004) proposed *overcommitment to work* occurs when employees seek high job demands and extend their work efforts beyond what is expected of the organization, all in an effort to obtain approval. A similar construct in terms of high commitment, *goal commitment,* refers to an "attachment to or determination to reach a goal" (Locke & Latham, 1990, p. 125). Employees with high goal commitment are characterized as persistent, resisting distractions, and keeping to the goal even in the face of obstacles that would, under all other circumstances, deter others (Bipp & Kleinbeck, 2011). These characterizations are not unlike what has been attributed to engaged employees; engaged employees are characterized as persistent even when faced with challenges, and can be so absorbed they lose track of time and filter out all distractions. Persistence to the point of not knowing when to stop or not stopping even when the organization wants you to becomes obsessive passion and a negative for the organization. Likewise, failing to pay attention to important issues, including personal needs, borders on workaholic behavior that cannot be considered positive or good.

Workaholics are considered over-involved in their work, essentially taking job involvement to an extreme (Ng et al., 2007) and developing an irrational commitment to excessive work (Cherrington, 1980). Job involvement and workaholism are positively correlated (Mudrack & Naughton, 2001), such that when employees become excessively involved in their jobs, they become compulsive, workaholics, and rigid in their thinking and ability to change (Mudrack, 2004). Employees with high job involvement tend to demonstrate obsessive-compulsive behaviors (Schwartz, 1982), but not necessarily to levels of impairment as with a personality disorder (Macdonald & de Silva, 1999). Like job involvement, although extra-role behaviors are beneficial to an organization

(P. Podsakoff & MacKenzie, 1997), when taken to the extreme such as demonstrated at the expense of the actual job requirements or in lieu of what is required on the job, they become negative.

How the Paradox Occurs

The organization plays a role in moving engagement from a good mental state that brings about positive outcomes to a state wherein the results are paradoxically negative for the organization. For example, just as pay-for-performance plans result in employees' overly focusing on their in-role job behaviors (i.e., only what is directly and formally expected; Deckop, Mangel, & Cirka, 1999), over-rewarding and overemphasizing engagement to get citizenship behaviors results in attention focused on extra-role behaviors to the detriment of in-role performance behaviors (Bergeron, 2007). Research has shown when workaholic behaviors are reinforced by the organization, employees are more likely to develop workaholic tendencies (e.g., Burke, 2001; Harpaz & Snir, 2003; Ng et al., 2007; Snir & Harpaz, 2004).

Similarly, individuals who become too focused on their own work and are rewarded for doing so fail to make contributions to teamwork necessary for successful team performance (Pfeffer, 1998). Overemphasis on individual employee engagement is likely to cause employees to refrain from helping their teammates (Deming, 1986; Pfeffer, 1998) because doing so takes away from their concentration, their mindful presence on their work, and their ability to express themselves in their work role—unless it is clear their work role subsumes being a collaborative team player. With the focus of performance appraisal in most countries and work settings on the individual as opposed to the team (Cable & Judge, 1994), few employees are likely to see their primary role as being a team player.

It is widely known in organizations that what you focus on or reward is what you get (Hitt, 1995). Thus, engaged employees who are reinforced for their engagement levels may fall into extreme goal commitment and excessive attention to extra-role behaviors because they are rewarded for these behaviors. Some might argue, however, that engagement is a motivational state much like intrinsic motivation or it actually incorporates intrinsic motivation (Chalofsky & Krishna, 2009; Salanova & Schaufeli, 2008; Schaufeli et al., 2008), and therefore, external rewards inhibit and reduce motivational drive (Deci, Koestner, & Ryan, 1999; Deci & Ryan, 1985). Even though engagement may share conceptual space with intrinsic motivation and is positively related ($r = .35$; Rich et al., 2010), it has been shown to be distinct from intrinsic motivation (Rich et al., 2010). Therefore, it is unlikely rewards or reinforcement for being engaged will reduce levels of engagement.

WHAT DOES THE DARK SIDE OF
ENGAGEMENT LOOK LIKE?

Panya works for Pine Investments and regularly helps others, offering to stay late or take on additional work that is not hers. She goes above and beyond on her own projects, ensuring customers are very happy with the solutions; they regularly provide positive ratings on her, sending in comments about how she remembers their kids' names and birthdays and about how she takes time to chat with them beyond the scheduled appointment slot.

Panya is known for championing new service products, especially the ones she likes. She works with marketing to make the brochures personal, almost as if she owns the product. Panya is well rewarded for her performance—she is considered one of the top paid employees and receives many accolades from the bosses. Panya would rate herself very engaged—she is energetic at work and energized by what she is doing. She is focused at work, feeling fulfilled by the accomplishments and from the meaningfulness she derives from helping others at work. Panya's engagement at work, however, makes others feel pressured to be as busy, excited, and as attached to the work role as she. Her teammates have stopped asking her for help because she gets so into the project that she takes over, forgetting that they asked for help, not asked her to do it for them. Panya is highly rewarded for being the last-minute hero—but the supervisors overlook how that takes away from the contribution of all the others on the team who worked just as hard but earlier and for longer periods before the due date. Additionally, Panya considers herself a workaholic in the positive sense—she loves her job and that is why she works intensely at it—but others view her work habits as competitive. Because she loves what she does, Panya tends to agree to everything that comes her way, creating a workload bottleneck at times, and difficulty for the boss to balance the workload across team members.

Recently, a project on which Panya put in overtime and excessive personal attention was canceled. Panya was not willing to let go of the project and accept the cancellation decision; after all, she was enjoying the project and felt that it was the right thing for the organization to do. Her inability to let go created a lot of difficulty for the team, the boss, and herself. Because she was so into the project, she could not see that it really was best for the organization to cancel the project. Panya thinks she is doing what the organization wants from her because they keep talking about how critical it is that employees are engaged, and she is rewarded for her high engagement scores.

Panya's work involves focusing on a variety of tasks, but because Panya becomes engaged at work in the tasks she finds most meaningful, she loses sight of the big picture and the need to get all the tasks done. This results in unintended workflow and workload problems. Because Panya is so absorbed in what she is doing at work that she fails to see what she is not doing and how her engagement is not always best for the organization.

Conclusion

Engagement is considered a positive mental state of motivation and thus far, positive outcomes have been associated with the construct. However, there is a dark side to engagement, an unintended paradox wherein engagement is not necessarily always good for organizations. Organizations, consultants, and researchers, thus far, have not considered the possibility that engagement needs to be managed appropriately, and fluctuations in levels of engagement can be productive and necessary at the individual, group, and organizational levels. Recent research on engagement and recovery suggest that some recognize ongoing engagement may not be possible or may not be healthy (e.g., ten Brummelhuis & Bakker, 2012).

Researchers can contribute to understanding engagement by examining the potential for unintended consequences of engaged employees, organizational policies, and actions that promote and reinforce engagement at the expense of managed workloads and what exactly too much engagement means. Thus far, little work exists clearly separating engagement from workaholism or passion. Longitudinal studies may help shed light on whether, over time, engagement leads to workaholism or whether harmonious passion over time leads to obsessive passion that then filters into either engagement and/or workaholism. From my own initial work, it seems there may be a fine distinction between workaholism and engagement.

Employees' Reflections

In one of my engagement consulting projects, an employee I interviewed reflected on workaholism and engagement:

There are times when I really have to look at myself and say okay, am I a workaholic, or am I? Is this just where I thrive? I think prior . . . I probably would have labeled myself as a workaholic, but now I think it's really your perspective. It's not about what I have to do, it's about what I want to do.

It may be that after much research, we might find that there is no dark side to engagement. However, like constructs introduced long before engagement, such as citizenship behaviors, more sounds better until we ponder whether there is a dark side and what it looks like.

Walk-Away Points

- Theoretical discourse has likened too much engagement to workaholism and obsessive passion; too much engagement has been related to burnout.
- For all intents and purposes, engagement is desirable in employees and can contribute to productive and positive results for the organization, but there is a dark side when engagement is not necessarily beneficial.
- Fluctuations and changes in engagement levels may be productive and necessary for both employees and their organizations.

11

SUMMING IT ALL UP

Where Do We Go From Here?

Grasping the ideas within an entire book is challenging, especially if one only reads a few chapters here and there. In this chapter, I summarize the general ideas and contributions of the book and offer perspectives on next steps in the employee engagement landscape.

Where Are We?

You Are Here: The Current State of the Field

In Parts I and II of the book, I reviewed where we are today with understanding employee engagement. The current definitions of engagement (e.g., Kahn, 1990; Macey & Schneider, 2008; Schaufeli, Salanova, et al., 2002) suggest that engaged employees (a) feel vigorous, demonstrating high levels of energy and persistence at work; (b) are dedicated, experiencing enthusiasm, pride, and significant in their work; (c) are absorbed in their work, to the point that they are intensely concentrating, lose track of time, and display an inability to stop working (like "good" workaholics); (d) are mindful and present in their work roles; (e) are expressive emotionally, physically, and authentically; (f) are either stable in their levels of engagement (Schaufeli, Salanova, et al., 2002) or fluctuate in their engagement levels from moment to moment (Kahn, 1990); and (g) experience their engagement in a process whereby their individual characteristics (e.g., personality) lead to them to feel engaged, which translates into performance behaviors on the job.

Employee engagement is different from other psychological constructs studied in the organizational sciences. It is a unique construct from job performance, organizational citizenship behavior, job involvement, job satisfaction, organizational commitment, intrinsic motivation, flow, and happiness. Different from these other constructs, employee engagement proposes employees invest themselves completely (emotionally, mentally, and physiologically) into their work roles and toward achieving the goals of the organization. With engagement, the head and the heart are aligned—individuals' harmonious passion follows their thinking and their thinking follows their

193

passion. They value their work and feel they are doing what makes them most fulfilled and internally rewarded, while intellectually they know they are doing work fitting of their skills and capabilities. Engaged employees transform their work from day-to-day tasks that may be mechanical, automatic, and in some cases dehumanizing (Haslam, 2006), into something from which they derive meaning and purpose, and the organization thrives. Finally, employee engagement may synergistically incorporate intrinsic motivation, flow, involvement, passion, and physiological arousal, which results in behavioral displays of their engagement in the form of performance, citizenship behavior, satisfaction, happiness, and commitment.

Understanding what engagement is and how it is different from other known and understood constructs within the organizational sciences allows researchers and consultants to explore how to encourage engagement within organizations. Organizations and employees themselves contribute to whether they enter into a state of engagement. For example, leadership approaches such as full range, transformational, empowering, supportive, and interpersonal and applications of emotional intelligence are organizational interventions supporting the promotion of engagement in followers. Organizational changes to the immediate work environment such as job redesign efforts in which attention is focused on providing core job dimensions of the job characteristics theory, job rotation and enrichment, and greater team interdependency in collectivistic societies can facilitate engagement. Additionally, employees gain psychological availability when provided with sufficient job resources offsetting the many job demands with which they struggle and are challenged. Most job resources come from the organization; however, others such as social connections and coworker support come from employees themselves. Likewise, enabling employees themselves to mentally job redesign through job crafting has been theorized to facilitate engagement.

With some ideas of how to help employees become engaged, there is still the challenge of what to do about those who simply are not. What prevents employees from being engaged at work? Many refer to disengagement to define what engagement is or why engaged employees are so valuable to the organization (usually framed using lost and gained finances), but disengagement itself is rarely, if ever, defined. Kahn (1990) is one of the few authors to explicitly define disengagement, and yet few researchers have taken up the charge to study and pursue what is disengagement and how it manifests itself in organizations. Burnout has been put forth as a possible construct capturing the idea of disengagement, but burnout fails to reflect a state that is not dysfunctional but is also not energetic. Reflections on my own findings from recent qualitative work, exploring the idea of disengagement and what it means for people at work, reveals that disengagement is different from burnout. Based on my research and on the theoretical and empirical work on engagement thus far, in Chapter 5 I offered a number of organizational and individual factors that appear to play a role in inhibiting employee engagement.

In Chapter 6 I offered a crash course in psychometrics, conveying what makes for a good measure of engagement and how to evaluate measures to determine if they are good. The consequences of poorly assessing engagement are grave for clarifying and understanding the construct. Namely, incorrect and/or less than accurate conclusions are drawn about engagement (or what we think is engagement), and correcting those conclusions later becomes very challenging, if not impossible. Poor assessment means not really measuring engagement but measuring something else in its stead. Organizational interventions attend to issues and changes other than what will have the intended consequence on engagement, and the domino effect continues. Having struggled myself when first starting in this field of study to find a good measure of engagement, and having been asked by colleagues, students, and clients to help them with assessing engagement, I decided it was essential to provide a thorough review of existing measures of engagement. The accurate measurement of employee engagement is an area in need of attention. Developing measures, accumulating evidence, and then tweaking to improve those measures is essential for understanding the construct of engagement. It is not yet clear whether engagement is a fluctuating state, stable and consistent over time, or the same across all cultures. Without proper measures and rigorous study methods, we will not be able to answer these questions.

Engaged employees create competitive advantage for organizations and the development of a culture for engagement is essential towards this end. In my consulting work, I am often asked whether employees can be selected for engagement—is there a measure or a way to choose who is most likely to be an engaged employee? Engagement has not yet been examined as a personality characteristic, nor assessed for its stability (or lack thereof). Researchers have not yet determined whether engagement is determined by situational characteristics, or perhaps an interaction between person and situation. Therefore, measuring a job candidate's engagement level to determine potential for stability and continuous engagement levels after hire is not a fruitful endeavor. It may be possible, though, to select employees based on other stable attributes research has shown are associated with engagement, such as conscientiousness (e.g., Inceoglu & Warr, 2011; H. Kim, Shin, & Swanger, 2009).

Where Do We Go From Here?

Future: A Path Forward

In Part III of the book, I focused on how employee engagement can be a competitive advantage for organizations by drawing attention to the future of the field. I proposed a number of research agendas that advance the scientific study of employee engagement, while creating a path for how organizations can consider fostering employee engagement to promote their employees' well-being as well as their own (Chapter 7 was devoted to creating an organizational climate and culture for engagement).

Part IV of the book reflects the new frontiers of employee engagement. In Chapter 9 I focused on engagement around the globe, reviewing what is currently known about engagement internationally, and more important, I exposed the gaps in our understanding and challenges with filling those gaps. I introduced the paradox of engagement, the idea that engagement may not always be a good thing for employees or their organizations, in Chapter 10, and I do not mean workaholism or burnout as others have suggested. Instead, I propose that the dark side of engagement, even as a good state for employees to be in, may not be in an organization's best interest to strive for consistent and continuous engagement from every employee at all times.

Measuring engagement—getting it right. In Chapter 6, I reviewed several measures of engagement. Although the Utrecht Work Engagement Scale (UWES; Schaufeli & Bakker, 2003) has been used quite a bit, recent studies examining the validity of the UWES question the short form (Wefald, Mills, Smith, & Downew, 21012) and whether the UWES (regardless which form) is measuring a different construct than existing measures of burnout (reverse scored; Cole, Walter, Bedeian, & O'Boyle, 2012). Thus, "low burnout equals engagement" may be what the UWES is actually assessing, but researchers have steered away from the idea of engagement as the opposite of burnout, including the UWES's authors Schaufeli and Bakker (see Schaufeli, Salanova, et al., 2002). Other measures such as the Job Engagement Scale (Rich, LePine, & Crawford, 2010) and Saks's (2006) job and organizational engagement scales have little accumulated validity evidence as of this date. Finally, nonacademic measures fail to provide psychometric evidence of their validity, and their proprietary nature renders them both non-verifiable and inaccessible. Thus, the opportunity exists for developing good measures of engagement; measures with accumulated validity evidence to support their use.

Using engagement to create thriving organizations. There is no lack of interest in understanding employee engagement; however, to date, it has most frequently been studied in the context of well-being and overall health of employees. Turning this focus upside down, in Chapter 8, I discussed how we can use employee engagement to create healthy-thriving organizations by introducing the idea of engagement contagion. Through the synergistic integration of emotional, cognitive, and behavioral contagion, I argue for engagement contagion as a means for how engaged employees create other engaged employees in the organization, eventually creating a healthy-thriving organization in which employees are engaged and self-reinforcing.

Cross-cultural studies of engagement. Although I noted there is no lack of interest in studying engagement, from a review of the literature, employee engagement appears to be largely a phenomenon within the United States. A number of studies have examined engagement in non-U.S. countries; however, the studies do not compare across cultures and most appear to adopt the current academic definitions of engagement without first examining if those definitions make sense. In a small handful of cases, researchers have compared scores across *countries*, but this is not necessarily the same as *cross-cultural* research. Chapter 9 was solely dedicated to shedding an international spotlight on employee engagement. The field of cross-cultural psychology is vast and trying to squeeze in a comprehensive review of all theories and relevant empirical findings would be impossible. Instead, I used two well-known taxonomies of culture to offer suggestions for how engagement may vary (or not) by culture, and developed specific propositions that can be studied across cultures.

The paradox of engagement. Regardless of where engagement has been studied, thus far it has been defined and examined as a positive concept that no organization can do without. In Chapter 10, I asked the question, "But what if engagement is not always a good thing for organizations?" I introduced the *dark side* of engagement, a paradox wherein engagement, otherwise thought to be the solution to all that ails an organization, comes at the expense of several other highly desirable organizational constructs. The dark side of engagement is not the same as "too engaged," which some researchers have argued is the same as workaholism, burnout, and limited cognitive processing. By incorporating the problem-solving signals that negative affectivity activates (George, 2010), engaged employees may become more aware of situations that need transforming and debates that need to be held to improve the work environment and work product. Whether there is such a thing as too much engagement or whether the dark side of engagement exists are empirical questions, ones that researchers can explore.

Other Considerations

The stability (or not) of engagement. A large gap in our understanding of engagement exists in not knowing whether engagement is a moment-to-moment, intense, and short-lived experience (e.g., emotion); a relatively stable state (e.g., mood); a very stable state (e.g., attitude); or a trait or individual difference characteristic (e.g., personality). Opportunities for future research exist in answering this fundamental question: What is the "time" associated with engagement? Although there are a couple of studies in which researchers used diary studies to capture engagement at various points in time, those studies did not seek to answer the questions of how and when engagement varied—the focus of the research was on whether resources and recovery time affect engagement measured once a day or once at the end of the week (Bakker & Bal, 2010; Petrou, Demerouti, Peeters, Schaufeli, & Hetland, 2012; Sonnentag, 2003; Xanthopoulou, Bakker, Demerouti, & Schaufeli, 2009; Xanthopoulou, Bakker, Heuven, Demerouti, & Schaufeli, 2008). Sonnentag, Dormann, and Demerouti (2010) provide a nice review of day-level and week-level studies conducted by themselves and their colleagues. These studies have been informative and advanced an understanding of how resources during the day relate to employees' responses to questions about their engagement. However, as recognized by the study authors, methodological issues such as controlling when during the day individuals note their engagement levels should be addressed and improved in future studies. Additionally, although these studies serve as a good start, the attention first needs to be on understanding the time aspect of engagement, how and whether it changes over time, and what causes those changes and when.

Theory of purposeful work behavior. In a recent publication, Barrick, Mount, and Li (2013) proposed a theory of purposeful work behavior, which captures a process model for purposeful work behavior. The authors suggest a motivational process results from the interaction of individual characteristics (i.e., personality) and situational characteristics (e.g., social and job environment), which leads to various work outcomes such as job satisfaction and performance behaviors (citizenship behavior, task performance). I have simplified the model in Figure 11.1 for illustration purposes.

Essentially, the model says the person by situation effects on motivation are channeled through high-level achievement goals and experienced meaningfulness derived from the work, resulting in motivated behavior. Barrick et al. (2013) propose that one's personality is a key determinant of motivated behavior when combined with and understood in the context of the situational constraints and offerings, resulting in a behavior set unique to each individual. When the situation allows for the full expression of one's

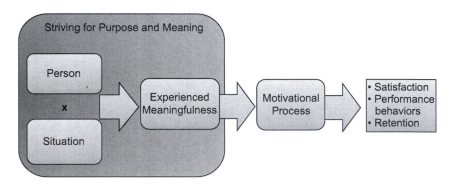

Figure 11.1 Adapted model from Barrick, Mount, and Li's (2013) Theory of Purposeful Work Behavior

personality, the more motivational drive is experienced—one can pursue one's goals as desired. The authors note that "a basic assumption in the theory of purposeful work behavior is that employee behavior is purposeful or directed toward the attainment of goals" (Barrick et al., 2013, p. 135). Goals, or personal agendas as the authors refer to them, whether conscious or not, are important in the model as they specify to what an individual is motivated toward. Personal agendas can include communion (affiliation), status, autonomy, or achievement, and each is associated with one or more specific personality traits and situational characteristics. For example, if one strives for status, extraversion becomes more relevant over conscientiousness, openness to experience, emotional stability, or agreeableness, and the situation must support task significance, feedback from others, and the opportunity for power and influence.

The model holds promise for potentially explaining engagement. Other models, such as my own research reviewed in Chapter 4, are similar to the Barrick et al. (2013) model in that they consider the importance of contextual variables, and the development of psychological meaningfulness and feelings of purpose, which translate into outcomes via motivational processes. A number of researchers seem to be converging on the idea that various factors of the environment and person explain their striving for meaning and purpose, which results in motivational behavior (e.g., Kahn & Fellows, 2013; Lent, 2013).

Building on previous theoretical models and empirical findings of engagement reviewed in this book, an all-encompassing model of engagement might look (in its simplest form) like Figure 11.2:

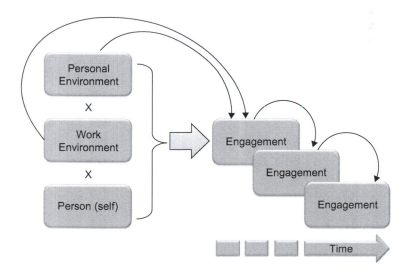

Figure 11.2 Proposed Model of Employee Engagement

The results of the interaction between personal environment, work environment, and person combine to predict engagement at work.

Personal environment refers to the environment around
the person, outside of the job:

- Social support and acceptance (e.g., family, friends)
- Life sustenance (consider the lower levels of Maslow's Hierarchy: adequate money for living, comfortable place to live both in terms of house/roof over the head and community/country, adequate food, physical safety, health)
- Cognitive load (too much on your mind prevents you from being able to think or focus)

Work environment refers to anything having to do with
the workplace itself:

- Leadership (relational, transactional, visionary)
- Organizational vision
- Fit—between your values and those of the job and organization
- Job dimensions (skill variety, task variety, autonomy when appropriate for culture)
- Meaningfulness (may include affiliation, meeting esteem needs, fulfilling ideals)
- Competence (ability to develop and demonstrate skills and capability)
- Growth (to build self-efficacy and keep learning)
- Reinforcement that engagement is desirable and highly regarded
- New and future oriented (work on something new as opposed to something that has no future)
- Resources such as equipment to do your job, time to do it, communications to understand the job requirements
- Social support and acceptance (e.g., coworker support, friends at work)
- Culture (country, ethnic or religious, and organizational)

Person (self) refers to what the person brings to the workplace:

- Sense of calling—called to do the work
- Personality
- Head and heart alignment (what I feel about the job coincides/aligns with how I think about the job; I'm doing the "right" thing)
- Identification with the occupation, organization, or being engaged (it is part of your identity, who you are—you are an "engaged" person)
- Need for belongingness—my engagement fits with the norms of the organization, therefore, I fit and belong

- Instrumental (Where am I going? What's my purpose? Engagement gets me there)
- Choice to be engaged

As individuals experience engagement, their feelings of personal alignment, fit, and competence, along with reinforcement that what they are doing is instrumental, meaningful, and achievable feeds back into the work environment and personal environment. Engaged employees choose to be engaged, and are reinforced both internally and externally for their engagement, which results in more engagement. Thus, the model is cyclical, reflecting to some degree the idea of an engagement process—a self-sustaining model of engagement. The model additionally incorporates the passage of time and the idea that engagement in one moment affects engagement in the next moment, but still recognize that engagement may come in chunks as opposed a single continuous stream of focus, energy, and thought.

Employees' Reflections

*I think someone who is truly engaged doesn't get there because someone else has facilitated that. I really believe that they get there because they have made a decision that this is for me and this is what I'm going to dig into because this is what I want to do and this is what I **choose** to do, and I see the possibilities.*

Conclusion

Even though work has been accumulating, researchers have their work cut out for them in demonstrating what exactly engagement is and is not, and whether or how it can be fostered, managed, and utilized in organizations. Progress in several fundamental areas must be made to move these efforts forward (e.g., measurement instruments). Table 11.1 reviews some of the areas of engagement in which progress has been made, as well as areas left to be explored, and the associated challenges or gaps still existing in those areas.

One area that has shown progress in the study of engagement is creating a bridge between practice and science. Newman and Harrison (2008) concluded academics are seeking ways to bridge the gap between how practitioners refer to engagement and what engagement might be if understood from an academic perspective (putting it into theoretical context with what is known from the theoretical and empirical works of

Table 11.1 Areas of Engagement With Their Respective Challenges and/or Gaps

Area	Challenges	Sub-challenges
Definition	Consensus	
	Capturing time component	Measurement
	Cross-cultural	Translation
	Maintaining uniqueness or distinctiveness	
	Reflecting static concept or dynamic process concept	Measuring constantly changing construct
	Trait engagement	
	Is it on a continuum?	
	Multifoci engagement?	Isolating the foci
Measurement	Improving existing measures	
	Creating new and better measures	
	Culturally-free measures	
	Multidimensional or unidimensional?	
	Long versus short	What is too long?
	Summing, averaging, or moment-based	Stability of engagement
Creating culture to foster engagement	Empirical evidence supporting effectiveness of solutions	Quasi-experimentation
		Too many variables
	Measuring change	
Disengagement	Defining	What is the tipping point?
		Does it become burnout?
	Measurement	
Shrinking Science-Practice Gap	Should it be shrunk? Are practice and science talking about the same concept?	Specificity on language in practice
		Utility of research
Contagion	Measurement	Isolating infection from other ways of becoming engaged
	How to encourage	
Dark Side	Measurement	What is the tipping point?
	Identifying negative consequences of dark side	

similar topics). Since 2008, quite a bit more progress has been made, and interest in the topic appears to be thriving and growing (if the number of publications, both books and empirical works, and conference presentations are any indication). However, questions still remain as to whether engagement as understood in the practice circles is what academicians are constructing it to be and whether that translation makes sense. Specifically, it may be that engagement is a concept that takes on more meaning than can be justified theoretically and/or empirically. Continued research on engagement will answer this question.

The study of employee engagement is still in its infancy. In this book, I have provided a comprehensive review of the theoretical and empirical works on employee engagement from a variety of perspectives, including academic and practice. It is my hope that the chapters in this book provide essential knowledge and understanding of engagement as we understand it today and, importantly, spark conversation, research, and challenges to the ideas to move the field forward toward the future.

Walk-Away Points

- We have developed a base of knowledge in employee engagement, as base that still has many holes. At this point, engagement appears to be a new construct, although shares conceptual space with other similar and related constructs.
- There may be a dark side to engagement that suggests that it is not the answer to all that ails organizations today.
- The advancement of our understanding of engagement would progress faster and farther if practice and academe were to join hands and collaborate more.
- Advancement of the field requires good measures, convergent on a clear definition, and evaluation studies of organizational interventions.
- Cross-cultural research is necessary to determine if engagement is a unique and relevant construct across the globe, or only unique to one or more cultures.

REFERENCES

Adelmann, P. K., & Zajonc, R. B. (1989). Facial efference and the experience of emotion. *Annual Review of Psychology, 40*, 249–280. doi:10.1146/annurev. ps.40.020189.001341

Agarwal, U. A., & Bhargava, S. (2013). Effects of psychological contract breach on organizational outcomes: Moderating role of tenure and educational levels. *Vikalpa: The Journal for Decision Makers, 38*(1), 13–25.

Agarwal, U. A., Datta, S., Blake-Beard, S., & Bhargava, S. (2012). Linking LMX, innovative work behaviour and turnover intentions: The mediating role of work engagement. *The Career Development International, 17*(3), 208–230. doi:10.1108/13620431211241063

Ajzen, I. (1991). The theory of planned behavior. *Organizational Behavior And Human Decision Processes, 50*(2), 179–211. doi:10.1016/0749-5978(91)90020-T

Ajzen, I. (2001). Nature and operation of attitudes. *Annual Review of Psychology, 52*, 27–58. doi:10.1146/annurev.psych.52.1.27

Alarcon, G. M., & Lyons, J. B. (2011). The relationship of engagement and job satisfaction in working samples. *Journal of Psychology: Interdisciplinary and Applied, 145*(5), 463–480. doi:10.1080/00223980.2011.584083

Albrecht, S. L. (2010). Employee engagement: 10 key questions for research and practice. In S. L. Albrecht (Ed.), *Handbook of employee engagement: Perspectives, issues, research and practice* (pp. 3–19). Northampton, MA: Edward Elgar.

Alderfer, C. P. (1972). *Existence, relatedness, and growth: Human needs in organizational settings.* New York, NY: The Free Press.

Allen, N. J., & Meyer, J. P. (1990). The measurement and antecedents of affective, continuance and normative commitment to the organization. *Journal of Occupational Psychology, 63*(1), 1–18. doi:10.1111/j.2044-8325.1990.tb00506.x

Allen, R. W., Madison, D. L., Porter, L. W., Renwick, P. A., & Mayes, B. T. (1979). Organizational politics. *California Management Review, 22*(1), 77–83.

Allport, G. W. (1961). *Pattern and growth in personality.* New York, NY: Holt, Rinehart and Winston.

Alpers, G. W., Adolph, D., & Pauli, P. (2011). Emotional scenes and facial expressions elicit different psychophysiological responses. *International Journal of Psychophysiology, 80*(3), 173–181. doi:10.1016/j.ijpsycho.2011.01.010

Amabile, T. M., Conti, R., Coon, H., Lazenby, J., & Herron, M. (1996). Assessing the work environment for creativity. *Academy of Management Journal, 39*(5), 1154–1184. doi:10.2307/256995

American Education Research Association, American Psychological Association, & National Council on Measurement in Education. (1999). *Standards for educational and psychological testing.* Washington, DC: American Educational Research Association.

Andersson, L. M., & Pearson, C. M. (1999). Tit for tat? The spiraling effect of incivility in the workplace. *Academy of Management Review, 24*(3), 452–471. doi:10.5465/AMR.1999.2202131

Andreassen, C., Ursin, H., & Eriksen, H. R. (2007). The relationship between strong motivation to work, "workaholism", and health. *Psychology & Health, 22*(5), 615–629. doi:10.1080/14768320600941814

Arendasy, M., Sommer, M., & Hergovich, A. (2007). Statistical judgment formation in personnel selection: A study in military aviation psychology. *Military Psychology, 19*(2), 119–136. doi:10.1080/08995600701323418

Aryee, S., Budhwar, P. S., & Chen, Z. (2002). Trust as a mediator of the relationship between organizational justice and work outcomes: Test of a social exchange model. *Journal of Organizational Behavior, 23*(3), 267–286. doi:10.1002/job.138

Aryee, S., Walumbwa, F. O., Zhou, Q., & Hartnell, C. A. (2012). Transformational leadership, innovative behavior, and task performance: Test of mediation and moderation processes. *Human Performance, 25*(1), 1–25. doi:10.10 80/08959285.2011.631648

Ashforth, B. E., & Kreiner, G. E. (2013). Profane or profound? Finding meaning in dirty work. In B. J. Dik, Z. S. Byrne, & M. F. Steger (Eds.), *Purpose and meaning in the workplace* (pp. 127–130). Washington, DC: American Psychological Association.

Ashforth, B. E., & Mael, F. (1989). Social identity theory and the organization. *The Academy of Management Review, 14*(1), 20–39. doi:10.2307/258189

Avolio, B. J. (1999). *Full leadership development: Building the vital forces in organizations.* Thousand Oaks, CA: Sage.

Avolio, B. J. (2011). *Full range leadership development* (2nd ed). Thousand Oaks, CA: Sage.

Avolio, B. J., & Bass. B. M. (1991). *The full range leadership development programs: Basic and advanced manuals.* Binghamton, NY: Bass, Avolio & Associates

Avolio, B. J., & Bass, B. M. (1994). *Evaluate the impact of transformational leadership training at individual, group, organizational and community levels* (Final Report to the W. K. Kellogg Foundation). Binghamton, NY: Binghamton University.

Avolio, B. J., Gardner, W. L., Walumbwa, F. O., Luthans, F., & May, D. R. (2004). Unlocking the mask: A look at the process by which authentic leaders impact follower attitudes and behaviors. *The Leadership Quarterly, 15*(6), 801–823. doi:10.1016/j.leaqua.2004.09.003

Azen, R., & Budescu, D. V. (2003). The dominance analysis approach for comparing predictors in multiple regression. *Psychological Methods, 8*(2), 129–148. doi:10.1037/1082-989X.8.2.129

Bailenson, J. N., & Yee, N. (2005). Digital chameleons: Automatic assimilation of nonverbal gestures in immersive virtual environments. *Psychological Science*, 16(10), 814–819. doi:10.1111/j.1467-9280.2005.01619.x

Bakker, A. B. (2009). Building engagement in the workplace. In R. J. Burke & C. L. Cooper (Eds.), *The peak performing organization* (pp. 50–72). Oxford, England: Routledge.

Bakker, A. B. (2010). Engagement and "job crafting": Engaged employees create their own great place to work. In S. L. Albrecht (Ed.), *Handbook of employee engagement: Perspectives, issues, research and practice* (pp. 229–244). Northampton, MA: Edward Elgar.

Bakker, A. B., & Bal, P. (2010). Weekly work engagement and performance: A study among starting teachers. *Journal of Occupational and Organizational Psychology*, 83(1), 189–206. doi:10.1348/096317909X402596

Bakker, A. B., & Demerouti, E. (2008). Towards a model of work engagement. *The Career Development International*, 13(3), 209–223. doi:10.1108/13620430810870476

Bakker, A. B., Demerouti, E., & Schaufeli, W. B. (2005). The crossover of burnout and work engagement among working couples. *Human Relations*, 58(5), 661–689. doi:10.1177/0018726705055967

Bakker, A. B., Hakanen, J. J., Demerouti, E., & Xanthopoulou, D. (2007). Job resources boost work engagement, particularly when job demands are high. *Journal of Educational Psychology*, 99(2), 274–284. doi:10.1037/0022-0663.99.2.274

Bakker, A. B., & Leiter, M. P. (2010). *Work engagement: A handbook of essential theory and research*. New York, NY: Psychology Press.

Bakker, A. B., Schaufeli, W. B., Leiter, M. P., & Taris, T. W. (2008). Work engagement: An emerging concept in occupational health psychology. *Work & Stress*, 22(3), 187–200. doi:10.1080/02678370802393649

Bakker, A. B., Tims, M., & Derks, D. (2012). Proactive personality and job performance: The role of job crafting and work engagement. *Human Relations*, 65(10), 1359–1378. doi:10.1177/0018726712453471

Baltes, B. B., Zhdanova, L. S., & Clark, M. A. (2011). Examining the relationships between personality, coping strategies, and work–family conflict. *Journal of Business and Psychology*, 26(4), 517–530. doi:10.1007/s10869-010-9207-0

Bargh, J. A., Chen, M., & Burrows, L. (1996). Automaticity of social behavior: Direct effects of trait construct and stereotype activation on action. *Journal of Personality and Social Psychology*, 71(2), 230–244. doi:10.1037/0022-3514.71.2.230

Barling, J., Weber, T., & Kelloway, E. K. (1996). Effects of transformational leadership training on attitudinal and financial outcomes: A field experiment. *Journal of Applied Psychology*, 81, 827–832. doi:10.1037/0021-9010.81.6.827

Barrick, M. R., Mount, M. K., & Li, N. (2013). The theory of purposeful work behavior: The role of personality, higher-order goals, and job characteristics. *The Academy of Management Review*, 38(1), 132–153. doi:10.5465/amr.2010.0479

Barsade, S. G. (2002). The ripple effects: Emotional contagion and its influence on group behavior. *Administrative Science Quarterly*, 47(4), 644–675. doi:10.2307/3094912

Bartone, P. T., Roland, R. R., Picano, J. J., & Williams, T. J. (2008). Psychological hardiness predicts success in U.S. Army Special Forces candidates. *International Journal of Selection And Assessment*, 16(1), 78–81. doi:10.1111/j.1468-2389. 2008.00412.x

Bass, B. M. (1985). *Leadership and performance beyond expectations*. New York, NY: The Free Press.

Bass, B. M. (1998). *Transformational leadership: Industrial, military, and educational impact*. Mahwah, NJ: Erlbaum.

Bass, B. M., & Avolio, B. J. (1990). *Transformational leadership development: Manual for the Multifactor Leadership Questionnaire*. Palo Alto, CA: Consulting Psychologist Press.

Bateman, T. S., & Crant, J. (1993). The proactive component of organizational behavior: A measure and correlates. *Journal of Organizational Behavior*, 14(2), 103–118. doi: 10.1002/job.4030140202

Bateman, T. S., Griffin, R. W., & Rubinstein, D. (1987). Social information processing and group-induced shifts in responses to task design. *Group & Organization Studies*, 12(1), 88–108. doi:10.1177/105960118701200107

Bateman, T. S., & Organ, D. W. (1983). Job satisfaction and the good soldier: The relationship between affect and employee "citizenship." *Academy of Management Journal*, 26(4), 587–595. doi:10.2307/255908

Baugher, J. E., & Roberts, J. (2004). Workplace hazards, unions, and coping styles. *Labor Studies Journal*, 29(2), 83–106.

Baumeister, R. F. (1991). *Meanings in life*. New York, NY: Guilford Press. doi:10.1207/s15327965pli0704_2

Baumeister, R. F., & Leary, M. R. (1995). The need to belong: Desire for interpersonal attachments as a fundamental human motivation. *Psychological Bulletin*, 117(3), 497–529. doi: 10.1037/0033-2909.117.3.497

Baumeister, R. F., & Vohs, K. D. (2002). The pursuit of meaningfulness in life. In C. R. Snyder & S. J. Lopez (Eds.), *The handbook of positive psychology* (pp. 608–619). New York, NY: Oxford University Press.

Bavelas, J. B., Black, A., Lemery, C. R., & Mullett, J. (1986). 'I show how you feel': Motor mimicry as a communicative act. *Journal of Personality and Social Psychology*, 50(2), 322–329. doi:10.1037/0022-3514.50.2.322

Becherer, R. C., Morgan, F. W., & Richard, L. M. (1982). The job characteristics of industrial salespersons: Relationships to motivation and satisfaction. *Journal of Marketing*, 46, 125–135. doi:10.2307/1251368

Becker, H. S. (1960). Notes on the concept of commitment. *American Journal of Sociology*, 66, 32–40. doi:10.1086/222820

Becker, T. E. (1992). Foci and bases of commitment: Are they distinctions worth making?. *Academy of Management Journal*, 35(1), 232–244. doi:10.2307/256481

Beehr, T. A., & Gupta, N. (1978). A note on the structure of employee withdrawal. *Organizational Behavior & Human Performance*, 21(1), 73–79.

Behson, S. J., Eddy, E. R., & Lorenzet, S. J. (2000). The importance of the critical psychological states in the job characteristics model: A meta-analytic and structural equations modeling examination. *Current Research in Social Psychology*, 5(12), 170–189.

Berg, J.M., Dutton, J.E., & Wrzesniewski, A. (2013). Job crafting and meaningful work. In B.J. Dik, Z.S. Byrne, & M.F. Steger (Eds.), *Purpose and meaning in the workplace* (pp. 81–104). Washington, DC: American Psychological Association.

Berg, J.M., Grant, A.M., & Johnson, V. (2010). When callings are calling: Crafting work and leisure in pursuit of unanswered occupational callings. *Organization Science*, 21(5), 973–994. doi:10.1287/orsc.1090.0497

Bergeron, D.M. (2007). The potential paradox of organizational citizenship behavior: Good citizens at what cost? *Academy of Management Review*, 32(4), 1078–1095. doi:10.5465/AMR.2007.26585791

Berlyne, D.E. (1966). Curiosity and exploration. *Science*, 153, 25–33. doi:10.1126/science.153.3731.25

Bhatnagar, J. (2012). Management of innovation: Role of psychological empowerment, work engagement and turnover intention in the Indian context. *The International Journal of Human Resource Management*, 23(5), 928–951. doi:10.1080/09585192.2012.651313

Bies, R.J. (1987). The predicament of injustice: The management of moral outrage. In L.L. Cummings & B.M. Staw (Eds.), *Research in organizational behavior* (Vol. 9, pp. 289–319). Greenwich, CT: JAI Press.

Bies, R.J., & Moag, J.S. (1986). Interactional justice: Communication criteria of fairness. In R.J. Lewicki, B.H. Sheppard, & M.H. Bazerman (Eds.), *Research on negotiation in organizations: Vol. 1.* (pp. 43–55). Greenwich, CT: JAI Press.

Bies, R.J., & Tripp, T.M. (2005). The study of revenge in the workplace: Conceptual, ideological, and empirical issues. In S. Fox & P.E. Spector (Eds.), *Counterproductive work behavior: Investigations of actors and targets* (pp. 65–81). Washington, DC: American Psychological Association. doi:10.1037/10893-003

Biggs, A., Brough, P., & Barbour, J.P. (2013). Strategic alignment with organizational priorities and work engagement: A multi-wave analysis. *Journal of Organizational Behavior*, Advanced online publication. doi:10.1002/job.1866

Binning, J.F., & Barrett, G.V. (1989). Validity of personnel decisions: A conceptual analysis of the inferential and evidential bases. *Journal of Applied Psychology*, 74(3), 478–494. doi:10.1037/0021-9010.74.3.478

Bipp, T., & Kleinbeck, U. (2011). The effect of neuroticism in the process of goal pursuit. *Personality and Individual Differences*, 51(4), 454–459. doi:10.1016/j.paid.2011.04.014

Biswas, S., & Bhatnagar, J. (2013). Mediator analysis of employee engagement: Role of perceived organizational support, P-O Fit, organizational commitment and job satisfaction. *Vikalpa: The Journal For Decision Makers*, 38(1), 27–40.

Blau, P.M. (1964). *Exchange and power in social life*. New York, NY: Wiley.

Borman, W.C., & Motowidlo, S.J. (1997). Task performance and contextual performance: The meaning for personnel selection research. *Human Performance*, 10(2), 99–109. doi:10.1207/s15327043hup1002_3

Bretz, R.D., Ash, R.A., & Dreher, G.F. (1989). Do people make the place? An examination of the attraction-selection-attrition hypothesis. *Personnel Psychology*, 42(3), 561–581. doi:10.1111/j.1744-6570.1989.tb00669.x

Britt, T.W. (1999). Engaging the self in the field: Testing the triangle model of responsibility. *Personality and Social Psychology Bulletin*, 25(6), 696–706.

Britt, T. W., & Bliese, P. D. (2003). Testing the stress–buffering effects of self engagement among soldiers on a military operation. *Journal of Personality, 71*(2), 245–266.

Britt, T. W., Mckibben, E. S., Greene-Shortridge, T. M., Odle-Dusseau, H. N., & Herleman, H. A. (2012). Self-engagement moderates the mediated relationship between organizational constraints and organizational citizenship behaviors via rated leadership. *Journal of Applied Social Psychology, 42*(8), 1830–1846. doi:10.1111/j.1559-1816.2012.00920.x

Brooke, P. P., Russell, D. W., & Price, J. L. (1988). Discriminant validation of measures of job satisfaction, job involvement, and organizational commitment. *Journal of Applied Psychology, 73*(2), 139–145. doi:10.1037/0021-9010.73.2.139

Brophy, J., Rohrkemper, M., Rashid, H., & Goldberger, M. (1983). Relationships between teachers' presentations of classroom tasks and students' engagement in those tasks. *Journal of Educational Psychology, 75*(4), 544–552. doi:10.1037/0022-0663.75.4.544

Brown, A., Kitchell, M., O'Neill, T., Lockliear, J., Vosler, A., Kubek, D., & Dale, L. (2001). Identifying meaning and perceived satisfaction within the context of work. *Work, 16*, 219–226.

Brown, K., & Ryan, R. M. (2003). The benefits of being present: Mindfulness and its role in psychological well-being. *Journal of Personality and Social Psychology, 84*(4), 822–848. doi:10.1037/0022-3514.84.4.822

Brown, S. B. (1996). A meta-analysis and review of organizational research on job involvement. *Psychological Bulletin, 20*, 235–255. doi:10.1037//0033-2909.120.2.235

Brown, W., & May, D. (2012). Organizational change and development: The efficacy of transformational leadership training. *Journal of Management Development, 31*(6), 520–536. doi:10.1108/02621711211230830

Brunetto, Y., Teo, S. T., Shacklock, K., & Farr-Wharton, R. (2012). Emotional intelligence, job satisfaction, well-being and engagement: explaining organisational commitment and turnover intentions in policing. *Human Resource Management Journal, 22*(4), 428–441. doi:10.1111/j.1748-8583.2012.00198.x

Buckingham, M., & Coffman, C. (1999). *First, break all the rules: What the world's greatest managers do differently.* New York, NY: Simon & Schuster

Bukowski, W. M., Motzoi, C., & Meyer, F. (2009). Friendship as process, function, and outcome. In K. H. Rubin, V. M. Bukowski, & B. Laursen (Eds.), *Handbook of peer interactions, relationships, and groups* (pg. 217–231). New York, NY: Guilford Press.

Burke, R. J. (2001). Workaholism in organizations: The role of organizational values. *Personnel Review, 30*(6), 637–645. doi:10.1108/EUM0000000005977

Burke, R. J. (2009). Working to live or living to work: Should individuals and organizations care? *Journal of Business Ethics, 84*, 167–172. doi:10.1007/s10551-008-9703-6

Burke, R. J. (2010). Flow, work satisfaction and psychological well-being at the workplace. *IUP Journal of Soft Skills, 4*(1/2), 37–48.

Burke, R. J., Burgess, Z., & Oberklaid, F. (2003). Workaholism and divorce among Australian psychologists. *Psychological Reports, 93*(1), 91–92.

Burke, R. J., & Matthiesen, S. (2004). Workaholism among Norwegian journalists: Antecedents and consequences. *Stress & Health: Journal of the*

International Society for the Investigation of Stress, 20(5), 301–308. doi:10.1002/smi.1025

Burke, R. J., Richardsen, A. M., & Martinussen, M. (2004). Workaholism among Norwegian senior managers: New research directions. *International Journal of Management*, 21(4), 415–426.

Burns, J. M. (1978). *Leadership*. New York: Harper and Row. doi: 10.1177/1745691610393980

Butler, J., Doherty, M. S., & Potter, R. M. (2007). Social antecedents and consequences of interpersonal rejection sensitivity. *Personality & Individual Differences*, 43(6), 1376–1385. doi:10.1016/j.paid.2007.04.006

Byrne, Z. S. & Cropanzano, R. (2001). History of organizational Justice: The founders speak. In R. Cropanzano (Ed.), *Justice in the Workplace: Vol. II. From theory to practice* (pp. 3–26). Mahwah, NJ: Erlbaum.

Byrne, Z. S., Dik, B. J., & Chiaburu, D. S. (2008). Alternatives to traditional mentoring in fostering career success. *Journal of Vocational Behavior*, 72(3), 429–442. doi:10.1016/j.jvb.2007.11.010

Byrne, Z. S., & Hochwarter, W. A. (2008). Perceived organizational support and performance. *Journal of Managerial Psychology*, 23(1), 54–72. doi:10.1108/02683940810849666

Byrne, Z. S., Mueller-Hanson, R. A., Cardador, J. M., Thornton III, G. C., Schuler, H., Frintrup, A., & Fox, S. (2004). Measuring achievement motivation: Tests of equivalency for English, German, and Israeli versions of the achievement motivation inventory. *Personality and Individual Differences*, 37, 203–217. doi:10.1016/j.paid.2003.08.012

Byrne, Z. S., Palmer, C. E., Smith, C. L., & Weidert, J. M. (2011). The engaged employee face of organizations. In M. A. Sarlak (Ed.), *The new faces of organizations in the 21st century* (Vol. 1, pp. 93–135). Canada: NAISIT Publishers.

Byrne, Z. S., Peters, J. M., & Drake, T. (2014). *Measurement of employee engagement: The Utrecht Work Engagement Scale versus the Job Engagement Scale*. Manuscript submitted for publication.

Byrne, Z. S., Peters, J. M., Rechlin, A., Smith, C. L., & Kedharnath, U. (2013). *Fostering employee engagement through job control and work-related leader support*. Manuscript submitted for publication.

Byrne, Z. S., Pitts, V. E., Wilson, C. M., & Steiner, Z. J. (2012). Trusting the fair supervisor: the role of supervisory support in performance appraisals. *Human Resource Management Journal*, 22(2), 129–147. doi:10.1111/j.1748-8583.2012.00193.x

Cable, D. M., & Judge, T. A. (1996). Person–organization fit, job choice decisions, and organizational entry. *Organizational Behavior and Human Decision Processes*, 67(3), 294–311. doi:10.1006/obhd.1996.0081

Campbell, A. (1976). Subjective measures of well-being. *American Psychologist*, 31(2), 117–124. doi:10.1037/0003-066X.31.2.117

Campbell, J. P. (1990). Modeling the performance prediction problem in industrial and organizational psychology. In M. D. Dunnette & L. M. Hough (Eds.), *Handbook of industrial and organizational psychology* (Vol. 1, 2nd ed., pp. 687–732). Palo Alto, CA: Consulting Psychologists Press.

Campbell, J. P., Dunnette, M. D., Lawler, E. E., & Weick, K. E. (1970). *Managerial behavior, performance, and effectiveness*. New York, NY: McGraw-Hill.

Campbell, J. P., McHenry, J. J., & Wise, L. L. (1990). Modeling job performance in a population of jobs. *Personnel Psychology*, *43*(2), 313–333. doi:10.1111/j.1744-6570.1990.tb01561.x

Cannon, M. D., & Edmondson, A. C. (2001). Confronting failure: antecedents and consequences of shared beliefs about failure in organizational work groups. *Journal of Organizational Behavior*, *22*(2), 161–177.

Cannon-Bowers, J. A., & Salas, E. (2001). Reflections on shared cognition. *Journal Of Organizational Behavior*, *22*(2), 195–202. doi:10.1002/job.82

Cannon-Bowers, J. A., Salas, E., & Converse, S. (1993). Shared mental models in expert team decision making. In N. J. Castellan (Ed.), *Individual and group decision making: Current issues* (pp. 221–246). Hillsdale, NJ: Erlbaum.

Carnegie Foundation for the Advancement of Teaching (2009). Retrieved http://classifications.carnegiefoundation.org/descriptions/community_engagement.php

Caruso, D. R., Mayer, J. D., & Salovey, P. (2002). Emotional intelligence and emotional leadership. In R. E. Riggio, S. E. Murphy, & F. J. Pirozzolo (Eds.), *Multiple intelligences and leadership* (pp. 55–74). Mahwah, NJ: Erlbaum.

Carver, C., & Scheier, M. (1998). *On the self regulation of behavior.* New York, NY: Cambridge University Press.

Cascio, W. F. (1998). *Applied psychology in human resource management.* Upper Saddle River, NJ: Prentice Hall.

Case, J. (1995). *Open-book management: The coming business revolution.* New York, NY: HarperBusiness

Chalofsky, N., & Krishna, V. (2009). Meaningfulness, commitment, and engagement: The intersection of a deeper level of intrinsic motivation. *Advances in Developing Human Resources*, *11*, 189–203. doi:10.1177/1523422309333147

Champoux, J. E. (1991). A multivariate test of the Job Characteristics Theory of Work Motivation. *Journal of Organizational Behavior*, *12*(5), 431–446. doi:10.1002/job.4030120507

Chan, A. W., Snape, E., & Redman, T. (2011). Multiple foci and bases of commitment in a Chinese workforce. *The International Journal of Human Resource Management*, *22*(16), 3290–3304. doi:10.1080/09585192.2011.586866

Chartrand, T. L., & Bargh, J. A. (1999). The chameleon effect: The perception–behavior link and social interaction. *Journal of Personality and Social Psychology*, *76*(6), 893–910. doi:10.1037/0022-3514.76.6.893

Chartrand, T. L., Maddux, W. W., & Lakin, J. L. (2005). Beyond the perception-behavior link: The ubiquitous utility and motivational moderators of nonconscious mimicry. In R. R. Hassin, J. S. Uleman, & J. A. Bargh (Eds.), *The new unconscious* (pp. 334–361). New York, NY: Oxford University Press.

Chatman, J. A. (1989). Improving interactional organizational research: A model of person-organization fit. *Academy of Management Review*, *14*(3), 333–349. doi:10.5465/AMR.1989.4279063

Chatman, J. A. (1991). Matching people and organizations: Selection and socialization in public accounting firms. *Administrative Science Quarterly*, *36*(3), 459–484. doi:10.2307/2393204

Chen, C.-C., & Chiu, S.-F. (2009). The mediating role of job involvement in the relationship between job characteristics and organizational citizenship behavior. *The Journal of Social Psychology*, *149*, 474–494. doi:10.3200/SOCP.149.4.474-494

Chen, Z., Zhang, X., & Vogel, D. (2011). Exploring the underlying processes between conflict and knowledge sharing: A work-engagement perspective. *Journal of Applied Social Psychology*, *41*(5), 1005–1033. doi:10.1111/j.1559-1816.2011.00745.x

Cheng, B., Jiang, D., & Riley, J.H. (2003). Organizational commitment, supervisory commitment and employee outcomes in the Chinese context: proximal hypothesis or global hypothesis? *Journal of Organizational Behavior*, *24*(3), 313–334. doi:10.1002/job.190

Cherniss, C., Grimm, L.G., & Liautaud, J.P. (2010). Process-designed training: A new approach for helping leaders develop emotional and social competence. *Journal Of Management Development*, *29*(5), 413–431. doi:10.1108/02621711011039196

Cherrington, D.J. (1980). *The work ethic*. New York, NY: American Management Association

Chiaburu, D. S. (2010). How do coworkers matter? Examining influences on peers' role definitions, attitudes, OCBs, and performance. *Dissertation Abstracts International Section A*, *70*

Christian, M. S., Garza, A. S., & Slaughter, J. E. (2011). Work engagement: A quantitative review and test of its relations with task and contextual performance. *Personnel Psychology*, *64*, 89–136. doi:10.1111/j.1744-6570.2010.01203.x

Chughtai, A., & Buckley, F. (2011). Work engagement: Antecedents, the mediating role of learning goal orientation and job performance. *The Career Development International*, *16*(7), 684–705. doi:10.1108/13620431111187290

CIPD. (2009). *Employee engagement*. Retrieved from www.cipd.co.uk/hr-topics/employee-engagement.aspx

Clore, G.L., Schwarz, N., & Conway, M. (1994). Affective causes and consequences of social information processing. In R.S. Wyer & T.K. Srull (Eds.), *Handbook of social cognition* (pp. 323–417). Hillsdale, NJ: Erlbaum.

Cochran, D.S., David, F.R., & Gibson, C. (2008). A framework for developing an effective mission statement. *Journal of Business Strategies*, *25*(2), 27–39.

Cohen, A. (2007). One nation, many cultures: A cross-cultural study of the relationship between personal cultural values and commitment in the workplace to in-role performance and organizational citizenship behavior. *Cross-Cultural Research: The Journal of Comparative Social Science*, *41*(3), 273–300.

Cole, M.S., Walter, F., Bedeian, A.G., & O'Boyle, E.H. (2012). Job burnout and employee engagement: A meta-analytic examination of construct proliferation. *Journal of Management*, *38*(5), 1550–1581. doi:10.1177/0149206311415252

Collins, S. (2007). Social workers, resilience, positive emotions and optimism. *Practice: Social Work in Action*, *19*(4), 255–269. doi:10.1080/09503150701728186

Conger, J.A., & Kanungo, R.N. (1988). The empowerment process: Integrating theory and practice. *Academy of Management Review*, *13*(3), 471–482. doi:10.5465/AMR.1988.4306983f

Constantine, M. G. (2001). Independent and interdependent self-construals as predictors of multicultural case conceptualization ability in counsellor trainees.

Counselling Psychology Quarterly, 14(1), 33–42. doi:10.1080/09515070 110059124

Cooper, C. L., & Cartwright, S. (1994). Healthy mind; healthy organization: A proactive approach to occupational stress. *Human Relations, 47*(4), 455–471. doi:10.1177/001872679404700405

Cortina, L. M., & Magley, V. J. (2009). Patterns and profiles of response to incivility in the workplace. *Journal of Occupational Health Psychology, 14*(3), 272–288. doi:10.1037/a0014934

Cortina, L. M., Magley, V. J., Williams, J., & Langhout, R. (2001). Incivility in the workplace: Incidence and impact. *Journal of Occupational Health Psychology, 6*(1), 64–80. doi:10.1037/1076-8998.6.1.64

Costa, P., & McCrae, R. R. (2009). The Five-Factor Model and the NEO Inventories. In J. N. Butcher (Ed.), *Oxford handbook of personality assessment* (pp. 299–322). New York, NY: Oxford University Press. doi:10.1093/oxfordhb/ 9780195366877.013.0016

Costa, P. T., & McCrae, R. R. (1992). The five-factor model of personality and its relevance to personality disorders. *Journal of Personality Disorders, 6*(4), 343–359. doi:10.1521/pedi.1992.6.4.343

Crawford, E. R., LePine, J. A., & Rich, B. (2010). Linking job demands and resources to employee engagement and burnout: A theoretical extension and meta-analytic test. *Journal of Applied Psychology, 95*(5), 834–848. doi:10.1037/a0019364

Cronbach, L. J. (1951). Coefficient alpha and the internal structure of tests. *Psychometrika, 16,* 297–334.

Cronbach, L. J., & Meehl, P. E. (1955). Construct validity in psychological tests. *Psychological Bulletin, 52,* 281–302. doi:10.1037/h0040957

Cross, S. E., & Gore, J. S. (2012). Cultural models of the self. In M. R. Leary & J. Tangney (Eds.), *Handbook of self and identity* (2nd ed., pp. 587–614). New York, NY: Guilford Press.

Crumpton, H., & Gregory, A. (2011). I'm not learning: The role of academic relevancy for low-achieving students. *The Journal of Educational Research, 104*(1), 42–53. doi:10.1080/00220670903567398

Csikszentmihalyi, M. (1990). *Flow: The psychology of optimal experience.* New York, NY: Harper Perennial.

Csikszentmihalyi, M. (1996). *Creativity: Flow and the psychology of discovery and invention.* New York: HarperCollins.

Csikszentmihalyi, M. (1997). *Finding flow: The psychology of engagement with everyday life.* New York, NY: Basic Books.

Csikszentmihalyi, M., & Kleiber, D. A. (1991). Leisure and self-actualization. In B. L. Driver, P. J. Brown, & G. L. Peterson (Eds.), *Benefits of Leisure* (pp. 91–102). State College, PA: Venture Publishing.

Csikszentmihalyi, M., & Rathunde, K. (1993). The measurement of flow in everyday life: Toward a theory of emergent motivation. *Nebraska Symposium on Motivation, 40,* 57–97.

Csikszentmihalyi, M., Abuhamdeh, S., & Nakamura, J. (2005). Flow. In A. Elliot & C. S. Dweck (Eds.), *Handbook of competence and motivation* (pp. 598–608). New York, NY: Guilford Press.

Dalal, R.S., Baysinger, M., Brummel, B.J., & LeBreton, J.M. (2012). The relative importance of employee engagement, other job attitudes, and trait affect as predictors of job performance. *Journal of Applied Social Psychology, 42,* E295–E325. doi:10.1111/j.1559-1816.2012.01017.x

Dalal, R.S., Brummel, B.J., Wee, S., & Thomas, L.L. (2008). Defining employee engagement for productive research and practice. *Industrial and Organizational Psychology: Perspectives on Science and Practice, 1*(1), 52–55. doi:10.1111/j.1754-9434.2007.00008.x

Dale Carnegie Organization (2007). *Beyond rules of engagement: How can organizational leaders build a culture that supports high engagement?* Retrieved from www.dalecarnegie.com/imap/white_papers/employee_engagement_white_paper/

Damasio, A. (1999). *The feeling of what happens: Body and emotion in the making of consciousness.* Fort Worth, TX: Harcourt College Publishers.

Dane, E. (2011). Paying attention to mindfulness and its effects on task performance in the workplace. *Journal of Management, 37*(4), 997–1018. doi:10.1177/0149206310367948

Danner, F., & Lonky, E. (1981). A cognitive-developmental approach to the effects of rewards on intrinsic motivation. *Child Development, 52*(3), 1043–1052. doi:10.2307/1129110

Davidov, E., Schmidt, P., & Schwartz, S.H. (2008). Bringing values back in: The adequacy of the European social survey to measure values in 20 countries. *Public Opinion Quarterly, 72*(3), 420–445. doi:10.1093/poq/nfn035

De Beer, L., Rothmann, S. Jr., & Pienaar, J. (2012). A confirmatory investigation of a job demands-resources model using a categorical estimator. *Psychological Reports, 111*(2), 528–544. doi:10.2466/01.03.10.PR0.111.5.528-544

Deci, E.L. (1975). *Intrinsic motivation.* New York, NY: Plenum.

Deci, E.L., Koestner, R., & Ryan, R.M. (1999). A meta-analytic review of experiments examining the effects of extrinsic rewards on intrinsic motivation. *Psychological Bulletin, 125,* 627–668. doi:10.1037/0033-2909.125.6.627

Deci, E.L., & Ryan, R.M. (1980). The empirical exploration of intrinsic motivational processes. In L. Berkowitz (Ed.), *Advances in experimental social psychology* (Vol. 13, pp. 39–80). New York, NY: Academic Press.

Deci, E.L., & Ryan, R.M. (1985). *Intrinsic motivation and self-determination in human behavior.* New York, NY: Plenum.

Deckop, J.R., Mangel, R., & Cirka, C.C. (1999). Getting more than you pay for: Organizational citizenship behavior and pay-for-performance plans. *Academy of Management Journal, 42*(4), 420–428. doi:10.2307/257012

Demerouti, E., Bakker, A.B., de Jonge, J., Janssen, P.M., & Schaufeli, W.B. (2001). Burnout and engagement at work as a function of demands and control. *Scandinavian Journal of Work, Environment & Health, 27*(4), 279–286. doi:10.5271/sjweh.615

Deming, W.E.(1986). *Out of the crisis.* Cambridge, MA: MIT Center for Advanced Engineering Study

Deutsch, M. (1985). *Distributive justice: A social-psychological perspective.* New Haven, CT: Yale University Press.

Diagnostic and statistical manual of mental disorders. (1994). *DSM-IV.* 4th ed. Washington, DC: American Psychiatric Association.

Dictionary of occupational titles. (1991). 4th ed., rev. 1991. Washington, D.C.: The Administration.

Dijksterhuis, A., & Nordgren, L. F. (2006). A Theory of unconscious thought. *Perspectives on Psychological Science*, *1*(2), 95–109. doi:10.1111/j.1745-6916.2006.00007.x

Dijksterhuis, A., & van Olden, Z. (2006). On the benefits of thinking unconsciously: Unconscious thought can increase post-choice satisfaction. *Journal of Experimental Social Psychology*, *42*(5), 627–631. doi:10.1016/j.jesp.2005.10.008

Dik, B. J., Byrne, Z. S., & Steger, M. J. (Editors, 2013). *Purpose and meaning in the workplace*. Washington, DC: American Psychological Association.

Dikkers, J. E., Jansen, P. W., de Lange, A. H., Vinkenburg, C. J., & Kooij, D. (2010). Proactivity, job characteristics, and engagement: A longitudinal study. *The Career Development International*, *15*(1), 59–77. doi:10.1108/13620431011020899

Duffy, E. (1957). The psychological significance of the concept of "arousal" or "activation." *Psychological Review*, *64*, 265–275. doi:10.1037/h0048837

Dunham, R. B., Smith, F. J., & Blackburn, R. S. (1977). Validation of the Index of Organizational Reactions with the JDI, the MSQ, and Faces Scales. *Academy of Management Journal*, *20*(3), 420–432. doi:10.2307/255415

Dvir, T., Eden, D., Avolio, B. J., & Shamir, B. (2002). Impact of transformational leadership on follower development and performance: A field experiment. *Academy of Management Journal*, *45*(4), 735–744. doi:10.2307/3069307

Eagly, A. H., & Chaiken, S. (1998). Attitude structure and function. In D. T. Gilbert, S. T. Fiske, G. Lindzey (Eds.), *The handbook of social psychology* (Vol. 1&2, 4th ed., pp. 269–322). New York, NY: McGraw-Hill.

Eagly, A. H., & Chaiken, S. (2007). The advantages of an inclusive definition of attitude. *Social Cognition*, *25*(5), 582–602.

Edwards, C. C. (2009). The pursuit of happiness. *Engineering & Technology*, *4*(4), 76–79. doi:10.1049/et.2009.0419

Eisenberger, R., Huntington, R., Hutchison, S., & Sowa, D. (1986). Perceived organizational support. *Journal of Applied Psychology*, *71*(3), 500–507. doi:10.1037/0021-9010.71.3.500

Eisenberger, R., Stinglhamber, F., Vandenberghe, C., Sucharski, I., & Rhoades, L. (2002). Perceived supervisor support: Contributions to perceived organizational support and employee retention. *Journal of Applied Psychology*, *87*, 565–573.

Ekman, P. (1992). Are there basic emotions? *Psychological Review*, *99*, 550–553. doi:10.1037/0033-295X.99.3.550

Erez, A., & Judge, T. A. (2001). Relationship of core self-evaluations to goal setting, motivation, and performance. *Journal of Applied Psychology*, *86*(6), 1270–1279. doi:10.1037/0021-9010.86.6.1270

Erez, M. (1994). Toward a model of cross-cultural industrial and organizational psychology. In H. C. Triandis, M. D. Dunnette, & L. M. Hough (Eds.), *Handbook of industrial and organizational psychology* (Vol. 4, 2nd ed., pp. 559–607). Palo Alto, CA: Consulting Psychologists Press.

Fairhurst, K., & May, C. (2006). What general practitioners find satisfying in their work: Implications for health care system reform. *Annals of Family Medicine*, *4*(6), 500–505. doi:10.1370/afm.565

Fairlie, P. (2011). Meaningful work, employee engagement, and other key employee outcomes: Implications for human resource development. *Advances in Developing Human Resources, 13*(4), 508–525. doi:10.1177/1523422311431679

Ferris, G. R., & Kacmar, K. (1992). Perceptions of organizational politics. *Journal of Management, 18*(1), 93–116.

Ferris, G. R., Frink, D. D., Beehr, T. A., & Gilmore, D. C. (1995). Political fairness and fair politics: The conceptual integration of divergent constructs. In R. S. Cropanzano & K. M. Kacmar (Eds.), *Organizational Politics, Justice, and Support: Managing the Social Climate of the Workplace.* (pp. 21–36). Westport, CT: Quorum Books.

Ferris, G. R., Russ, G. S., & Fandt, P. M. (1989). Politics in organizations. In R. A. Giacalone & P. Rosenfeld (Eds.), *Impression management in the organization* (pp. 143–170). Hillsdale, NJ: Lawrence Erlbaum Associates, Inc.

Fine, G., & Holyfield, L. (1996). Secrecy, trust, and dangerous leisure: Generating group cohesion in voluntary organizations. *Social Psychology Quarterly, 59*(1), 22–38. doi:10.2307/2787117

Fine, M. (1983). The social context and a sense of injustice: The option to challenge. *Representative Research in Social Psychology, 13,* 15–33.

Fine, S., Horowitz, I., Weigler, H., & Basis, L. (2010). Is character good enough? The effects of situational variables on the relationship between integrity and counterproductive work behaviors. *Human Resource Management Review, 20,* 73–84.

Fineman, S. (1983). Work meanings, non-work, and the taken-for-granted. *Journal of Management Studies, 20*(2), 143–157.

Fisher, C. D. (1978). The effects of personal control, competence, and extrinsic reward systems on intrinsic motivation. *Organizational Behavior and Human Performance, 21,* 273–288. doi:10.1016/0030-5073(78)90054-5

Fiske, A., Kitayama, S., Markus, H., & Nisbett, R. E. (1998). The cultural matrix of social psychology. In D. T. Gilbert, S. T. Fiske, & G. Lindzey (Eds.), *The handbook of social psychology* (Vol. 1 & 2, 4th ed., pp. 915–981). New York, NY: McGraw-Hill.

Fiske, S. T., & Taylor, S. E. (1991). *Social cognition* (2nd ed.). New York, NY: McGraw-Hill.

Flade, P. (2003). Great Britain's workforce lacks inspiration. *Gallup Management Journal Online,* 1–3.

Forest, J., Mageau, G. A., Sarrazin, C., & Morin, E. M. (2011). "Work is my passion": The different affective, behavioural, and cognitive consequences of harmonious and obsessive passion toward work. *Canadian Journal of Administrative Sciences, 28*(1), 17–30. doi:10.1002/cjas.170

Francaro, K. E. (2007). The consequences of micromanaging. *Contract Management, 47*(7), 4–8.

Frank, L. L., & Hackman, J. (1975). A failure of job enrichment: The case of the change that wasn't. *Journal of Applied Behavioral Science, 11*(4), 413–436. doi:10.1177/002188637501100404

Frankl, V. E. (1984). *Man's search for meaning* (3rd ed.). New York, NY: First Washington Square Press. (Original work published in 1963).

Frankl, V. E. (1967). *Psychotherapy and existentialism: Selected papers on logotherapy.* New York: Washington Square Press.

Frankl, V. E. (1978). *The unheard cry for meaning: Psychotherapy and human-ism*. New York, NY: Washington Square Press. http://dx.doi.org/10.1037/h0086035

Fredrickson, B. L. (2001). The role of positive emotions in positive psychology: The broaden-and-build theory of positive emotions. *American Psychologist, 56*, 218–226. doi:10.1037/0003-066X.56.3.218

Fredrickson, B. L., Tugade, M. M., Waugh, C. E., & Larkin, G. R. (2003). What good are positive emotions in crisis? A prospective study of resilience and emotions following the terrorist attacks on the United States on September 11th, 2001. *Journal Of Personality And Social Psychology, 84*(2), 365–376. doi:10.1037/0022-3514.84.2.365

Freeney, Y. M., & Tiernan, J. (2009). Exploration of the facilitators of and barri-ers to work engagement in nursing. *International Journal of Nursing Studies, 46*(12), 1557–1565. doi:10.1016/j.ijnurstu.2009.05.003

Frese, M., Kring, W., Soose, A., & Zempel, J. (1996). Personal initiative at work: Differences between East and West Germany. *Academy of Management Jour-nal, 39*, 37–63.

Friedman, H. S., Riggio, R. E., & Casella, D. F. (1988). Nonverbal skill, personal charisma, and initial attraction. *Personality and Social Psychology Bulletin, 14*(1), 203–211. doi:10.1177/0146167288141020

Friedman, S. D., Christensen, P., & DeGroot, J. (1998). Work and life: the end of the zero-sum game. *Harvard Business Review, 76*(6), 119–129.

Frijda, N. H. (1987). Emotion, cognitive structure, and action tendency. *Cogni-tion & Emotion, 1*, 115–143. doi:10.1080/02699938708408043

Frijda, N. H. (1988). The laws of emotion. *American Psychologist, 43*(5), 349–358. doi:10.1037/0003-066X.43.5.349

Gagné, M., Senécal, C. B., & Koestner, R. (1997). Proximal job characteristics, feelings of empowerment, and intrinsic motivation: A multidimensional model. *Journal of Applied Social Psychology, 27*(14), 1222–1240. doi:10.1111/j.1559-1816.1997.tb01803.x

Gallup Organization. (2002, April 15). The high cost of disengaged employees. *Gallup Management Journal,* 1–2. Retrieved from http://gmj.gallup.com

Gallup Organization. (2013a). *State of the American workplace: Employee engagement insights for U.S. business leaders*. Retrieved from www.gallup.com/strategicconsulting/163007/state-american-workplace.aspx

Gallup Organization. (2013b). *State of the global workplace: Employee engage-ment insights for business leaders worldwide*. Retrieved from www.gallup.com/file/strategicconsulting/164735/State%20of%20the%20Global%20Workplace%20Report%202013.pdf

Ganster, D. C. (1995). Interventions for building healthy organizations: Sugges-tions from the stress research literature. In L. R. Murphy, J. Jr. Hurrell, S. L. Sauter, & G. Keita (Eds.), *Job stress interventions* (pp. 323–336). Washington, DC: American Psychological Association. doi:10.1037/10183-021

Garczynski, A. M., Waldrop, J. S., Rupprecht, E. A., & Grawitch, M. J. (2013). Differentiation between work and nonwork self-aspects as a predictor of presenteeism and engagement: Cross-cultural differences. *Journal of Occupa-tional Health Psychology, 18*(4), 417–429. doi:10.1037/a0033988

Gebauer, J., Lowman, D., & Gordon, J. (2008). *Closing the engagement gap: How great companies unlock employee potential for superior results*. New York, NY: Portfolio.

George, J. M. (1990). Personality, affect, and behavior in groups. *Journal of Applied Psychology, 75*(2), 107–116. doi:10.1037/0021-9010.75.2.107

George, J. M. (2002). Affect regulation in groups and teams. In. R. G. Lord, R. J. Klimoski, & R. Kanfer (Eds.), *Emotions in the workplace: Understanding the structure and role of emotions in organizational behavior* (p.182–217). San Francisco, CA: Jossey-Bass

George, J. M. (2009). The illusion of will in organizational behavior research: Nonconscious processes and job design. *Journal of Management, 35*(6), 1318–1339. doi:10.1177/0149206309346337

George, J. M. (2010). More engagement is not necessarily better: The benefits of fluctuating levels of engagement. In S. L. Albrecht (Ed.), *Handbook of employee engagement: Perspectives, issues, research and practice* (pp. 253–263). Northampton, MA: Edward Elgar Publishing.

George, J. M., & Brief, A. P. (1992). Feeling good-doing good: A conceptual analysis of the mood at work-organizational spontaneity relationship. *Psychological Bulletin, 112*(2), 310–329. doi:10.1037/0033-2909.112.2.310

Gillet, N., Huart, I., Colombat, P., & Fouquereau, E. (2013). Perceived organizational support, motivation, and engagement among police officers. *Professional Psychology: Research And Practice, 44*(1), 46–55. doi:10.1037/a0030066

Glaser, J., & Kihlstrom, J. F. (2005). Compensatory automaticity: Unconscious volition is not an oxymoron. In R. R. Hassin, J. S. Uleman, & J. A. Bargh (Eds.), *The new unconscious* (pp. 171–195). New York, NY: Oxford University Press.

Goffman, E. (1961). *Encounters: Two studies in the sociology of interaction*. Indianapolis, IN: Bobbs-Merrill.

Graen, G. B., & Uhl-Bien, M. (1995). Relationship-based approach to leadership: Development of leader-member exchange (LMX) theory of leadership over 25 years: Applying a multi-level multi-domain perspective. *The Leadership Quarterly, 6*(2), 219–247. doi:10.1016/1048-9843(95)90036-5

Graham, H., Howard, K. J., & Dougall, A. (2012). The growth of occupational health psychology. In R. J. Gatchel & I. Z. Schultz (Eds.), *Handbook of occupational health and wellness* (pp. 39–59). New York, NY: Springer Science + Business Media. doi:10.1007/978-1-4614-4839-6_3

Green, K. W. (2010). Impact of recession-based workplace anxiety. *International Journal of Management & Enterprise Development, 9*(3), 213–232.

Gregory, B. T., Albritton, M., & Osmonbekov, T. (2010). The mediating role of psychological empowerment on the relationships between P–O fit, job satisfaction, and in-role performance. *Journal of Business and Psychology, 25*(4), 639–647. doi:10.1007/s10869-010-9156-7

Griffin, M. A., Parker, S. K., & Neal, A. (2008). Is behavioral engagement a distinct and useful construct? *Industrial and Organizational Psychology: Perspectives on Science and Practice, 1*(1), 48–51. doi:10.1111/j.1754-9434.2007.00007.x

Gronlund, N. E., & Linn, R. L. (1990). *Measurement and Evaluation in Teaching* (6th ed.). New York, NY: Macmillan.

Groysberg, B., & Slind, M. (2012). Leadership is a conversation. *Harvard Business Review*, 90(6), 76–84.

Gruenfeld, D. H., & Hollingshead, A. B. (1993). Sociocognition in work groups: The evolution of group integrative complexity and its relation to task performance. *Small Group Research*, 24(3), 383–405. doi:10.1177/1046496493243006

Guest, R. H. (1964). Better utilization of skills through job design. *Management of Personnel Quarterly*, 3(3), 3–11.

Guion, R. M., & Gibson, W. M. (1988). Personnel selection and placement. *Annual Review of Psychology*, 39, 349–374. doi:10.1146/annurev.ps.39.020188.002025

Guion, R. M., & Landy, F. J. (1972). The meaning of work and the motivation to work. *Organizational Behavior & Human Performance*, 7(2), 308–339. doi:10.1016/0030-5073(72)90020-7

Gundling, E., & Zanchettin, A. (2007). *Global diversity: Winning customers and engaging employees within world markets*. Boston, MA: Nicholas Brealey International.

Hackman, J., & Lawler, E. E., III. (1971). Employee reactions to job characteristics. *Journal of Applied Psychology*, 55(3), 259–286.

Hackman, J., & Oldham, G. R. (1975). Development of the Job Diagnostic Survey. *Journal of Applied Psychology*, 60(2), 159–170. doi:10.1037/h0076546

Hackman, J., & Oldham, G. R. (1976). Motivation through the design of work: Test of a theory. *Organizational Behavior & Human Performance*, 16(2), 250–279.

Hakanen, J. J., Bakker, A. B. & Schaufeli, W. B. (2006). Burnout and work engagement among teachers. *Journal of School Psychology, 43*, 495-513.

Hakanen, J. J., Perhoniemi, R., & Toppinen-Tanner, S. (2008). Positive gain spirals at work: From job resources to work engagement, personal initiative and work-unit innovativeness. *Journal of Vocational Behavior*, 73(1), 78–91. doi:10.1016/j.jvb.2008.01.003

Hakanen, J. J., Schaufeli, W. B., & Ahola, K. (2008). The Job Demands-Resources model: A three-year cross-lagged study of burnout, depression, commitment, and work engagement. *Work & Stress*, 22(3), 224–241. doi:10.1080/02678370802379432

Halbesleben, J. B., Harvey, J., & Bolino, M. C. (2009). Too engaged? A conservation of resources view of the relationship between work engagement and work interference with family. *Journal of Applied Psychology*, 94(6), 1452–1465. doi:10.1037/a0017595

Halbesleben, J. B., & Wheeler, A. R. (2008). The relative roles of engagement and embeddedness in predicting job performance and intention to leave. *Work & Stress*, 22(3), 242–256. doi:10.1080/02678370802383962

Halbesleben, J. B., Wheeler, A. R., & Shanine, K. K. (2013). The moderating role of attention-deficit/hyperactivity disorder in the work engagement–performance process. *Journal of Occupational Health Psychology*, 18(2), 132–143. doi:10.1037/a0031978

Hall, D. T. (1996). Implications: The new role of the career practitioner. In D. T. Hall & Associates (Eds.), *The career is dead, long live the career, a relational approach to careers* (pp. 314–336). San Francisco, CA: Jossey-Bass.

Hallberg, U., & Schaufeli, W.B. (2006). "Same same" but different: Can work engagement be discriminated from job involvement and organizational commitment? *European Journal of Psychology, 11*, 119–127.

Hansen, A.M., Byrne, Z.S., & Kiersch, C.E. (in press). How interpersonal leadership relates to employee engagement. *Journal of Managerial Psychology.*

Hardin, C.D., & Higgins, E. (1996). Shared reality: How social verification makes the subjective objective. In R.M. Sorrentino & E. Higgins (Eds.), *Handbook of motivation and cognition, Vol. 3: The interpersonal context* (pp. 28–84). New York, NY: Guilford Press.

Harpaz, I., & Snir, R. (2003). Workaholism: Its definition and nature. *Human Relations, 56*(3), 291–319. doi:10.1177/0018726703056003613

Harris, G.E., & Cameron, J.E. (2005). Multiple dimensions of organizational identification and commitment as predictors of turnover intentions and psychological well-being. *Canadian Journal of Behavioural Science/Revue Canadienne Des Sciences Du Comportement, 37*(3), 159–169. doi:10.1037/h0087253

Harrison, A. (2012). 5 steps to employee engagement: Improving your goals for organizational success. *Public Relations Tactics, 19*(11), 10.

Harrison, D.A., Newman, D.A., & Roth, P.L. (2006). How important are job attitudes? Meta-analytic comparisons of integrative behavioral outcomes and time sequences. *Academy of Management Journal, 49*(2), 305–325. doi:10.5465/AMJ.2006.20786077

Harter, J.K., Schmidt, F.L., & Hayes, T.L. (2002). Business-unit-level relationship between employee satisfaction, employee engagement, and business outcomes: A meta-analysis. *Journal of Applied Psychology, 87*(2), 268–279.

Haslam, N. (2006). Dehumanization: An integrative review. *Personality and Social Psychology Review, 10*, 252–264. doi:10.1207/s15327957pspr1003_4

Hassan, A., & Ahmed, F. (2011). Authentic Leadership, Trust and Work Engagement. *World Academy of Science, Engineering & Technology, 80*, 750–756.

Hatfield, E., Cacioppo, J.T., & Rapson, R.L. (1993). Emotional Contagion. *Current Directions In Psychological Science, 2*(3), 96–99. doi:10.1111/1467-8721.ep10770953

Hatfield, E., Cacioppo, J.T., & Rapson, R.L. (1994). *Emotional contagion.* New York, NY: Cambridge University Press.

Hatfield, E., Hsee, C.K., Costello, J., & Weisman, M. (1995). The impact of vocal feedback on emotional experience and expression. *Journal of Social Behavior & Personality, 10*(2), 293–312.

Hay Group. (2010). *The road to performance: Leveraging employee research to achieve business success.* Retrieved from https://www.haygroup.com/ww/downloads/details.aspx?ID=20768

Heil, G., Bennis, W., & Stephens, D.C. (2000). *Douglas McGregor, revisited: Managing the human side of the enterprise.* New York, NY: John Wiley.

Heine, S.J., Kitayama, S., Lehman, D.R., Takata, T., Ide, E., Leung, C., & Matsumoto, H. (2001). Divergent consequences of success and failure in Japan and North America: An investigation of self-improving motivations and malleable selves. *Journal of Personality and Social Psychology, 81*(4), 599–615. doi:10.1037/0022-3514.81.4.599

Herndon, F. (2008). Testing mindfulness with perceptual and cognitive factors: External vs. internal encoding, and the Cognitive Failures Questionnaire. *Personality and Individual Differences, 44*(1), 32–41. doi:10.1016/j.paid.2007.07.002

Hershcovis, M., Turner, N., Barling, J., Arnold, K. A., Dupré, K. E., Inness, M., LeBlanc, M. M., & Sivanathan, N. (2007). Predicting workplace aggression: A meta-analysis. *Journal of Applied Psychology, 92*(1), 228–238. doi:10.1037/0021-9010.92.1.228

Herzberg, F., Mausner, B., & Snyderman, B. B. (1959). *The motivation to work.* New York, NY: Wiley.

Hilgard, E. R. (1987). *Psychology in America: A historical survey.* San Diego, CA: Harcourt Brace Jovanovich.

Hirschfeld, R. R., & Thomas, C. H. (2008). Representations of trait engagement: Integration, additions, and mechanisms. *Industrial and Organizational Psychology: Perspectives on Science and Practice, 1*(1), 63–66. doi:10.1111/j.1754-9434.2007.00011.x

Hitt, W. D. (1995). The learning organization: Some reflections on organizational renewal. *Leadership & Organization Development Journal, 16*(8), 17–25. doi:10.1108/01437739510097996

Ho, V. T., Wong, S., & Lee, C. (2011). A tale of passion: Linking job passion and cognitive engagement to employee work performance. *Journal of Management Studies, 48*(1), 26–47. doi:10.1111/j.1467-6486.2009.00878.x

Hobfoll, S. E. (1989). Conservation of resources: A new attempt at conceptualizing stress. *American Psychologist, 44*(3), 513–524. doi:10.1037/0003-066X.44.3.513

Hobfoll, S. E., & Shirom, A. (2001). Conservation of resources theory: Applications to stress and management in the workplace. In R. T. Golembiewski (Ed.), *Handbook of organizational behavior* (2nd ed., pp. 57–80). New York, NY: Marcel Dekker.

Hobson, C. J., Delunas, L., & Kesic, D. (2001). Compelling evidence of the need for corporate work/life balance initiatives: Results from a national survey of stressful life-events. *Journal of Employment Counseling, 38*(1), 38–44.

Hofstede, G. (1980). Motivation, leadership, and organization: Do American theories apply abroad? *Organizational Dynamics, 9*, 42–63.

Hofstede, G. (1983). Dimensions of national cultures in fifty countries and three regions. In J. B. Deregowski, S. Dziurawiec, & R. C. Annis (Eds.), *Expiscations in cross-cultural psychology* (pp. 335–355). Lisse, the Netherlands: Swets & Zeitlinger.

Hofstede, G. (2001). *Culture's consequences: Comparing values, behaviors, institutions, and organizations across nations* (2nd ed). Thousand Oaks, CA: Sage Publications.

Hofstede, G., & Bond, M. (1988). The Confucius connection: From cultural roots to economic growth. *Organizational Dynamics, 16*(4), 5–21.

Hofstede, G., & Bond, M. H. (1984). Hofstede's culture dimensions: An independent validation using Rokeach's Value Survey. *Journal of Cross-Cultural Psychology, 15*(4), 417–433. doi:10.1177/0022002184015004003

Holahan, C. J., & Moos, R. H. (1985). Life stress and health: Personality, coping, and family support in stress resistance. *Journal of Personality and Social Psychology, 49*(3), 739–747. doi:10.1037/0022-3514.49.3.739

Holman, D. J., Axtell, C. M., Sprigg, C., Totterdell, P., & Wall, T. D. (2010). The mediating role of job characteristics in job redesign interventions: A serendipitous quasi-experiment. *Journal of Organizational Behavior*, *31*(1), 84–105. doi:10.1002/job.631

Hoppock, R. (1935). *Job satisfaction*. New York, NY: Harper & Row.

Howard, J. H., Rechnitzer, P. A., & Cunningham, D. A. (1975). Coping with job tension-effective and ineffective methods. *Public Personnel Management*, *4*(5), 317–325

Howard, L. W., & Cordes, C. L. (2010). Flight from unfairness: Effects of perceived injustice on emotional exhaustion and employee withdrawal. *Journal of Business and Psychology*, *25*(3), 409–428. doi:10.1007/s10869-010-9158-5

Howell, J. M., & Frost, P. J. (1989). A laboratory study of charismatic leadership. *Organizational Behavior and Human Decision Processes*, *43*(2), 243–269. doi:10.1016/0749-5978(89)90052-6

Hsee, C. K., Hatfield, E., Carlson, J. G., & Chemtob, C. (1990). The effect of power on susceptibility to emotional contagion. *Cognition And Emotion*, *4*(4), 327–340. doi:10.1080/02699939008408081

Hu, L., & Bentler, P. M. (1999). Cutoff criteria for fit indexes in covariance structure analysis: Conventional criteria versus new alternatives. *Structural Equation Modeling*, *6*, 1–55.

Hulin, C. L., & Judge, T. A. (2003). Job attitudes. In W. C. Borman, D. R. Ilgen, & R. J. Klimoski (Eds.), *Handbook of psychology: Industrial and organizational psychology* (Vol. 12, pp. 255–276). Hoboken, NJ: Wiley.

Hutchins, E. (1991). The social organization of distributed cognition. In L. B. Resnick, J. M. Levine, & S. D. Teasley (Eds.), *Perspectives on socially shared cognition* (pp. 283–307). Washington, DC: American Psychological Association. doi:10.1037/10096-012

Ickes, W., & Gonzalez, R. (1994). "Social" cognition and social cognition: From the subjective to the intersubjective. *Small Group Research*, *25*(2), 294–315. doi:10.1177/1046496494252008

Ilgen, D. R., & Klein, H. J. (1989). Organizational behavior. *Annual Review of Psychology*, *40*, 327–351. doi:10.1146/annurev.ps.40.020189.001551

Inceoglu, I., & Warr, P. (2011). Personality and job engagement. *Journal of Personnel Psychology*, *10*(4), 177–181. doi:10.1027/1866-5888/a000045

Irvine, D. (2009, May 8). "Employee engagement: What it is and why you need it." Retrieved from www.businessweek.com/bwdaily/dnflash/content/may2009/db2009058_952910.htm

Isen, A. M. (2000). Positive affect and decision making. In M. Lewis & J. M. Haviland-Jones (Eds.), *Handbook of emotion* (pp. 417–435). New York, NY: Guilford Press.

Iyengar, S. S., & DeVoe, S. E. (2003). Rethinking the value of choice: Considering cultural mediators of intrinsic motivation. In V. Murphy-Berman & J. J. Berman (Eds.), *Cross-cultural differences in perspectives on the self* (pp. 146–191). Lincoln: University of Nebraska Press.

Iyengar, S. S., & Lepper, M. R. (1999). Rethinking the value of choice: A cultural perspective on intrinsic motivation. *Journal of Personality and Social Psychology*, *76*, 349–366.

Jacob, R. G., Thayer, J. F., Manuck, S. B., Muldoon, M. F., Tamres, L. K., Williams, D. M., . . . Gatsonis, C. (1999). Ambulatory blood pressure responses and the circumplex model of mood: A 4-day study. *Psychosomatic Medicine*, *61*(3), 319–333.

Janssen, O. (2000). Job demands, perceptions of effort-reward fairness and innovative work behaviour. *Journal of Occupational and Organizational Psychology*, *73*(3), 287–302. doi:10.1348/096317900167038

Javidan, M., House, R. J., & Dorfman, P. W. (2004). A nontechnical summary of GLOBE findings. In R. J. House, P. J. Hanges, M. Javidan, P. W. Dorfman, & V. Gupta (Eds.), *Culture, leadership, and organizations: The GLOBE study of 62 societies* (pp. 29–48). Thousand Oaks, CA: Sage.

Jin, Y., Hopkins, M. M., & Wittmer, J. S. (2010). Linking human capital to competitive advantages: Flexibility in a manufacturing firm's supply chain. *Human Resource Management*, *49*(5), 939–963. doi:10.1002/hrm.20385

Johnson, J. W., & LeBreton, J. M. (2004). History and use of relative importance indices in organizational research. *Organizational Research Methods*, *7*, 238–257.

Jones, A. P., & James, L. R. (1979). Psychological climate: Dimensions and relationships of individual and aggregated work environment perceptions. *Organizational Behavior and Human Performance*, *23*, 201–250.

Judge, T. A., & Bono, J. E. (2000). Five-factor model of personality and transformational leadership. *Journal of Applied Psychology*, *85*, 751–765. doi: 10.1037/0021-9010.85.5.751

Judge, T. A., Bono, J. E., Erez, A., & Locke, E. A. (2005). Core Self-evaluations and job and life satisfaction: The role of self-concordance and goal attainment. *Journal of Applied Psychology*, *90*(2), 257–268. doi:10.1037/0021-9010.90.2.257

Judge, T. A., Locke, E. A., & Durham, C. C. (1997). The dispositional causes of job satisfaction: a core evaluations approach. *Research in Organizational Behavior*, *19*, 151–189.

Judge, T. A., Thoresen, C. J., Bono, J. E., & Patton, G. K. (2001). The job satisfaction–job performance relationship: A qualitative and quantitative review. *Psychological Bulletin*, *127*(3), 376–407. doi:10.1037/0033-2909.127.3.376

Justis, R. T. (1975). Leadership effectiveness: A contingency approach. *Academy of Management Journal*, *18*(1), 160–167. doi:10.2307/255636

Kâğitçibaşi, Ç. (1987). Individual and group loyalties: Are they compatible? In Ç. Kâğitçibaşi (Ed.), *Growth and progress in cross-cultural psychology* (pp. 94–103). Berwyn, PA: Swets North America.

Kâğitçibaşi, Ç. (1994). A critical appraisal of individualism and collectivism: Toward a new formulation. In U. Kim, H. C. Triandis, Ç. Kâğitçibaşi, S. Choi, & G. Yoon (Eds.), *Individualism and collectivism: Theory, method, and applications* (pp. 52–65). Thousand Oaks, CA: Sage.

Kabasakal, H., Dastmalchian, A., & Imer, P. (2011). Organizational citizenship behavior: A study of young executives in Canada, Iran, and Turkey. *The International Journal of Human Resource Management*, *13*, 2703–2729. doi:10.1080/09585192.2011.599943

Kahn, W. A. (1990). Psychological conditions of personal engagement and disengagement at work. *Academy of Management Journal*, *33*, 692–724.

Kahn, W. A. (1992). To be fully there: Psychological presence at work. *Human Relations*, *45*(4), 321–349. doi:10.1177/00187267920450040

Kahn, W. A., & Fellows, S. (2013). Employee engagement and meaningful work. In B. J. Dik, Z. S. Byrne, & M. F. Steger (Eds.), *Purpose and meaning in the workplace* (pp. 105–126). Washington, DC: American Psychological Association.

Kanfer, R. (1990). Motivation theory and industrial and organizational psychology. In M. D. Dunnette & L. M. Hough (Eds.), *Handbook of industrial and organizational psychology* (Vol. 1, pp. 75–170). Palo Alto, CA: Consulting Psychologists Press.

Kanste, O. (2011). Work engagement, work commitment and their association with well-being in health care. *Scandinavian Journal of Caring Sciences, 25*(4), 754–761. doi:10.1111/j.1471-6712.2011.00888.x

Kanter, R. (1988). When a thousand flowers bloom: structural, collective, and social conditions for innovation in organization. *Research In Organizational Behavior, 10*, 169–213.

Kanungo, R. N. (1982). Measurement of job and work involvement. *Journal of Applied Psychology, 67*, 341–249. doi:10.1037//0021-9010.67.3.341

Karasek, R. A. (1979). Job demands, job decision latitude, and mental strain: Implications for job redesign. *Administrative Science Quarterly, 24*(2), 285–308.

Karatepe, O. M. (2013). Perceptions of organizational politics and hotel employee outcomes: The mediating role of work engagement. *International Journal of Contemporary Hospitality Management, 25*(1), 82–104.

Karatepe, O. M., Keshavarz, S., & Nejati, S. (2012). Do core self-evaluations mediate the effect of coworker support on work engagement? A study of hotel employees in Iran. *Journal of Hospitality And Tourism Management, 17*(1), 61–71.

Karl, K. A., O'Leary-Kelly, A. M., & Martocchio, J. J. (1993). The impact of feedback and self-efficacy on performance in training. *Journal of Organizational Behavior, 14*(4), 379–394.

Katz, D. (1964). The motivational basis of organizational behavior. *Behavioral Science, 9*(2), 131–146. doi:10.1002/bs.3830090206

Kendon, A. (1970). Movement coordination in social interaction: Some examples described. *Acta Psychologica, Amsterdam, 32*(2), 101–125. doi:10.1016/0001-6918(70)90094-6

Kenexa Research Institute. (2009). The impact of employee engagement. Retrieved from www.kenexa.com/getattachment/8c36e336-3935-4406-8b7b-777f1afaa57d/The-Impact-of-Employee-Engagement.aspx

Kim, B., Williams, L., & Gill, D. L. (2003). A cross-cultural study of achievement orientation and intrinsic motivation in young USA and Korean athletes. *International Journal of Sport Psychology, 34*(2), 168–184.

Kim, H. J., Shin, K. H., & Swanger, N. (2009). Burnout and engagement: A comparative analysis using the Big Five personality dimensions. *International Journal of Hospitality Management, 28*(1), 96–104.

King, L. A., Hicks, J. A., Krull, J. L., & Del Gaiso, A. K. (2006). Positive affect and the experience of meaning in life. *Journal of Personality and Social Psychology, 90*(1), 179–196. doi:10.1037/0022-3514.90.1.179

Klimoski, R., & Mohammed, S. (1994). Team mental model: Construct or metaphor? *Journal of Management, 20*(2), 403. doi:10.1016/0149-2063(94)90021-3

Koch, S., & Leary, D. E. (1985). *A century of psychology as science*. Washington, DC: American Psychological Association. doi:10.1037/10117-000

Korsgaard, M., Schweiger, D. M., & Sapienza, H. J. (1995). Building commitment, attachment, and trust in strategic decision-making teams: The role of procedural justice. *Academy of Management Journal, 38*(1), 60–84. doi:10.2307/256728

Kottke, J. L., & Sharafinski, C. E. (1988). Measuring perceived supervisory and organizational support. *Educational and Psychological Measurement, 48*, 1075–1079.

Kożusznik, M., Rodríguez, I., & Peiró, J. M. (2012). Cross-national outcomes of stress appraisal. *Cross Cultural Management, 19*(4), 507–525. doi:10.1108/13527601211269996

Kramer, R. M. (1994). The sinister attribution error: Paranoid cognition and collective distrust in organizations. *Motivation And Emotion, 18*(2), 199–230. doi:10.1007/BF02249399

Kramer, R. M. (1999). Trust and distrust in organizations: Emerging perspectives, enduring questions. *Annual Review of Psychology, 50*, 569–598. doi:10.1146/annurev.psych.50.1.569

Kristof-Brown, A. L., Zimmerman, R. D., & Johnson, E. C. (2005). Consequences of individuals' fit at work: A meta-analysis of person–job, person–organization, person–group, and person–supervisor fit. *Personnel Psychology, 58*(2), 281–342. doi:10.1111/j.1744-6570.2005.00672.x

Kühnel, J., Sonnentag, S., & Westman, M. (2009). Does work engagement increase after a short respite? The role of job involvement as a double-edged sword. *Journal of Occupational and Organizational Psychology, 82*(3), 575–594. doi:10.1348/096317908X349362

Kurman, J. (2001). Self-regulation strategies in achievement settings: Culture and gender differences. *Journal of Cross-cultural Psychology, 32*, 491–503.

Lacey, J. L., Bateman, D. E., & VanLehn, R. (1953). Autonomic response specificity: An experimental study. *Psychomatic Medicine, 15*, 8–21.

LaFrance, M., & Broadbent, M. (1976). Group rapport: Posture sharing as a nonverbal indicator. *Group & Organization Studies, 1*(3), 328–333. doi:10.1177/105960117600100307

Lakin, J. L., & Chartrand, T. L. (2003). Using nonconscious behavioral mimicry to create affiliation and rapport. *Psychological Science, 14*(4), 334–339. doi:10.1111/1467-9280.14481

Lam, S. S. K., Hui, C., & Law, K. S. (1999). Organizational citizenship behavior: Comparing perspectives of supervisor and subordinates across four international samples. *Journal of Applied Psychology, 84*, 594–601.

Lambert, S. J. (1991). The combined effects of job and family characteristics on the job satisfaction, job involvement, and intrinsic motivation of men and women workers. *Journal of Organizational Behavior, 12*, 341–363. doi:10.1002/job.4030120408

Latané, B. (1997). Dynamic social impact: The societal consequences of human interaction. In C. McGarty & S. Haslam (Eds.), *The message of social psychology: Perspectives on mind in society* (pp. 200–220). Malden, MA: Blackwell Publishing.

Latané, B., & L'Herrou, T. (1996). Spatial clustering in the conformity game: Dynamic social impact in electronic groups. *Journal of Personality and Social Psychology, 70*(6), 1218–1230. doi:10.1037/0022-3514.70.6.1218

Lauver, K.J., & Kristof-Brown, A. (2001). Distinguishing between employees' perceptions of person—job and person—organization fit. *Journal of Vocational Behavior, 59*(3), 454–470. doi:10.1006/jvbe.2001.1807

Lavigna, B. (2013). Improving employee engagement—the special case of the public service. *PA Times, 36*(1), 11–12.

Lawler, E.E., & Hall, D.T. (1970). Relationship of job characteristics to job involvement, satisfaction, and intrinsic motivation. *Journal of Applied Psychology, 54*(4), 305–312. doi:10.1037/h0029692

Lawler, E.E., Hackman, J., & Kaufman, S. (1973). Effects of job redesign: A field experiment. *Journal of Applied Social Psychology, 3*(1), 49–62. doi:10.1111/j.1559-1816.1973.tb01294.x

Lazarus, R.S. (1991), *Emotion and adaptation.* New York, NY: Oxford University Press.

Lazarus, R.S., & Folkman, S. (1984). *Stress, appraisal, and coping.* New York, NY: Springer.

LeBreton, J.M., Hargis, M.B., Griepentrog, B., Oswald, F.L., & Ployhart, R.E. (2007). A multidimensional approach for evaluating variables in organizational research and practice. *Personnel Psychology, 60*(2), 475–498. doi:10.1111/j.1744-6570.2007.00080.x

Lee, A.Y., Aaker, J.L., & Gardner, W.L. (2000). The pleasures and pains of distinct self-construals: The role of interdependence in regulatory focus. *Journal of Personality and Social Psychology, 78*, 1122–1134.

Lee, K., & Allen, N.J. (2002). Organizational citizenship behavior and workplace deviance: The role of affect and cognitions. *Journal of Applied Psychology, 87*(1), 131–142. doi:10.1037/0021-9010.87.1.131

Lee, W., Reeve, J., Xue, Y., & Xiong, J. (2012). Neural differences between intrinsic reasons for doing versus extrinsic reasons for doing: An fMRI study. *Neuroscience Research, 73*(1), 68–72. doi:10.1016/j.neures.2012.02.010

Lench, H.C., Flores, S.A., & Bench, S.W. (2011). Discrete emotions predict changes in cognition, judgment, experience, behavior, and physiology: A meta-analysis of experimental emotion elicitations. *Psychological Bulletin, 137*, 834–855. doi:10.1037/a0024244

Lent, R.W. (2013). Promoting meaning and purpose at work: A social-cognitive perspective. In B.J. Dik, Z.S. Byrne, & M.F. Steger (Eds.), *Purpose and meaning in the workplace* (pp. 151–170). Washington, DC: American Psychological Association.

LePine, J.A., Erez, A., & Johnson, D.E. (2002). The nature and dimensionality of organizational citizenship behavior: A critical review and meta-analysis. *Journal of Applied Psychology, 87*(1), 52–65. doi:10.1037/0021-9010.87.1.52

Lepper, M.R., Sethi, S., Dialdin, D., & Drake, M. (1997). Intrinsic and extrinsic motivation: A developmental perspective. In S.S. Luthar, J.A. Burack, D. Cicchetti, J.R. Weisz (Eds.), *Developmental psychopathology: Perspectives on adjustment, risk, and disorder* (pp. 23–50). New York, NY: Cambridge University Press.

Lerner, J.S., & Keltner, D. (2000). Beyond valence: Toward a model of emotion-specific influences on judgment and choice. *Cognition & Emotion, 14*, 473–493. doi:10.1080/026999300402763

Lester, P.B., Hannah, S.T., Harms, P.D., Vogelgesang, G.R., & Avolio, B.J. (2011). Mentoring impact on leader efficacy development: A field experiment. *Academy of Management Learning & Education, 10*(3), 409–429. doi:10.5465/amle.2010.0047

Levine, J.M., Resnick, L.B., & Higgins, E. (1993). Social foundations of cognition. *Annual Review of Psychology, 44*, 585–612. doi:10.1146/annurev.ps.44.020193.003101

Lewin, K. (1946). Action research and minority problems. *Journal of Social Issues, 2*, 434–46. doi:10.1111/j.1540-4560.1946.tb02295.x

Lewin, K. (1947). Frontiers in group dynamics. II. Channels of group life; social planning and action research. *Human Relations, 1*, 143–153. doi:10.1177/001872674700100201

Liao, F., Yang, L., Wang, M., Drown, D., & Shi, J. (2013). Team-member exchange and work engagement: Does personality make a difference? *Journal of Business & Psychology, 28*(1), 63–77. doi:10.1007/s10869-012-9266-5

Linnenbrink, E.A., & Pintrich, P.R. (2010). Achievement goal theory and affect: An asymmetrical bidirectional model. *Educational Psychologist, 37*(2), 69–78. doi:10.1207/S1532698SEP3702_2

Locke, E.A. (1976). The nature and causes of job satisfaction. In M.D. Dunnette (Ed.), *Handbook of industrial and organizational psychology* (pp. 1297–1349). Chicago, IL: Rand McNally College.

Locke, E.A., & Latham, G.P. (1990). *A theory of goal setting & task performance.* Englewood Cliffs, NJ: Prentice Hall.

Locke, E.A., Smith, P., Kendall, L.M., Hulin, C.L., & Miller, A.M. (1964). Convergent and discriminant validity for areas and methods of rating job satisfaction. *Journal of Applied Psychology, 48*(5), 313–319. doi:10.1037/h0043202

Lodahl, T.M., & Kejner, M. (1965). The definition and measurement of job involvement. *Journal of Applied Psychology, 49*(1), 24–33.

Luria, G., & Torjman, A. (2009). Resources and coping with stressful events. *Journal of Organizational Behavior, 30*(6), 685–707. doi:10.1002/job.v30:610.1002/job.551

Luthans, F., Kemmerer, B., Paul, R., & Taylor, L. (1987). The impact of a job redesign intervention on salespersons' observed performance behaviors: A field experiment. *Group & Organization Studies, 12*(1), 55–72. doi:10.1177/105960118701200105

Luthans, F., & Peterson, S.J. (2002). Employee engagement and manager self-efficacy: Implications for managerial effectiveness and development. *Journal of Management Development, 5*, 376–387.

Maas, H., & Spinath, F.M. (2012). Personality and coping with professional demands: A behavioral genetics analysis. *Journal of Occupational Health Psychology, 17*(3), 376–385. doi:10.1037/a0027Ml

Macdonald, A.M., & de Silva, P. (1999). The assessment of obsessionality using the Padua Inventory: Its validity in a British non-clinical sample. *Personality and Individual Differences, 27*(6), 1027–1046. doi:10.1016/S0191-8869(99)00036-7

Macey, W. H., & Schneider, B. (2008). The meaning of employee engagement. *Industrial and Organizational Psychology: Perspectives on Science and Practice*, *1*, 3–30.

Macey, W. H., Schneider, B., Barbera, K. M., & Young, S. A. (2009). *Employee engagement: Tools for analysis, practice, and competitive advantage*. Chichester, England: Blackwell.

Macgowan, M. J. (2000). Evaluation of a measure of engagement for group work. *Research on Social Work Practice*, *10*(3), 348–361.

Machlowitz, M. (1980). *Workaholics: Living with Them, Working with Them*. Reading, MA: Addison-Wesley.

Maddux, J. E. (2002). Stopping the "madness": Positive psychology and the deconstruction of the illness ideology and the DSM. In C. R. Snyder, & S. J. Lopez (Eds.), *Handbook of positive psychology* (pp. 13–25). New York, NY: Oxford University Press.

Mael, F. A., & Tetrick, L. E. (1992). Identifying organizational identification. *Educational And Psychological Measurement*, *52*(4), 813–824. doi: 10.1177/0013164492052004002

Maguire, M. A. (1983). The effects of context on attitude measurement: The case of job satisfaction. *Human Relations*, *36*(11), 1013–1030. doi:10.1177/001872678303601104

Markus, H. (1977). Self-schemata and processing information about the self. *Journal of Personality and Social Psychology*, *35*(2), 63–78. doi:10.1037/0022-3514.35.2.63

Markus, H., & Kitayama, S. (1991). Culture and the self: Implications for cognition, emotion, and motivation. *Psychological Review*, *98*(2), 224–253.

Markus, H., Kitayama, S., & Heiman, R. J. (1996). Culture and 'basic' psychological principles. In E. Higgins & A. W. Kruglanski (Eds.), *Social psychology: Handbook of basic principles* (pp. 857–913). New York, NY: Guilford Press.

Maslach, C. (1982). *Burnout: The cost of caring*. Englewood Cliffs, NJ: Prentice Hall.

Maslach, C. (2003). Job burnout: new directions in research and intervention. *Current Directions in Psychological Science*, *12*(5), 189–193. doi:10.1111/1467-8721.01258

Maslach, C., & Jackson, S. E. (1981). The measurement of experienced burnout. *Journal of Occupational Behavior*, *2*(2), 99–113.

Maslach, C., & Jackson, S. E. (1984). Burnout in organizational settings. *Applied Social Psychology Annual*, *5*, 133–153.

Maslach, C., & Leiter, M. P. (1997). *The truth about burnout: How organizations cause personal stress and what to do about it*. San Francisco, CA: Jossey-Bass.

Maslach, C., Schaufeli, W. B., & Leiter, M. P. (2001). Job burnout. *Annual Review of Psychology*, *52*, 397–422.

Maslow, A. H. (1943). A theory of human motivation. *Psychological Review*, *50*(4), 370–396. doi:10.1037/h0054346

Maslow, A. H. (1968). *Towards a psychology of being*. New York, NY: Van Nostrand.

Maslow, A. H. (1998). *Maslow on management*. New York, NY: Wiley.

Matthews, D. J. (2010, February). Trust me: Credible leadership delivers results. *Chief Learning Officer*, 28–31.

Mauno, S., Kinnunen, U., & Ruokolainen, M. (2007). Job demands and resources as antecedents of work engagement: A longitudinal study. *Journal of Vocational Behavior*, 70(1), 149–171. doi:10.1016/j.jvb.2006.09.002

Mauno, S., Kinnunen, U., Mäkikangas, A., & Nätti, J. (2005). Psychological consequences of fixed-term employment and perceived job insecurity among health care staff. *European Journal of Work and Organizational Psychology*, 14(3), 209–237. doi:10.1080/13594320500146649

May, D. R., Gilson, R. L., & Harter, L. M., (2004), The psychological conditions of meaningfulness, safety and availability and the engagement of the human spirit at work. *Journal of Occupational and Organizational Psychology. 77*, 11–37.

Mayer, J. D., Caruso, D. R., & Salovey, P. (2000). Selecting a measure of emotional intelligence: The case for ability scales. In R. Bar-On & J. A. Parker (Eds.), *The handbook of emotional intelligence: Theory, development, assessment, and application at home, school, and in the workplace* (pp. 320–342). San Francisco, CA: Jossey-Bass.

Mayer, J. D., & Salovey, P. (1995). Emotional intelligence and the construction and regulation of feelings. *Applied & Preventive Psychology*, 4(3), 197–208. doi:10.1016/S0962-1849(05)80058-7

McAllister, D. J. (1995). Affect- and cognition-based trust as foundations for interpersonal cooperation in organizations. *Academy of Management Journal*, 38(1), 24–59. doi:10.2307/256727

McCulloch, M. C., & Turban, D. B. (2007). Using person—organization fit to select employees for high-turnover jobs. *International Journal of Selection and Assessment*, 15(1), 63–71. doi:10.1111/j.1468-2389.2007.00368.x

McGregor, I., & Little, B. R. (1998). Personal projects, happiness, and meaning: On doing well and being yourself. *Journal of Personality and Social Psychology*, 74(2), 494–512. doi:10.1037/0022-3514.74.2.494

McHugo, G. J., Lanzetta, J. T., Sullivan, D. G., Masters, R. D., & Englis, B. G. (1985). Emotional reactions to a political leader's expressive displays. *Journal of Personality and Social Psychology*, 49(6), 1513–1529. doi:10.1037/0022-3514.49.6.1513

McMillan, L. W., & O'Driscoll, M. P. (2006). Exploring new frontiers to generate an integrated definition of workaholism. In R. J. Burke (Ed.), *Research companion to working time and work addiction* (pp. 89–107). Northampton, MA: Edward Elgar.

McPhail, S. M. (2007) (Ed). *Alternative validation strategies: Developing new and leveraging existing validity evidence*. Hoboken, NJ: Wiley.

Medlin, B., & Green, K. W. (2009). Enhancing performance through goal setting, engagement, and optimism. *Industrial Management & Data Systems, 109*, 943–956.

Meglino, B. M., Ravlin, E. C., & Adkins, C. L. (1989). A work values approach to corporate culture: A field test of the value congruence process and its relationship to individual outcomes. *Journal of Applied Psychology*, 74(3), 424–432. doi:10.1037/0021-9010.74.3.424

Mehrabian, A., & Ksionzky, S. (1970). Models for affiliative and conformity behavior. *Psychological Bulletin*, 74(2), 110–126. doi:10.1037/h0029603

Menguc, B., Auh, S., Fisher, M., & Haddad, A. (2013). To be engaged or not to be engaged: The antecedents and consequences of service employee engagement. *Journal of Business Research, 66*, 2163–2170.

Meurs, J. A., & Perrewé, P. L. (2011). Cognitive activation theory of stress: An integrative theoretical approach to work stress. *Journal of Management, 37*(4), 1043–1068. doi:10.1177/0149206310387303

Meyer, J. P., & Allen, N. J. (1991). A three-component conceptualization of organizational commitment. *Human Resource Management Review, 1*(1), 61–90.

Meyer, J. P., & Gagné, M. (2008). Employee engagement from a self-determination theory perspective. *Industrial and Organizational Psychology: Perspectives on Science and Practice, 1*(1), 60–62. doi:10.1111/j.1754-9434.2007.00010.x

Meyer, J. P., Gagné, M., & Parfyonova, N. M. (2010). Toward an evidence-based model of engagement: What we can learn from motivation and commitment research. In S. L. Albrecht (Ed.), *Handbook of employee engagement: Perspectives, issues, research and practice* (pp. 62–73). Northampton, MA: Edward Elgar.

Michela, J. L., & Vena, J. (2012). A dependence-regulation account of psychological distancing in response to major organizational change. *Journal of Change Management, 12*(1), 77–94. doi:10.1080/14697017.2011.652376

Miles, R. H. (2001). Beyond the age of Dilbert: Accelerating corporate transformations by rapidly engaging all employees. *Organizational Dynamics, 29*(4), 313–321.

Miller, J. G., & Bersoff, D. M. (1994). Cultural influences on the moral status of reciprocity and the discounting of endogenous motivation. *Personality and Social Psychology Bulletin, 20*(5), 592–602. doi:10.1177/0146167294205015

Miller, R. B., Greene, B. A., Montalvo, G. P., Ravindran, B., & Nichols, J. D. (1996). Engagement in academic work: The role of learning goals, future consequences, pleasing others, and perceived ability. *Contemporary Educational Psychology, 21*, 388–422.

Misumi, J. (1989). Research on leadership and group decision in Japanese organisations. *Applied Psychology: An International Review, 38*(4), 321–336. doi:10.1111/j.1464-0597.1989.tb01211.x

Misumi, J. (1995). The development in Japan of the performance-maintenance (PM) theory of leadership. *Journal of Social Issues, 51*(1), 213–228. doi:10.1111/j.1540-4560.1995.tb01319.x

Misumi, J., & Peterson, M. F. (1985a). *The behavioral science of leadership: An interdisciplinary Japanese research program.* Ann Arbor: University of Michigan Press.

Misumi, J., & Peterson, M. F. (1985b). The performance-maintenance (PM) theory of leadership: Review of a Japanese research program. *Administrative Science Quarterly, 30*(2), 198–223. doi:10.2307/2393105

Mone, E. M., & London, M. (2010). *Employee engagement through effective performance management: A practical guide for managers.* New York, NY: Routledge/Taylor & Francis Group.

Moneta, G. B. (2004). The flow model of intrinsic motivation in Chinese: Cultural and personal moderators. *Journal of Happiness Studies, 5*, 181–217.

Moreland, J. (2013). Improving job fit can improve employee engagement and productivity. *Employment Relations Today, 40*(1), 57–62. doi:10.1002/ert.21400

Moreland, R. L., Argote, L., & Krishnan, R. (1996). Socially shared cognition at work: Transactive memory and group performance. In J. L. Nye & A. M. Brower (Eds.), *What's social about social cognition? Research on socially shared cognition in small groups* (pp. 57–84). Thousand Oaks, CA: Sage.

Morin, A. S., Vandenberghe, C., Boudrias, J., Madore, I., Morizot, J., & Tremblay, M. (2011). Affective commitment and citizenship behaviors across multiple foci. *Journal of Managerial Psychology, 26*(8), 716–738. doi:10.1108/02683941111181798

Morin, E. M. (1995). Organizational effectiveness and the meaning of work. In T. C. Pauchant & Associates (Eds.), *In search of meaning: Managing for the health of our organizations, our communities, and the natural world* (pp. 29–64). San Francisco, CA: Jossey-Bass.

Mostert, K., & Rothmann, S. (2006). Work-related well-being in the South African police service. *Journal of Criminal Justice, 34*(5), 479–491. doi:10.1016/j.jcrimjus.2006.09.003

Motowidlo, S. J. (2003). Job performance. In W. C. Borman, D. R. Ilgen, & R. J. Klimoski (Eds.), *Handbook of psychology: Industrial and organizational psychology* (Vol. 12, pp. 39–53). Hoboken, NJ: Wiley.

Motowidlo, S. J., & van Scotter, J. R. (1994). Evidence that task performance should be distinguished from contextual performance. *Journal of Applied Psychology, 79*(4), 475–480. doi:10.1037/0021-9010.79.4.475

Mowday, R. T., Steers, R. M., & Porter, L. W. (1979). The measurement of organizational commitment. *Journal of Vocational Behavior, 14*(2), 224–247. doi:10.1016/0001-8791(79)90072-1

Mudrack, P. E. (2004). Job involvement, obsessive-compulsive personality traits, and workaholic behavioral tendencies. *Journal of Organizational Change Management, 17*(5), 490–508. doi:10.1108/09534810410554506

Mudrack, P. E., & Naughton, T. J. (2001). The assessment of workaholism as behavioral tendencies: Scale development and preliminary empirical testing. *International Journal of Stress Management, 8*(2), 93–111. doi:10.1023/A:1009525213213

Murphy, K. R. (1989). Dimensions of job performance. In R. F. Dillon & J. W. Pellegrino (Eds.), *Testing: Theoretical and applied perspectives* (pp. 218–247). New York, NY: Praeger Publishers.

Murphy, K. R. (1994). Toward a broader conception of jobs and job performance: Impact of changes in the military environment on the structure, assessment, and prediction of job performance. In M. G. Rumsey, C. B. Walker, & J. Harris (Eds.), *Personnel selection and classification* (pp. 85–102). Hillsdale, NJ: Erlbaum.

Myers, I. B., & McCauley, M. H. (1985). *Manual: A guide to the development and use of the Myers-Briggs type indicator.* Palo Alto, CA: Consulting Psychologist Press.

Nakamura, J., & Csikszentmihalyi, M. (2002). The concept of flow. In C. R. Snyder & S. J. Lopez (Eds.), *Handbook of positive psychology* (pp. 89–105). New York, NY: Oxford University Press.

Ncube, F., & Jerie, S. (2012). Leveraging employee engagement for competitive advantage in the hospitality industry. A comparative study of hotels A and B in Zimbabwe. *Journal of Emerging Trends in Economics & Management Sciences, 3*(4), 380–388.

Newman, D. A., & Harrison, D. A. (2008). Been there, bottled that: Are state and behavioral work engagement new and useful construct "wines"? *Industrial and Organizational Psychology: Perspectives on Science and Practice, 1,* 31–35. doi:10.1111/j.1754-9434.2007.00003.x

Ng, T. H., Sorensen, K. L., & Feldman, D. C. (2007). Dimensions, antecedents, and consequences of workaholism: a conceptual integration and extension. *Journal of Organizational Behavior, 28*(1), 111–136.

Nielsen, K., Randall, R., Yarker, J., & Brenner, S-O. (2008). The effects of transformational leadership on followers' perceived work characteristics and psychological well-being: A longitudinal study. *Work & Stress, 22,* 16–32. doi: 10.1080/02678370801979430

Nikolaou, I. (2003). Fitting the person to the organisation: Examining the personality-job performance relationship from a new perspective. *Journal of Managerial Psychology, 18*(7), 639–648. doi:10.1108/02683940310502368

Nunnally, J. C., & Bernstein, I. (1994). *Psychometric theory* (3rd ed.). New York, NY: McGraw-Hill.

Oates, W. (1968). On being a "workaholic." *Pastoral Psychology, 19*(8), 16–20. doi:10.1007/BF01785472

Ochsner, K. N. (2007). How thinking controls feeling: A social cognitive neuroscience approach. In E. Harmon-Jones & P. Winkielman (Eds.), *Social neuroscience: Integrating biological and psychological explanations of social behavior* (pp. 106–133). New York, NY: Guilford Press.

Okurame, D. E. (2012). Linking work–family conflict to career commitment: The moderating effects of gender and mentoring among Nigerian civil servants. *Journal of Career Development, 39*(5), 423–442. doi:10.1177/089484 5310391903

Oldham, G. R., & Hackman, J. (1980). Work design in the organizational context. *Research In Organizational Behavior, 2,* 247–279.

Olesen, C., White, D., & Lemmer, I. (2007). Career models and culture change at Microsoft. *Organization Development Journal, 25*(2), P31–P35.

O'Reilly, C. A., & Chatman, J. (1986). Organizational commitment and psychological attachment: The effects of compliance, identification, and internalization on prosocial behavior. *Journal of Applied Psychology, 71*(3), 492–499. doi:10.1037/0021-9010.71.3.492

Organ, D. W. (1977). A reappraisal and reinterpretation of the satisfaction-causes-performance hypothesis. *Academy of Management Review, 2,* 46–53. doi:10.5465/AMR.1977.4409162

Organ, D. W. (1988). *Organizational citizenship behavior: The good soldier syndrome.* Lexington, MA: Lexington Books/D.C. Heath and Com.

Organ, D. W. (1997). Organizational citizenship behavior: It's construct clean-up time. *Human Performance, 10,* 85–97.

Organ, D. W., & Ryan, K. (1995). A meta-analytic review of attitudinal and dispositional predictors of organizational citizenship behavior. *Personnel Psychology, 48*(4), 775–802. doi:10.1111/j.1744-6570.1995.tb01781.x

Ostroff, C., Kinicki, A. J., & Muhammad, R. S. (2013). Organizational culture and climate. In N. W. Schmitt, S. Highhouse, & I. B. Weiner (Eds.), *Handbook of Psychology, Vol. 12. Industrial and organizational psychology* (2nd ed., pp. 643–676). Hoboken, NJ: Wiley.

Ostroff, C., Kinicki, A. J., & Tamkins, M. M. (2003). Organizational culture and climate. In W. C. Borman, D. R. Ilgen, & R. J. Klimoski (Eds.), *Handbook of psychology: Industrial and organizational psychology* (Vol. 12, pp. 565–593). Hoboken, NJ: Wiley.

O'Toole, R., & Dubin, R. (1968). Baby feeding and body sway: An experiment in George Herbert Mead's "taking the role of the other." *Journal of Personality and Social Psychology, 10*(1), 59–65. doi:10.1037/h0026387

Ouweneel, E., Schaufeli, W. B., & Le Blanc, P. M. (2013). Believe, and you will achieve: Changes over time in self-efficacy, engagement, and performance. *Applied Psychology: Health & Well-Being, 5*(2), 225–247. doi:10.1111/aphw.12008

Oyserman, D., Coon, H. M., & Kemmelmeier, M. (2002). Rethinking individualism and collectivism: Evaluation of theoretical assumptions and meta-analyses. *Psychological Bulletin, 128*(1), 3–73.

Park, C. L. (2010). Making sense of the meaning literature: An integrative review of meaning making and its effects on adjustment to stressful life events. *Psychological Bulletin, 136*(2), 257–301. doi:10.1037/a0018301

Parry, K. W., & Sinha, P. N. (2005). Researching the trainability of transformational organizational leadership. *Human Resource Development International, 8*(2), 165–183. doi:10.1080/13678860500100186

Paullay, I. M., Alliger, G. M., & Stone-Romero, E. F. (1994). Construct validation of two instruments designed to measure job involvement and work centrality. *Journal of Applied Psychology, 79*(2), 224–228. doi:10.1037/0021-9010.79.2.224

Pearce, I. A. (1982). The company mission as a strategic tool. *Sloan Management Review, 23*(3), 15–24.

Pedhazur, E., & Schmelkin, L. (1991). *Measurement, design, and analysis: An integrated approach.* Hillsdale, NJ: Erlbaum.

Perschel, A. (2010). Work-life flow: How individuals, Zappos, and other innovative companies achieve high engagement. *Global Business & Organizational Excellence, 29*(5), 17–30.

Petrou, P., Demerouti, E., Peeters, M. W., Schaufeli, W. B., & Hetland, J. (2012). Crafting a job on a daily basis: Contextual correlates and the link to work engagement. *Journal of Organizational Behavior, 33*(8), 1120–1141. doi:10.1002/job.1783

Pfeffer, J. (1998). *The human equation: Building profits by putting people first.* Boston, MA: Harvard Business School Press.

Pfieffelmann, B., Wagner, S. H., & Libkuman, T. (2010). Recruiting on corporate web sites: Perceptions of fit and attraction. *International Journal of Selection and Assessment, 18*(1), 40–47. doi:10.1111/j.1468-2389.2010.00487.x

Philp, M., Egan, S., & Kane, R. (2012). Perfectionism, over commitment to work, and burnout in employees seeking workplace counselling. *Australian Journal of Psychology, 64*(2), 68–74. doi:10.1111/j.1742-9536.2011.00028.x

Ployhart, R. E. (2008). The measurement and analysis of motivation. In R. Kanfer, G. Chen, & R. D. Pritchard (Eds.), *Work motivation: Past, present, and future* (pp. 17–61). New York, NY: Routledge/Taylor & Francis Group.

Ployhart, R. E. (2012). The psychology of competitive advantage: An adjacent possibility. *Industrial and Organizational Psychology: Perspectives on Science And Practice, 5*(1), 62–81. doi:10.1111/j.1754-9434.2011.01407.x

Podsakoff, N. P., Whiting, S. W., Podsakoff, P. M., & Blume, B. D. (2009). Individual- and organizational-level consequences of organizational citizenship behaviors: A meta-analysis. *Journal of Applied Psychology, 94*(1), 122–141. doi:10.1037/a0013079

Podsakoff, P. M., & MacKenzie, S. B. (1997). Impact of organizational citizenship behavior on organizational performance: A review and suggestions for future research. *Human Performance, 10*(2), 133–151. doi:10.1207/s15327043hup 1002_5

Podsakoff, P. M., MacKenzie, S. B., Lee, J., & Podsakoff, N. P. (2003). Common method biases in behavioral research: A critical review of the literature and recommended remedies. *Journal of Applied Psychology, 88*(5), 879–903. doi:10.1037/0021-9010.88.5.879

Porter, L. W., & Lawler, E. E. III. (1968). *Managerial attitudes and performance.* Homewood, IL: Irwin-Dorsey.

Pratt, M., & Ashforth, B. (2003). Fostering meaningfulness in working and at work. In K. Cameron, J. E. Dutton, & R. E. Quinn (Eds.), *Positive organizational scholarship: Foundations of a new discipline* (pp. 309–327). San Francisco, CA: Berrett-Koehler.

Pratt, M. G., Pradies, C., & Lepisto, D. A. (2013). Doing well, doing good, and doing with: Organizational practices for effectively cultivating meaningful work. In B. J. Dik, Z. S. Byrne, & M. F. Steger (Eds.), *Purpose and meaning in the workplace* (pp. 173–196). Washington, DC: American Psychological Association.

Prieto, L. L., Soria, M. S., Martinez, I. M., & Schaufeli, W. (2008). Extension of the job demands-resources model in the prediction of burnout and engagement among teachers over time. *Psicothema, 20*(3), 354–360.

Provine, R. R. (1986). Yawning as a stereotyped action pattern and releasing stimulus. *Ethology, 72*(2), 109–122. doi:10.1111/j.1439-0310.1986.tb00611.x

Pryce-Jones, J. (2011). Has the recession made us less happy at work? *Manager: British Journal of Administrative Management,* (73), 26–27.

Quick, J., & Tetrick, L. E. (2011). *Handbook of occupational health psychology* (2nd ed.). Washington, DC: American Psychological Association.

Quick, J. C., Murphy, L. R., & Hurrell, J. J. Jr. (Eds.). (1992). *Stress & well-being at work: Assessments and interventions for occupational mental health.* Washington, DC: American Psychological Association

Rabinowitz, S., & Hall, D. T. (1977). Organizational research on job involvement. *Psychological Bulletin, 84,* 265–268. doi:10.1037//0033-2909.84.2.265

Rafferty, A. E., & Griffin, M. A. (2004). Dimensions of transformational leadership: Conceptual and empirical extensions. *The Leadership Quarterly, 15,* 329–354.

Rampersad, H. (2006). Self-examination as the road to sustaining employee engagement and personal happiness. *Performance Improvement, 45*(8), 18–25. doi:10.1002/pfi.005

Rau, B. L., & Hyland, M. M. (2003). Corporate teamwork and diversity statements in college recruitment brochures: Effects on attraction. *Journal of Applied Social Psychology, 33*(12), 2465–2492. doi:10.1111/j.1559-1816.2003.tb02776.x

Ravichandran, K. K., Arasu, R. R., & Kumar, S. S. (2011). The impact of emotional intelligence on employee work engagement behavior: An empirical study. *International Journal of Business & Management*, 6(11), 157–169. doi:10.5539/ijbm.v6n11p157

Ray, E. B., & Ray, G. B. (1986). Teaching conflict management skills in corporate training: A perspective-taking approach. *Communication Education*, 35(3), 288–290. doi:10.1080/03634528609388351

Reinhardt, B. (1996). Factors affecting coefficient alpha: A mini Monte Carlo study. In B. Thompson (Ed.), *Advances in social science methodology* (pp. 3–20). Greenwich, CT: JAI Press.

Reis, H. T., Sheldon, K. M., Gable, S. L., Roscoe, J., & Ryan, R. M., (2000). Daily well-being: The role of autonomy, competence, and relatedness. *Personality and Social Psychology Bulletin*, 26(4), 419–435. doi: 10.1177/0146167200266002

Rentsch, J. R. (1990). Climate and culture: Interaction and qualitative differences in organizational meanings. *Journal of Applied Psychology*, 75, 668–681.

Resick, C. J., Baltes, B. B., & Shantz, C. (2007). Person-organization fit and work-related attitudes and decisions: Examining interactive effects with job fit and conscientiousness. *Journal of Applied Psychology*, 92(5), 1446–1455. doi:10.1037/0021-9010.92.5.1446

Resnick, L. B., Levine, J. M., & Teasley, S. D. (1991). *Perspectives on socially shared cognition*. Washington, DC: American Psychological Association. doi:10.1037/10096-000

Rheinberg, F. (2008). Intrinsic motivation and flow. In J. Heckhausen & H. Heckhausen (Eds.), *Motivation and action*, (pp. 323–348). New York, NY: Cambridge University. doi:10.1017/CBO9780511499821.014

Rich, B. L., LePine, J. A., & Crawford, E. R. (2010). Job engagement: Antecedents and effects on job performance. *Academy of Management Journal*, 53, 617–635. doi:10.5465/AMJ.2010.51468988

Richardsen, A. M., Burke, R. J., & Martinussen, M. (2006). Work and health outcomes among police officers: The mediating role of police cynicism and engagement. *International Journal of Stress Management*, 13, 555–574.

Robinson, D., Perryman, S., & Hayday, S. (2004). *The drivers of employee engagement*. London, UK: Institute for Employment Studies.

Roe, R. A. (1999). Work performance: A multiple regulation perspective. In C. L. Cooper & I. T. Robertson (Eds.), *International review of industrial and organizational psychology* (Vol. 14, pp. 231–335). New York, NY: Wiley.

Roe, R. A., Zinovieva, I. L., Dienes, E., & Ten Horn, L. (2000). A comparison of work motivation in Bulgaria, Hungary, and the Netherlands: Test of a model. *Applied Psychology: An International Review*, 49, 658–687. doi: 10.1111/1464-0597.00039

Roethlisberger, F. J., & Dickson, W. J. (1939). *Management and the worker: An account of a research program conducted by the Western Electric Company, Hawthorne Works, Chicago*. Cambridge, MA: Harvard University Press.

Rogers, C. (1959). A theory of therapy, personality, and interpersonal relationships as developed in the client-centered framework. In S. Koch (Ed.), *Psychology: A study of science* (Vol. 3, pp. 184–256). New York, NY: McGraw-Hill.

Rogers, C. (1961a). *On becoming a person*. Boston, MA: Houghton Mifflin.

Rogers, C.R. (1961b). The process equation of psychotherapy. *American Journal of Psychotherapy*, 15, 27–45.

Ronen, S., & Shenkar, O. (1985). Clustering countries on attitudinal dimensions: A review and synthesis. *Academy of Management Review*, 10(3), 435–454. doi: 10.5465/AMR.1985.4278955

Ronen, S., & Shenkar, O. (2013). Mapping world cultures: Cluster formation, sources and implications. *Journal of International Business Studies*, 44(9), 867–897. doi:10.1057/jibs.2013.42

Rossi, A.M., Perrewé, P.L., & Sauter, S.L. (Eds.). (2006). *Stress and quality of working life: Current perspectives in occupational health*. Charlotte, NC: Information Age Publishing

Rosso, B., Dekas, K., & Wrzesniewski, A. (2010). On the meaning of work: A theoretical integration and review. *Research in Organizational Behavior*, 30, 91–127. doi:10.1016/j.riob.2010.09.001

Rothbard, N.P. (2001). Enriching or depleting? The dynamics of engagement in work and family roles. *Administrative Science Quarterly*, 46(4), 655–684. doi: 10.2307/3094827

Rothmann, S.S., & Joubert, J.M. (2007). Job demands, job resources, burnout and work engagement of managers at a platinum mine in the North West Province. *South African Journal of Business Management*, 38(3), 49–61.

Russell, J.A. (1991). Culture and the categorization of emotions. *Psychological Bulletin*, 110, 426–450. doi:10.1037/0033-2909.110.3.426

Ryan, R. M. (1982). Control and information in the intrapersonal sphere: An extension of cognitive evaluation theory. *Journal Of Personality And Social Psychology*, 43(3), 450–461. doi:10.1037/0022-3514.43.3.450

Ryan, R.M., & Deci, E.L. (2000). Self-determination theory and the facilitation of intrinsic motivation, social development, and well-being. *American Psychologist*, 55, 68–78.

Saks, A.M. (2006). Antecedents and consequences of employee engagement. *Journal of Managerial Psychology*, 27, 600–619.

Saks, A.M., & Ashforth, B.E. (2002). Is job search related to employment quality? It all depends on the fit. *Journal of Applied Psychology*, 87(4), 646–654. doi:10.1037/0021-9010.87.4.646

Salancik, G.R., & Pfeffer, J. (1978). A social information processing approach to job attitudes and task design. *Administrative Science Quarterly*, 23(2), 224–253. doi:10.2307/2392563

Salanova, M., & Schaufeli, W.B. (2008). A cross-national study of work engagement as a mediator between job resources and proactive behavior: A cross-national study. International *Journal of Human Resources Management*, 19, 116–131.

Salanova, M., Lorente, L., Chambel, M.J., & Martínez, I.M. (2011). Linking transformational leadership to nurses' extra-role performance: The mediating role of self-efficacy and work engagement. *Journal of Advanced Nursing*, 67(10), 2256–2266. doi:10.1111/j.1365-2648.2011.05652.x

Salovey, P., Caruso, D., & Mayer, J.D. (2004). Emotional intelligence in practice. In P. Linley & S. Joseph (Eds.), *Positive psychology in practice* (pp. 447–463). Hoboken, NJ: Wiley.

Salovey, P., & Mayer, J. D. (1989). Emotional intelligence. *Imagination, Cognition and Personality, 9*(3), 185–211.

Sapolsky, R. M. (2004). *Why zebras don't get ulcers: The acclaimed guide to stress, stress-related diseases, and coping* (3rd ed.). New York, NY: Holt

Scarlett, K. (2009). What is engagement? Retrieved from www.scarlettsurveys.com/employee_engagement.cfm

Schaufeli, W. B., & Bakker, A. (2003, November). *Utrecht Work Engagement Scale: Preliminary manual* (Version 1). Unpublished document, Utrecht University, Utrecht, the Netherlands.

Schaufeli, W. B., & Bakker, A. B. (2004). Job demands, job resources and their relationship with burnout and engagement: a multi-sample study. *Journal of Organizational Behavior, 25*, 293–315. doi:10.1002/job.248

Schaufeli, W. B., Bakker, A. B., & Salanova, M. (2006). The measurement of work engagement with a short questionnaire: A cross-national study. *Educational and Psychological Measurement, 66*, 701–716.

Schaufeli, W. B., & Enzmann, D. (1998). *The burnout companion to study and practice: A critical analysis.* London, England: Taylor & Francis.

Schaufeli, W. B., Martínez, I. M., Marques Pinto, A., Salanova, M., & Bakker, A. B. (2002). Burnout and engagement in university students: A cross national study. *Journal of Cross-Cultural Psychology, 33*, 464–481. doi:10.1177/0022022102033005003

Schaufeli, W. B., Salanova, M., González-Romá. V., & Bakker, A. B. (2002). The measurement of engagement and burnout: A two sample confirmatory factor analytic approach. *Journal of Happiness Studies, 3*, 71–92.

Schaufeli, W. B., Taris, T. W., & Bakker, A. B. (2006). Dr. Jekyll and Mr. Hyde: On the differences between work engagement and workaholism. In R. Burke (Ed.), *Research companion to working time and work addiction* (pp. 193–252). Northampton, England: Edward Elgar.

Schaufeli, W. B., Taris, T. W., & van Rhenen, W. (2008). Workaholism, burnout, and work engagement: Three of a kind or three different kinds of employee well-being? *Applied Psychology: An International Review, 57*(2), 173–203. doi:10.1111/j.1464-0597.2007.00285.x

Scheflen, A. E. (1964). The significance of posture in communication systems. *Psychiatry: Journal for the Study of Interpersonal Processes, 27*(4), 316–331.

Schein, E. H. (1990). Organizational culture. *American Psychologist, 45*, 109–119.

Schein, E. H. (2000). Sense and nonsense about culture and climate. In N. M. Ashkanasy, C. P. M. Wilderom, & M. F. Peterson (Eds.), *Handbook of organizational culture & climate* (pp. xxiii–xxx). Thousand Oaks, CA: Sage.

Schleicher, D. J., Watt, J. D., & Greguras, G. J. (2004). Reexamining the job satisfaction-performance relationship: The complexity of attitudes. *Journal of Applied Psychology, 89*, 165–177. doi:10.1037/0021-9010.89.165

Schneider, B. (1987). The people make the place. *Personnel Psychology, 40*(3), 437–453. doi:10.1111/j.1744-6570.1987.tb00609.x

Schneider, B. (1990). The climate for service: An application of the climate construct. In B. Schneider (Ed.), *Organizational climate and culture* (pp. 383–412). San Francisco, CA: Jossey-Bass.

Schneider, B. (2000). The psychological life of organizations. In N. M. Ashkanasy, C. P. M. Wilderom, & M. F. Peterson (Eds.), *Handbook of organizational culture & climate* (pp. xvii–xxi). Thousand Oaks, CA: Sage.

Schohat, L. M., & Vigoda-Gadot, E. (2010). "Engage me once again": Is employee engagement for real, or is it "same lady—different dress"? In S. L. Albrecht (Ed.), *Handbook of employee engagement: Perspectives, issues, research and practice* (pp. 98–107). Northampton, MA: Edward Elgar Publishing.

Schwartz, H. S. (1982). Job involvement as obsession-compulsion. *Academy of Management Review, 7*(3), 429–432. doi:10.5465/AMR.1982.4285355

Schwartz, S. H. (1992). Universals in the content and structure of values: Theoretical advances and empirical tests in 20 countries. In M. P. Zanna (Ed.), *Advances in experimental social psychology* (Vol. 25, pp. 1–65). San Diego, CA: Academic Press. doi:10.1016/S0065-2601(08)60281-6

Schwartz, S. H., & Bilsky, W. (1987). Toward a universal psychological structure of human values. *Journal of Personality and Social Psychology, 53*(3), 550–562. doi:10.1037/0022-3514.53.3.550

Schwartz, S. H., & Bilsky, W. (1990). Toward a theory of the universal content and structure of values: Extensions and cross-cultural replications. *Journal of Personality and Social Psychology, 58*(5), 878–891. doi:10.1037/0022-3514.58.5.878

Scott, K. S., Moore, K. S., & Miceli, M. P. (1997). An exploration of the meaning and consequences of workaholism. *Human Relations, 50*(3), 287–314. doi:10.1023/A:1016986307298

Scott, S. G., & Bruce, R. A. (1994). Determinants of innovative behavior: a path model of individual innovation in the workplace. *Academy of Management Journal, 37*(3), 580–607. doi:10.2307/256701

Scroggins, W. A. (2008). The relationship between employee fit perceptions, job performance, and retention: Implications of perceived fit. *Employee Responsibilities and Rights Journal, 20*(1), 57–71. doi:10.1007/s10672-007-9060-0

Scroggins, W. A., & Benson, P. G. (2007). Self-concept–job fit: Expanding the person–job fit construct and implications for retention management. In D. J. Svyantek (Series Ed.) & D. J. Svyantek & E. McChrystal (Vol. Eds.), *Research in Organizational Science: Vol. 2. Refining familiar constructs: Alternative views in OB, HR and I/O* (pp. 211–232). Charlotte, NC: Information Age Publishers

Seijts, G. H., & Crim, D. (2006). What engages employees the most or, The Ten C's of employee engagement. *Ivey Business Journal, 70*(4), 1–5.

Sekaran, U. (1981). Are U.S. organizational concepts and measures transferable to another culture? An empirical investigation. *Academy of Management Journal, 24*, 409–417.

Sekiguchi, T., & Huber, V. L. (2011). The use of person–organization fit and person–job fit information in making selection decisions. *Organizational Behavior & Human Decision Processes, 116*(2), 203–216. doi:10.1016/j.obhdp.2011.04.001

Seligman, M. E., & Schulman, P. (1986). Explanatory style as a predictor of productivity and quitting among life insurance sales agents. *Journal of Personality and Social Psychology, 50*(4), 832–838. doi:10.1037/0022-3514.50.4.832

Seligman, M. P., & Csikszentmihalyi, M. (2000). Positive psychology: An introduction. *American Psychologist, 55*(1), 5–14. doi:10.1037/0003-066X.55.1.5

Seybold, K., & Salomone, P. R. (1994). Understanding workaholism: A review of causes and counseling approaches. *Journal of Counseling & Development, 73*(1), 4–9.

Shamir, B. (1991). The charismatic relationship: Alternative explanations and predictions. *The Leadership Quarterly, 2*(2), 81–104. doi:10.1016/1048-9843(91)90024-V

Sheldon, K. M., & Elliot, A. J. (1998). Not all personal goals are personal: Comparing autonomous and controlled reasons for goals as predictors of effort and attainment. *Personality and Social Psychology Bulletin, 24*(5), 546–557. doi:10.1177/0146167298245010

Sheldon, K. M., & Elliot, A. J. (1999). Goal striving, need satisfaction, and longitudinal well-being: The self-concordance model. *Journal of Personality and Social Psychology, 76*(3), 482–497. doi:10.1037//0022-3514.76.3.482

Shepard, J. M. (1972). Alienation as a process: Work as a case in point. *Sociological Quarterly, 13*(2), 161–173.

Sherif, C. W. (1963). Social categorization as a function of latitude of acceptance and series range. *The Journal of Abnormal and Social Psychology, 67*(2), 148–156. doi:10.1037/h0043022

Shipman, W. G., Heath, H. A., & Oken, D. (1970). Response specificity among muscular and autonomic variables. *Archives of General Psychiatry, 23*, 369–374.

Shore, L. M., Randel, A. E., Chung, B. G., Dean, M. A., Holcombe Ehrhart, K., & Singh, G. (2011). Inclusion and diversity in work groups: A review and model for future research. *Journal of Management, 37*(4), 1262–1289. doi:10.1177/0149206310385943

SHRM Foundation. (n.d.). *Employee Engagement: Your Competitive Advantage* [Executive brief]. Alexandria, VA: Author. Retrieved from www.shrm.org/about/foundation/products/documents/engagement%20briefing-final.pdf

Siegrist, J. (1996). Adverse health effects of high-effort/low-reward conditions. *Journal of Occupational Health Psychology, 1*(1), 27–41. doi:10.1037/1076-8998.1.1.27

Siegrist, J., Starke, D., Chandola, T., Godin, I., Marmot, M., Niedhammer, I., & Peter, R. (2004). The measurement of effort-reward imbalance at work: European comparisons. *Social Science & Medicine, 58*(8), 1483–1499. doi:10.1016/S0277-9536(03)00351-4

Singelis, T. M., Triandis, H. C., Bhawuk, D., & Gelfand, M. J. (1995). Horizontal and vertical dimensions of individualism and collectivism: A theoretical and measurement refinement. *Cross-Cultural Research: The Journal of Comparative Social Science, 29*(3), 240–275. doi:10.1177/106939719502900302

Skarlicki, D. P., & Folger, R. (1997). Retaliation in the workplace: The roles of distributive, procedural, and interactional justice. *Journal of Applied Psychology, 82*(3), 434–443.

Skinner, E. A., & Belmont, M. J. (1993). Motivation in the classroom: Reciprocal effects of teacher behavior and student engagement across the school year. *Journal of Educational Psychology, 85*(4), 571–581. doi:10.1037/0022-0663.85.4.571

Sloan, M. M. (2012). Unfair treatment in the workplace and worker well-being: The role of coworker support in a service work environment. *Work and Occupations*, 39(1), 3–34. doi:10.1177/0730888411406555

Snir, R., & Harpaz, I. (2004). Attitudinal and demographic antecedents of workaholism. *Journal of Organizational Change Management*, 17(5), 520–536. doi:10.1108/09534810410554524

Song, S.-H., & Olshfski, D. (2008). Friends at work: A comparative study of work attitudes in Seoul City government and New Jersey state government. *Administration & Society*, 40(2), 147–169. doi: 10.1177/0095399707312827

Sonnentag, S. (2003). Recovery, work engagement, and proactive behavior: A new look at the interface between nonwork and work. *Journal of Applied Psychology*, 88(3), 518–528. doi:10.1037/0021-9010.88.3.518

Sonnentag, S., Dormann, C., & Demerouti, E. (2010). Not all days are created equal: The concept of state work engagement. In A.B. Bakker & M.P. Leiter (Eds.), *Work engagement: A handbook of essential theory and research* (pp. 25–38). New York, NY: Psychology Press.

Sosik, J.J., & Jung, D.I. (2010). *Full range leadership development: Pathways for people, profit, and planet*. New York, NY: Psychology Press.

Sosik, J.J., Juzbasich, J., & Chun, J. (2011). Effects of moral reasoning and management level on ratings of charismatic leadership, in-role and extra-role performance of managers: A multi-source examination. *The Leadership Quarterly*, 22(2), 434–450. doi:10.1016/j.leaqua.2011.02.015

Sousa-Lima, M., Michel, J.W., & Caetano, A. (2013). Clarifying the importance of trust in organizations as a component of effective work relationships. *Journal of Applied Social Psychology*, 43(2), 418–427. doi:10.1111/j.1559-1816.2013.01012.x

Spector, P.E., Allen, T.D., Poelmans, S.Y., Lapierre, L.M., Cooper, C.L., O'Driscoll, M., & . . . Widerszal-Bazyl, M. (2007). Cross-national differences in relationships of work demands, job satisfaction, and turnover intentions with work-family conflict. *Personnel Psychology*, 60(4), 805–835. doi:10.1111/j.1744-6570.2007.00092.x

Spence, J.T., & Robbins, A.S. (1992). Workaholism: Definition, measurement, and preliminary results. *Journal of Personality Assessment*, 58(1), 160–179.

Stack, J. (1994). *The great game of business: Unlocking the power and profitability of open-book management*. New York, NY: Currency/Doubleday.

Staw, B.M., Sutton, R.I., & Pelled, L.H. (1994). Employee positive emotion and favorable outcomes at the workplace. *Organization Science*, 5(1), 51–71.

Steele, J.P., Rupayana, D.D., Mills, M.J., Smith, M.R., Wefald, A., & Downey, R.G. (2012). Relative importance and utility of positive worker states: A review and empirical examination. *Journal of Psychology: Interdisciplinary and Applied*, 146(6), 617–650. doi:10.1080/00223980.2012.665100

Steinmetz, H., Park, Y., & Kabst, R. (2011). The relationship between needs and job attitudes in South Korea and Germany. *Journal of Managerial Psychology*, 26(7), 623–644. doi:10.1108/02683941111164517

Stevens, M. (2013). Driving employee engagement for business success. *In Practice*, 35(2), 91–93. doi:10.1136/inp.f192

Storm, K.K., & Rothmann, S.S. (2003). A psychometric analysis of the Maslach Burnout Inventory-General Survey in the South African police service.

South African Journal of Psychology, 33(4), 219–226. doi:10.1177/0081 24630303300404

Studer, B., & Clark, L. (2011). Place your bets: Psychophysiological correlates of decision-making under risk. *Cognitive, Affective & Behavioral Neuroscience, 11*(2), 144–158. doi:10.3758/s13415-011-0025-2

Suh, T., Houston, M. B., Barney, S. M., & Kwon, I. G. (2011). The impact of mission fulfillment on the internal audience: Psychological job outcomes in a services setting. *Journal of Service Research, 14*(1), 76–92. doi:10.1177/ 1094670510387915

Suinn, R. M. (1984). Visual motor behavior rehearsal: The basic technique. *Scandinavian Journal of Behaviour Therapy, 13*(3), 131–142. doi:10.1080/ 16506078409455701

Sullivan, M. J., & Conway, M. (1989). Negative affect leads to low-effort cognition: Attributional processing for observed social behavior. *Social Cognition, 7*(4), 315–337. doi:10.1521/soco.1989.7.4.315

Tajfel, H. (1978). Social categorization, social identity, and social comparison. In H. Tajfel (Ed.), *Differentiation between social groups: Studies in the social psychology of intergroup relations* (pp. 61–76). New York, NY: Academic Press.

Tajfel, H., Billig, M. G., Bundy, R. P., & Flament, C. (1971). Social categorization and intergroup behaviour. *European Journal Of Social Psychology, 1*(2), 149–178. doi:10.1002/ejsp.2420010202

Tajfel, H., & Turner, J. C. (1979). An integrative theory of intergroup conflict. In W. Austin & S. Worchel (Eds.), *The social psychology of intergroup relations* (33–47). Monterey, CA: Brooks/Cole.

Tan, H. H., & Tan, C. S. (2000). Toward the differentiation of trust in supervisor and trust in Organization. *Genetic, Social, and General Psychology Monographs, 126*(2), 241–260.

Tannen, D. (1990). *You just don't understand: Women and men in conversation.* New York, NY: William Morrow & Co.

Taris, T. W., van Horn, J. E., Schaufeli, W. B., & Schreurs, P. G. (2004). Inequity, burnout and psychological withdrawal among teachers: A dynamic exchange model. *Anxiety, Stress & Coping: An International Journal, 17*(1), 103–122. doi:10.1080/1061580031000151620

Teece, D. J. (2010). Business models, business strategy and innovation. *Long Range Planning: International Journal of Strategic Management, 43*(2–3), 172–194. doi: 10.1016/j.lrp.2009.07.003

ten Brummelhuis, L. L., & Bakker, A. B. (2012). Staying engaged during the week: The effect of off-job activities on next day work engagement. *Journal of Occupational Health Psychology, 17*(4), 445–455. doi:10.1037/a0029213

Tetrick, L. E., Quick, J., & Gilmore, P. L. (2012). Research in organizational interventions to improve well-being: Perspectives on organizational change and development. In C. Biron, M. Karanika-Murray, & C. Cooper (Eds.), *Improving organizational interventions for stress and well-being: Addressing process and context* (pp. 59–76). New York, NY: Routledge/Taylor & Francis Group.

Thierry, H. (1990). Intrinsic motivation reconsidered. In U. Kleinbeck, H-H. Quast, H. Thierry, & H. Häcker (Eds.), *Work motivation* (pp. 67–82). Hillsdale, NJ: Erlbaum.

Thompson, B. (2004). *Exploratory and confirmatory factor analysis: Understanding concepts and applications*. Washington, DC: American Psychological Association. doi:10.1037/10694-000

Tims, M., & Bakker, A. B. (2010) Job crafting: Towards a new model of individual job redesign. *South African Journal of Industrial Psychology, 36*, 1–9.

Tims, M., Bakker, A. B., & Derks, D. (2013). The impact of job crafting on job demands, job resources, and well-being. *Journal of Occupational Health Psychology, 18*(2), 230–240. doi:10.1037/a0032141

Torelli, C. J., & Shavitt, S. (2010). Culture and concepts of power. *Journal of Personality and Social Psychology, 99*(4), 703–723. doi:10.1037/a0019973

Tremblay, M., Cloutier, J., Simard, G., Chênevert, D., & Vandenberghe, C. (2010). The role of HRM practices, procedural justice, organizational support and trust in organizational commitment and in-role and extra-role performance. *The International Journal of Human Resource Management, 21*(3), 405–433. doi:10.1080/09585190903549056

Trépanier, S., Fernet, C., Austin, S., Forest, J., & Vallerand, R. J. (2013). Linking job demands and resources to burnout and work engagement: Does passion underlie these differential relationships? *Motivation And Emotion*. doi:10.1007/s11031-013-9384-z

Treviño, L. K., & Brown, M. E. (2005). The role of leaders in influencing unethical behavior in the workplace. In R. E. Kidwell, Jr., & C. L. Martin (Eds.), *Managing organizational deviance* (pp. 69–88). Thousand Oaks, CA: Sage.

Triandis, H. C. (1994). *Culture and social behavior*. New York, NY: McGraw-Hill.

Triandis, H. C. (1995). *Individualism & collectivism*. Boulder, CO: Westview Press.

Triandis, H. C., Leung, K., Villareal, M. J., & Clack, F. L. (1985). Allocentric versus idiocentric tendencies: Convergent and discriminant validation. *Journal of Research in Personality, 19*(4), 395–415. doi:10.1016/0092-6566(85)90008-X

Triandis, H. C., McCusker, C., Betancourt, H., Iwao, S., Leung, K., Salazar, J., . . . Zaleski, Z. (1993). An etic-emic analysis of individualism and collectivism. *Journal of Cross-Cultural Psychology, 24*(3), 366–383. doi:10.1177/0022022193243006

Tsoumbris, P., & Xenikou, A. (2010). Commitment profiles: The configural effect of the forms and foci of commitment on work outcomes. *Journal of Vocational Behavior, 77*(3), 401–411. doi:10.1016/j.jvb.2010.07.006

Tuckey, M. R., Dollard, M. F., & Bakker, A. B. (2012). Empowering leaders optimize working conditions for engagement: A multilevel study. *Journal of Occupational Health Psychology, 17*(1), 15–27. doi:10.1037/a0025942

Uleman, J. S., & Bargh, J. A. (1989). *Unintended thought*. New York, NY: Guilford Press.

Ulrich, D., & Lake, D. (1991). Organization capability: creating competitive advantage. *Executive, 5*(1), 77–92. doi:10.5465/AME.1991.4274728

Ursin, H., & Eriksen, H. R. (2004). The cognitive activation theory of stress. *Psychoneuroendocrinology, 29*(5), 567–592. doi:10.1016/S0306-4530(03)00091-X

Utay, J., & Utay, C. (1999). The ABC's of rapport building: An organizing strategy for training counselors. *Psychology: A Journal of Human Behavior, 36*(1), 34–39.

Vacha-Haase, T. (1998). Reliability generalization: Exploring variance in measurement error affecting score reliability across studies. *Educational and Psychological Measurement, 58*(1), 6–20. doi:10.1177/0013164498058001002

Vallerand, R. J. (2008). On the psychology of passion: In search of what makes people's lives most worth living. *Canadian Psychology, 49*, 1–13. doi:10.1037/0708-5591.49.1.1

Vallerand, R. J., & Houlfort, N. (2003). Passion at work: Toward a new conceptualization. In S. W. Gilliland, D. D. Steiner, & D. P. Skarlicki (Eds.), *Emerging perspectives on values in organizations* (pp. 175–204). Greenwich, CT: Information Age Publishing.

Van Ameringen, M., Mancini, C., & Oakman, J. M. (1998). The relationship of behavioral inhibition and shyness to anxiety disorder. *Journal of Nervous and Mental Disease, 186*(7), 425–431. doi:10.1097/00005053-199807000-00007

van Baaren, R. B., Holland, R. W., Kawakami, K., & van Knippenberg, A. (2004). Mimicry and prosocial behavior. *Psychological Science, 15*(1), 71–74. doi:10.1111/j.0963-7214.2004.01501012.x

van Baaren, R. B., Maddux, W. W., Chartrand, T. L., de Bouter, C., & van Knippenberg, A. (2003). It takes two to mimic: Behavioral consequences of self-construals. *Journal of Personality and Social Psychology, 84*(5), 1093–1102. doi:10.1037/0022-3514.84.5.1093

van Beek, I., Taris, T. W., & Schaufeli, W. B. (2011). Workaholic and work engaged employees: Dead ringers or worlds apart? *Journal of Occupational Health Psychology, 16*(4), 468–482. doi:10.1037/a0024392

van den Heuvel, M., Demerouti, E., Schreurs, B. J., Bakker, A. B., & Schaufeli, W. B. (2009). Does meaning-making help during organizational change?: Development and validation of a new scale. *The Career Development International, 14*(6), 508–533. doi:10.1108/13620430910997277

Van Dyne, L., & LePine, J. A. (1998). Helping and voice extra-role behaviors: Evidence of construct and predictive validity. *Academy of Management Journal, 41*(1), 108–119. doi:10.2307/256902

Van Eerde, W., & Thierry, H. (1996). Vroom's expectancy models and work-related criteria: A meta-analysis. *Journal of Applied Psychology, 81*(5), 575–586.

Van Knippenberg, D., & Sleebos, E. (2006). Organizational identification versus organizational commitment: self-definition, social exchange, and job attitudes. *Journal of Organizational Behavior, 27*(5), 571–584. doi:10.1002/job.359

Van Scotter, J., Motowidlo, S. J., & Cross, T. C. (2000). Effects of task performance and contextual performance on systemic rewards. *Journal of Applied Psychology, 85*(4), 526–535. doi:10.1037/0021-9010.85.4.526

Van Wijhe, C. I., Peeters, M. W., & Schaufeli, W. B. (2011). To stop or not to stop, that's the question: About persistence and mood of workaholics and work engaged employees. *International Journal of Behavioral Medicine, 18*(4), 361–372. doi:10.1007/s12529-011-9143-z

Vandenberghe, C., Bentein, K., & Stinglhamber, F. (2004). Affective commitment to the organization, supervisor, and work group: Antecedents and outcomes. *Journal of Vocational Behavior, 64*(1), 47–71. doi:10.1016/S0001-8791(03)00029-0

Vansteenkiste, M., Neyrinckck, B., Niemiec, C. P., Soenens, B., De Witte, H., & Van den Broeck, A. (2007). On the relations among work value orientations, psychological need satisfaction and job outcomes: A self-determination theory approach. *Journal of Occupational and Organizational Psychology, 80*, 251–277. doi:10.1348/096317906X111024

Vasalampi, K., Salmela-Aro, K., & Nurmi, J. (2009). Adolescents' self-concordance, school engagement, and burnout predict their educational trajectories. *European Psychologist, 14*(4), 332–341. doi:10.1027/1016-9040.14.4.332

Vecina, M. L., Chacón, F., Sueiro, M., & Barrón, A. (2012). Volunteer engagement: Does engagement predict the degree of satisfaction among new volunteers and the commitment of those who have been active longer? *Applied Psychology: An International Review, 61*(1), 130–148. doi:10.1111/j.1464-0597.2011.00460.x

Veurink, S. A., & Fischer, R. (2011). A refocus on foci: A multidimensional and multi-foci examination of commitment in work contexts. *New Zealand Journal of Psychology, 40*(3), 160–167.

Viljoen, H. G. (1989). The socially-oriented psycho-analytic theories. In W. F. Meyer, C. Moore, & H. G. Viljoen (Eds.), *Personality theories—from Freud to Frankl* (pp. 116–144). Johannesburg, South Africa: Lexicon.

Vincent-Höper, S., Muser, C., & Janneck, M. (2012). Transformational leadership, work engagement, and occupational success. *Career Development International, 17*(7), 663–682. doi:10.1108/13620431211283805

Vozar, R. (2012). Employee engagement. *Smart Business Chicago, 10*(1), 20.

Vroom, V. H. (1964). *Work and motivation.* Oxford, England: Wiley.

Walker, C. R. (1950). The problem of the repetitive job. *Harvard Business Review, 28*, 54–58.

Walumbwa, F. O., Avolio, B. J., & Zhu, W. (2008). How transformational leadership weaves its influence on individual job performance: The role of identification and efficacy beliefs. *Personnel Psychology, 61*(4), 793–825.

Walumbwa, F. O., Christensen, A. L., & Muchiri, M. K. (2013). Transformational leadership and meaningful work. In B. J. Dik, Z. S. Byrne, & M. F. Steger (Eds.), *Purpose and meaning in the workplace* (pp. 197–215). Washington, DC: American Psychological Association. doi:10.1037/14183-010

Walumbwa, F. O., Morrison, E. W., & Christensen, A. L. (2012). Ethical leadership and group in-role performance: The mediating roles of group conscientiousness and group voice. *The Leadership Quarterly, 23*(5), 953–964. doi:10.1016/j.leaqua.2012.06.004

Wang, D.-S., & Hsieh, C.-C. (2013). The effect of authentic leadership on employee trust and employee engagement. *Social Behavior & Personality: An International Journal, 41*(4), 613–624. doi:10.2224/sbp.2013.41.4.613

Wang, X., Shi, Z., Ng, S., Wang, B., & Chan, C. W. (2011). Sustaining engagement through work in postdisaster relief and reconstruction. *Qualitative Health Research, 21*(4), 465–476. doi:10.1177/1049732310386049

Warr, P., Cook, J., & Wall, T. (1979). Scales for the measurement of some work attitudes and aspects of psychological well-being. *Journal of Occupational Psychology, 52*(2), 129–148. doi:10.1111/j.2044-8325.1979.tb00448.x

Wefald, A., & Downey, R. (2009). Job engagement in organizations: Fad, fashion, or folderol? *Journal of Organizational Behavior, 30*(1), 141–145.

Wefald, A. J., Mills, M. J., Smith, M. R., & Downey, R. G. (2012). A Comparison of three job engagement measures: Examining their factorial and criterion-related validity. *Applied Psychology: Health & Well-Being, 4*(1), 67–90. doi:10.1111/j.1758-0854.2011.01059.x

White, R. W. (1959). Motivation reconsidered: The concept of competence. *Psychological Review, 66*, 297–333. doi:10.1037/h0040934

Williams, L. J., & Anderson, S. E. (1991). Job satisfaction and organizational commitment as predictors of organizational citizenship and in-role behaviors. *Journal of Management, 17*(3), 601–617. doi:10.1177/014920639101700305

Wilson, T. D. (2002). *Strangers to ourselves: Discovering the adaptive unconscious.* Cambridge, MA: Belknap Press/Harvard University Press.

Wilson, T. D., Dunn, D. S., Bybee, J. A., Hyman, D. B., & Rotondo, J. A. (1984). Effects of analyzing reasons on attitude–behavior consistency. *Journal of Personality and Social Psychology, 47*(1), 5–16. doi:10.1037/0022-3514.47.1.5

Wilson, T. D., & Kraft, D. (1993a). Why do I love thee?: Effects of repeated introspections about a dating relationship on attitudes toward the relationship. *Personality and Social Psychology Bulletin, 19*(4), 409–418. doi: 10.1177/0146167293194006

Wilson, T. D., & Kraft, D. (1993b). "Why do I love thee? Effects of repeated introspections about a dating relationship on attitudes toward the relationship": Erratum. *Personality and Social Psychology Bulletin, 19*(6), 759. doi:10.1177/0146167293196012

Wilson, T. D., & Schooler, J. W. (1991). Thinking too much: Introspection can reduce the quality of preferences and decisions. *Journal of Personality and Social Psychology, 60*(2), 181–192. doi:10.1037/0022-3514.60.2.181

Wozniak, D. (2013). The road to employee engagement. *Credit Union Magazine, 79*(2), 44.

Wright, C. (2012). Getting serious about employee engagement in 2012! *Power Engineering, 116*(4), C3.

Wright, T. A., & Staw, B. M. (1999). Affect and favorable work outcomes: Two longitudinal tests of the happy-productive worker thesis. *Journal of Organizational Behavior, 20*(1), 1–23. doi:10.1002/(SICI)1099-1379(199901)20: 1<1::AID-JOB885>3.0.CO;2-W

Wrzesniewski, A., Berg, J. M., & Dutton, J. E. (2010). Turn the job you have into the job you want. *Harvard Business Review, 88*(6), 114–117.

Wrzesniewski, A., & Dutton, J. E. (2001). Crafting a job: Revisioning employees as active crafters of their work. *Academy of Management Review, 26*(2), 179–201. doi:10.5465/AMR.2001.4378011

Wrzesniewski, A., Dutton, J. E., & Debebe, G. (2003). Interpersonal sensemaking and the meaning of work. In R. M. Kramer & B. M. Staw (Eds.), *Research in organizational behavior: An annual series of analytical essays and critical reviews* (Vol. 25, pp. 93–135). Oxford, England: Elsevier Science Ltd.

Xanthopoulou, D., Bakker, A. B., Demerouti, E., & Schaufeli, W. B. (2007). The role of personal resources in the job demands-resources model. *International Journal of Stress Management, 14*(2), 121–141. doi:10.1037/1072-5245.14. 2.121

Xanthopoulou, D., Bakker, A. B., Demerouti, E., & Schaufeli, W. B. (2009). Reciprocal relationships between job resources, personal resources, and work engagement. *Journal of Vocational Behavior, 74*(3), 235–244. doi:10.1016/ j.jvb.2008.11.003

Xanthopoulou, D., Bakker, A. B., Heuven, E., Demerouti, E., & Schaufeli, W. B. (2008). Working in the sky: A diary study on work engagement among flight attendants. *Journal of Occupational Health Psychology, 13*(4), 345–356. doi:10.1037/1076-8998.13.4.345

Xu, J., & Thomas, H. C. (2011). How can leaders achieve high employee engagement? *Leadership and Organization Development Journal, 32*, 399–416. doi: 101437731111134661

Yamada, D.C. (2000). The phenomenon of "workplace bullying" and the need for status-blind hostile work environment protection. *Georgetown Law Journal, 88*, 475–537.

Yan, X., & Su, J. (2013). Core self-evaluations mediators of the influence of social support on job involvement in hospital nurses. *Social Indicators Research, 113*(1), 299–306. doi:10.1007/s11205-012-0093-x

Yukl, G. A. (2010). *Leadership in organizations.* Upper Saddle River, NJ: Pearson Prentice Hall.

Zajonc, R. B. (2008). Feeling and thinking: Preferences need no inferences. In R. H. Fazio & R. E. Petty (Eds.), *Attitudes: Their structure, function, and consequences* (pp. 143–168). New York, NY: Psychology Press.

Zajonc, R. B., & Adelmann, P. K. (1987). Cognition and communication: A story of missed opportunities. *Social Science Information/Sur Les Sciences Sociales, 26*(1), 3–30. doi:10.1177/053901887026001001

Zhu, W., Avolio, B. J., & Walumbwa, F. O. (2009). Moderating role of follower characteristics with transformational leadership and follower work engagement. *Group Organization Management, 34*, 590–619.

INDEX